CADUCEUS

CADUCEUS

A New Perspective on Historical Knowledge
and the Spirituality of Man

Robert Hamilton

Apollo Publications
Mayfair House
14-18 Heddon Street
Mayfair
London
W1B 4DA
www.thelightattheendofthetunnel.net

Cover Art
Original art copyright © 2007 by Robert Hamilton
Production by Alison Hamilton and SwingerDesign
Printed in Great Britain by Cpod, Trowbridge, Wiltshire

ISBN 978 0 9560681 0 1

British Library Cataloguing in Publication Data.
A catalogue record for this book is available from the British Library.

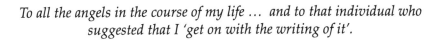

To all the angels in the course of my life … and to that individual who suggested that I 'get on with the writing of it'.

A special thank you to my editor Richard Preston.

Preface

In 1996 I experienced a spiritual 'event'; a literally illuminating and en*light*ening experience, which seemed to be the result of a process of meditation and re-education that I had previously imposed upon myself. This event had a profound and lasting effect on me.

Prior to this I had not been satisfied with the explanations of history and development of mankind and it was before and after this experience that I set out on the quest to fill in the gaps that I felt existed. In my study, across many disciplines including science, religion, philosophy and history, I sought, not only to make sense of the experience, but also explore further this new-found knowledge. In addition to the academic study, I felt it was essential that I travelled to many sites of antiquity to confirm for myself much of what I had read and also to form my own opinions. The result is this text which I have long felt compelled to write, and which forms a statement both of my physical and spiritual experience and of all the knowledge that I have imbibed. This book is the culmination of some fifteen years of intensive study and travel, and a book which I myself would like to have read at the beginning of my 'quest'.

The book does not intend to compromise any religious system or scientific tenet. However, I feel that it is essential to view the past in another light and better understand it in order to fulfil the destinies of our future. We need not, and should not, be satisfied with the reliance on convenient definitive boxes provided by traditional academics, superficial spirituality and its resultant complacency, or deferment regarding the true nature of our being.

I would like to stress that I myself am not an academic or member of an academic institution, nor am I a spiritual or religious zealot. Being self-employed for most of my working life has given me the chance to read and travel extensively. What I have come to know and believe, and what is presented in this book, I have really stumbled upon. While it may not be a book of original thought, I feel it is a work of original perspective on historical knowledge and man's spirituality.

R.H.

22.9.2008

Contents

The Caduceus Symbol

This ancient symbol dates back to the Greeks, and is best known for being carried by the Greek god Hermes, messenger of the gods and escorter of souls.

It is formed by a staff entwined by two serpents shaped like a double helix with wings and a sphere mounted above it. Its origins are uncertain but it was probably adopted by the Greeks from Mesopotamia. For a number of years now, the caduceus has been used by the medical profession as its symbol.

The symbolism is divided among the component parts: the staff symbolises authority carried by messengers; the wings denote information and transformation; the serpents are depicted in Judaeo-Christian traditions as a source of delivery of wisdom; and the double helix shape represents creation and life. The whole symbol, therefore, represents the authority to deliver vital information or wisdom to assist and enlighten.

In the Hermetic tradition the caduceus symbolises spiritual awakening and has parallels with the Kundalini serpents of Hindu mysticism.

Introduction

It is difficult to begin with a clear statement of the view that this philosophical work sets out to establish, or its relation to what others have written previously.

Philosophy, that is the use of reason and argument in seeking truth and knowledge, aims at a universality which comprises particulars but which cannot be expressed fully until each of the particulars has been concluded, thereby providing the universality desired. It is therefore necessary to find how the constituent parts function as a whole before defining each part in detail.

Nonetheless, the contents can be easily summarised in terms of format. The sequence of chapters is, to a degree, quasi-autobiographical in that the order of the chapters presented here and the knowledge gathered for them are loosely based on how I came to this spiritual 'event' (referred to in the preface). In the years previous to the 'event', I had sought to find explanations for what seemed to me to be gaps in the history and development of mankind and the way traditional ideas on this had not been questioned before. In addition to academic study in science, religion, philosophy and history, I visited many ancient sites as the book will show.

It seems now that the information gathered over these fifteen years or so assisted greatly in, or was perhaps essential for, opening the mind to new perspectives that perhaps in turn allowed this profound and enlightening experience to happen to me.

Summary of chapters
Chapter 1 looks at the acknowledged scientific tenets of today and identifies the 'gaps', and sometimes unfounded assumptions, that exist in many of these. It points out that these tenets cannot be described as absolute. Many of the leading scientists were more than men of formulae

and were often more profoundly contemplative, and in one case more concerned with metaphysical matters, than is readily accepted. This chapter covers four eminent scientists far apart in history: Stephen Hawking, Albert Einstein, Isaac Newton and Charles Darwin.

Chapter 2 examines the anomalies and inconsistencies in ancient history, revealed in the study of ancient maps, megalithic structures, astronomy and ancient mythologies, to further challenge traditional thought and knowledge. These anomalies are found in different parts of the world, including the Middle East, Africa, South and North America and Asia, and among many different cultures of antiquity, often with links between them.

Chapter 3 follows on from the previous chapter to consider the possibilities of a very ancient civilisation that may have existed many thousands of years before ours, drawing on accounts of ancient cultures and other sources.

Chapter 4 develops the parallels of the mythologies of ancient cultures where we look at various religions and spiritual texts from across many religious cultures such as Judaism, Christianity, Islam, Hinduism, Buddhism and others. (It is because of this that I have chosen to use CE (Common Era) instead of AD (Anno Domini) and replace BC (Before Christ) with BCE (Before Common Era or Christian Era) throughout *Caduceus*. The numbering and value of years within both systems are identical.)

This transcendent view is not only to provide some insight into these spiritual texts, and to show parallels, but also to highlight the constant and consistent reference to a spiritual experience and to the significance of the element of 'light' throughout.

Chapter 5 seeks to further this argument by highlighting some works of great and acknowledged thinkers of the world (such as Goethe, Dante, Nietzsche, Jung and Plato) who have shown, in various ways, references to a spiritual event of a certain kind and also its association with 'light'.

Chapter 6 describes the experience of my own spiritual event, providing contemporary commentary and experiences, bringing to light the main points from the previous two chapters. This chapter also discusses evidence of the same experience by the forerunners and originators of the religions and spiritual thought discussed in Chapter 4.

Chapter 7 explores the remarkable similarities between elements of this experience and that of the Near-death experience and includes a summary of a discussion with Dr Raymond Moody, author of *Life after Life*, who coined the phrase 'Near-death experience'.

Chapter 8 draws together assertions from the book and comments on the current state of the world in relation to spiritual matters, and how the individual might have an influence on the world to come.

The purpose of the book

It is my hope that this book will provide a new perspective on our world history and spirituality and initiate a change in how we approach the whole matter of life and living.

Many readers will agree that all is not well with the world as we know it today. There are global conflicts as a consequence of borders that cut across tribal lands and cultures of antiquity imposed by the 'colonialists' of the last few centuries. There is evidence of this in all regions of the world but predominantly within Africa and, most recently, in relation to the Kurds of the Middle East. We find brother fighting brother for land bestowed on us all, and if religion is not offered as the root cause it is used as an excuse for ulterior motives, predominantly economic and financial gain. These are among the many negatives in our superficial and material world that plague and distract us from the true essence of life, a complete knowledge of the Self.

More importantly, our souls, hearts and minds are not in the most contented of states. Whilst some of us are able to function at a purely automatic and intuitive level, there are many who desire a better and fuller understanding of themselves, of who they are and why. Indeed, there are many individuals who do sense something greater but have difficulty in identifying the starting point from which they can begin to penetrate through the mysteries of life. There are many, like myself, who are not content with blind religious faith, on the one hand, or partial scientific explanation on the other, and are compelled to get to some 'truth'.

Other books on a similar theme

There have been many publications such as *The Celestine Prophecy* and others which, whilst they have been successful and afford some value to the individual, have tended to appease our souls merely temporarily, if at all. Much like diet plans, they are employed for a short period until the next fad comes along. My text will, to some degree, delve into similar matters of the spirit as they do; however, my aim is to provide substance and foundation: food for thought on why we are driven to such activity and introspection in order to achieve a contentedness and peace within the soul that can be of greater depth and permanency.

We will seek to severely question and deconstruct our traditional understanding, ideas and knowledge of the history of humankind, instilled in us over centuries and to reassemble it using alternative theories on the evolution and development of man and our civilisation, in a way that produces a more complete and accurate perspective. It is only with this wider knowledge that we can truly progress both as individuals and as a world population with a global consciousness. Today, there is reason for optimism that this can indeed be achieved, as is evidenced by the 'green' movement, which shows that across the countries of the world a conscientious and united momentum for change can be created.

Having studied and travelled extensively over some fifteen years, my reasoning and conclusions were not reached with a gullible mind, nor do I expect the reader to react to the book in such a way. Rather, the intention of this book is to be simple, straightforward and succinct.

I have tried to base my assertions on fact, provide evidence and use as many relevant references as possible. While *Caduceus* is not a text of great length, I have tried to avoid – as in many books with subject matters similar to parts of this book – indulging in the writer's own personal experiences and commentaries. Here we concentrate on facts and references, with the sources cited so that the reader may investigate, whatever their matter of interest, in as greater detail as he or she so wishes.

A parallel with the Rosetta stone

At the same time, this is not intended as a definitive text. Subject matter such as science, for instance, is well beyond the purview of *Caduceus*. Indeed, it would be a rather lengthy book that delved into greater detail on the variety of topics mentioned in the different chapters.

For want of a better description, this text should be viewed as a Rosetta stone. The Rosetta stone is perhaps the most famous piece of rock in the world and has become a symbol for the mysteries and anomalies of antiquity and our endeavours to decipher them. It was the means by which, thanks to Jean-François Champollion in the 1820s, Egyptian hieroglyphics could actually be read for the first time. On this particular stone there was a single passage translated into three languages: Egyptian hieroglyphics, Demotic (ancient Egyptian) and Greek. With the understanding of Greek and Demotic (by understanding of the Coptic language), and then paralleling the meaning to the hieroglyphics, the message on the stone was finally revealed and hence the ability to read the texts of the Egyptians and further our understanding of this great and ancient culture was initiated.

This text aims to present all that we have known combined with alternative and equally viable theories that blend academic thinking and spirituality. These alternative theories, I stress, will be founded on substance, fact which will be cross referenced and, at the point of conclusion, should provide a fuller understanding of the evolution of man and from whence we came. At the very least, we should be better comforted by the depth and profundity of it all. The means by which *Caduceus* will unravel the mysteries, anomalies and the preconceived ideas of traditional education is through the presentation of ancient text and contemporary commentaries, in addition to looking at the hard evidence.

Unity of knowledge and universal history
This concept of the combination of disciplines is neither new nor original. It has been suggested previously by the biologist and scientist Edward O. Wilson in his book *Consilience - The Unity of Knowledge.* In the first chapter, Wilson wrote that its central tenet, as Einstein knew, is the unification of knowledge and that when we have unified enough certain knowledge, we will begin to understand who we are and why we are here.

Francis Fukuyama advances a similar concept in detail in his work *The End of History and the Last Man,* with reference to the renowned philosophers Kant and Hegel. Of Kant's *An Idea for a Universal History from a Cosmopolitan Point of View,* he writes:

> Kant suggested that history would have an end point, that is to say, a final purpose that was implied in man's current potentialities

and which made the whole of history intelligible ... It also provided a standard by which one could undertake the tremendous effort of abstraction required to separate what was essential in this evolution from the great mass of facts about events that constitute the raw material of history.

Of Hegel, he comments:

[He] defined his project as the writing of a Universal History which would provide "the exhibition of spirit [i.e. collective human consciousness] in the process of working out the knowledge of that which it is potentially.

Hegel, Fukuyama asserts, was the first historicist philosopher – that is a philosopher who believed in the essential historical relativity of the truth. Hegel maintained that all human consciousness was limited by the particular social and cultural conditions of man's surrounding environment – or, as we say, by 'the times'. Past thought, whether of ordinary people or great philosophers or scientists, was not true absolutely or 'objectively', but only relative to the historical or cultural horizon within which that person lived.

Hegel also suggested an end of history, however not in an apocalyptic sense, as Fukuyama goes on to write:

Hegel, however, had defined history as the progress of man to higher levels of rationality and freedom, and this process has a logical terminal point in the achievement of absolute self-consciousness ... a final form of society that was free from contradictions, and whose achievement would terminate the historical process.

It is beyond the scope of this book to discuss such a universal history in more detail; however, it is my hope that this will encourage a fresh approach to knowledge, history and pre-history of the human race. A knowledge which may provide a basis for dismissing unjustified prejudices and is more global and all-encompassing in relation to our origins and who and why we are presently.

I have tried to introduce a visual representation of this universal history with my design of the front cover of *Caduceus*. This complex symbolism envisages the overlapping of history and symbol. We see the cross of Christianity, which is also seen in aboriginal North American and the Mayan world (prior to Christianity), representing the four corners of the earth. The serpents of the caduceus symbol manoeuvre over the 'cross' and entwine themselves through the 'Eye of Horus' or the 'Eye of Consciousness' of the Egyptians, the cornea of which consists of the 'dualistic' symbol of the Buddhist Yin and Yang. These are all overlaid upon the Mayan calendar from which there is an emission of light. The reason for the use of this latter characteristic will become clearer as you read *Caduceus*. Whilst I could have made my image of the serpents and staff more sophisticated and refined, I refused the possibility of such change since this enhances the complexity of the symbolism and incorporates 'the rough and the smooth'; an analogy to this life itself.

In challenging some assertions of our traditional understanding, *Caduceus* may well be criticised by some academics, as has happened previously with texts that 'go against the grain'. The amount of evidence provided here should provoke the questions: When will such a number of anomalies cease being referred to as mere coincidences? How many coincidences form enough evidence and how much evidence equals proof, or at least substantive food for thought?

In summary of the above, therefore, there are essentially three parts to *Caduceus*:

i. That which we have known;
ii. That which we should know – the combination of the academic and the spiritual; and
iii. The reconciliation of these two parts.

This is not unlike the Buddhist concept of duality as symbolised by the Yin and the Yang. Having grasped this idea, understanding that which is to be achieved subsequently is *Atman* – reconciliation, oneness, bringing individual and global dichotomy and disharmony to an end.

1

The Scientific Fraternity

There are moments when one feels free from one's own identification with the human limitations and inadequacies. At such moments one imagines that one stands on some spot of a small planet gazing in amazement at the cold yet profoundly moving beauty of the eternal, the unfathomable; life and earth floe into one and there is neither evolution nor destiny; only Being.

Albert Einstein (1879–1955)

For over two thousand years, going back to the ancient Greek civilisation, scholars and scientists have spent their lives seeking both to provide answers of some kind to the question of why we exist and, at the same time, to define the laws of Nature. Most of their scientific thinking is outside the purview of *Caduceus* and the reason for including just a few of them in this text is to challenge current preconceived ideas and to show that these individuals of assiduous endeavour were concerned with more than mere numbers and formulae. They were also transcendent minds who incorporated religious and metaphysical contemplation in the course of their lives and, in some instances, included it in their work.

This chapter seeks to show that these particular individuals and their science need not be viewed as incompatible with religious belief of some kind or at variance with the notion of an omniscient entity; that science and religion are not mutually exclusive. It is difficult to comprehend the dichotomy existing between the evolutionists and the creationists and why neither side has been able to concede that it could be a little bit of both. It is my view that science explains, rather than denounces, that which has been created. As Albert Einstein said in 1921,

'Relativity is a purely scientific matter and has nothing to do with religion.' This was in response to the question of what effect relativity would have on religion posed by Randall Thomas Davidson, the then Archbishop of Canterbury. Einstein went on to say, 'Relativity theory is an abstract science. It fits into every world view.' There should be no reason why Einstein's response could not be applied to Newton's Theory of Gravity or the Big Bang theory.

Within the context of this book and the possible lack of relevance of writing about the majority of scientists of past centuries, I intend to concentrate on the most accessible and acceptable scientific theories the more recent past from four scientists of eminence:

Stephen Hawking (his commentary on): The Big Bang theory,
Isaac Newton: The Theory of Gravity,
Albert Einstein: The Theory of Relativity,
Charles Darwin: The Theory of Evolution

The Big Bang theory

The Big Bang theory is generally thought of today as the standard cosmological model of our universe. It purports to show that some 13.7 billion years ago all matter and energy originated in 'singularity', a point of infinite density and temperature. Ever since the Big Bang, the universe has been expanding and cooling down.

There are three main strands of evidence to support Big Bang theory. Firstly, galaxies are moving away from us at speeds proportional to their distance, suggesting expansion from a single point. Secondly, the universe is pervaded with 'cosmic microwave background radiation', presumed to be a faint afterglow of Big Bang energy. Thirdly, the amount of the most common chemical elements that astronomers observe in space correspond closely to the extrapolations of Big Bang theory.

Now, whilst one might accept this as possible – or even probable – it is by no means empirical or satisfactory or indeed conclusive. The biggest question that arises here is: What came before the Big Bang? And to this science has apparently no answer. Stephen Hawking, in his book *A Briefer History of Time* seems to admit that it is not possible to provide an answer and he claims that, in any case, it is not relevant to the theory:

> We know only what has happened since the Big Bang, we cannot determine what happened beforehand. As far as we are concerned, events before the Big Bang can have no consequences and so should not form part of a scientific model of the universe. We should therefore cut them out of the model and say that the Big Bang was the beginning of time. This means that questions such as who set up the conditions for the Big Bang are not questions that science addresses.
>
> *A Briefer History of Time*

This statement seems unacceptable to the extent that scientific theory presents an assertion, claiming rather emphatically that this is how it all began and forms the 'beginning of time'. However, because no definite answer can be provided as to the real origin of things before the Big Bang then – arbitrarily – we shall start at some later point of time and designate that as the beginning; that is the scientific explanation and all that happens thereafter is scientific fact!

General Theory of Relativity

The Theory of Special Relativity (Albert Einstein: 1905) is summed up by the well-known formula E=mc2, which expresses the equivalence of mass and energy, E being energy, m mass and c the speed of light. If the energy of an object increases, so does its mass, that is, its resistance to acceleration, or change in speed. Einstein's theory was based on the idea that the laws of science should be the same for all observers no matter how they are moving, in the absence of gravitational phenomena.

Einstein followed this with his Theory of General Relativity (1915) which included gravity in the equation. His theory is based on the idea that the laws of science should be the same for all observers, no matter how they are moving. It explains the force of gravity in terms of the curvature of a four-dimensional space-time.

As Einstein said:

> It follows from the theory of relativity that mass and energy are both different manifestations of the same thing – a somewhat unfamiliar conception for the average man. Furthermore, E=mc2, in which energy is put equal to mass multiplied with the square of the velocity of light, showed that a very small amount of mass may be converted into a very large amount of energy ... the mass and energy in fact were equivalent.

It is difficult to argue this point but it does seem to be rather at variance with Newton's Theory of Gravity, which preceded Einstein's Theory of Relativity and which has been scientifically accepted for over three centuries.

Stephen Hawking highlights this point that there is an inconsistency between the two theories and that, despite Einstein's 1915 Theory of General Relativity, the differences for practical purposes are quite small:

> Einstein's 1905 theory of relativity is called a special relativity. That is because, though it was very successful in explaining that the speed of light was the same to all observers and in explaining what happens when things move at speeds close to the speed of light, it was inconsistent with the Newtonian theory of gravity. Newton's theory says that at any given time objects are attracted to each other with a force that depends on the distance between them at that time ... Einstein made a number of unsuccessful attempts between 1908 and 1914 to find a theory of gravity that was consistent with special relativity. Finally in 1915 he proposed the even more revolutionary theory we now call the general theory of relativity.
>
> *A Briefer History of Time*

Hawking's conclusion is that the two theories are not in practice as consistent as is often thought. He states, 'However, we still use Newton's theory for most practical purposes because *the difference* between its predictions and those of general relativity is very small in the situations that we normally deal with.'

He also comments that the process of constructing a complete theory of the universe 'at one go' is not really possible and that scientific progress may come from 'partial theories' that are limited in scope.

As Hawking explains, it is very difficult to construct a complete unified theory of everything in the universe all at one go. So, instead, science has made progress by finding partial theories that describe a limited range of happenings and by neglecting other effects and approximating them by certain numbers.

These admissions from two of our greatest scientists and theorists do not seem particularly convincing overall and do not motivate an individual to accept the firm embrace of science as a way of full and tangible understanding of the universe we live in.

Quantum mechanics: 'God does not play dice'

There seems to be an even greater lack of conviction and agreement when we look at the great scientific development of the day, that of quantum mechanics. Quantum mechanics introduces an unavoidable element of unpredictability or randomness into scientific theories.

Einstein objected to this very strongly, despite the important role he had played in the development of these ideas. In fact, he was awarded the Nobel Prize for his contribution to quantum theory. Nevertheless, he never accepted that the universe was governed by chance: his feelings were summed up in his famous statement, 'God does not play dice'.

Einstein was also known to have been sceptical of its implications. 'The more success the quantum theory has,' he said, 'the sillier it looks. How non-physicists would scoff if they were able to follow the odd course of developments!'

He also confesses that he had been unable to pursue work on quantum theory with any real enthusiasm. As he puts it, 'Lecturing on quantum theory is not for me. Though I have laboured much with it, I have gained little insight into it.'

In a letter to the Royal Society in March 1927, Einstein comments, 'It is only in quantum theory that Newton's differential method becomes inadequate and indeed strict causality fails us. But the last word has not yet been said.'

The two theories, therefore, that of relativity and quantum mechanics co-exist uncomfortably without a common base. The theory of quantum mechanics was derived from Einstein and his Theory of Relativity but this great thinker was unable to be fully convinced about this theory that is so revered today. Yet they remain theories, described as such and in use today even if at source they are not congruent with each other.

'No' to omniscient entity – 'Yes' to other dimensions

The world of physics has now, therefore, ended up with these two bodies of laws: general relativity for the universe at large and quantum mechanics/theory for the micro world. In recent years, there have been a number of efforts to unify the Theory of General Relativity with Quantum Theory. This unification is nothing less than the Holy Grail of physicists today and the latest attempt, Quantum Gravity, is an area of research to try to find a way of achieving this.

There is, however, no one body of theory that is agreed upon for Quantum Gravity.

This theory itself describes the gravitational interactions of matter and energy in the way in which matter and energy are described by quantum theory. In most, but not all, theories of quantum gravity, gravity is also 'quantized'. Since the contemporary theory of gravity, general relativity, describes gravitation as the curvature of space-time by matter and energy, a quantization of gravity implies some sort of quantization of space-time itself – which has so far proved difficult.

One of the greatest new hopes of physicists today rests on what is variously described as String theory, Superstring theory and M-theory. This is way outside the scope of this book, however, String theory has changed over the years and has given rise to several new theories. While these String theories initially appeared mathematically different from each other, they were apparently connected and fundamentally the same, possessing multi-dimensional supergravity in common. Due to these connections and overlap, it was believed that the String theories that existed were all aspects of a single underlying theory. The name 'M-theory' was ascribed to this collection of theories.

Should such a unifying String theory be found where a set of equations can make two presently incompatible theories compatible it may well be mathematically elegant but, in practice, useless.

We live in what is described as four-dimensional space, which consists of three space dimensions and one time dimension. Stephen Hawking suggests that for String theories to work they need to be consistent only if there are many dimensions, indeed between ten and twenty-six instead of the usual four. This sounds to me more like the realms of science fiction! Some String theories go even further and suggest that there are many different universes or many different regions of a single universe, each with its own initial configuration and, perhaps, with its own set of laws of science.

What is fascinating in this line of development is that the scientific thinking which is largely dismissive of an omniscient entity, a God or Creator, can nevertheless contemplate the existence of other dimensions and universes. Surely this new stance demands as great a leap of faith as the other older one? Incidentally, it is interesting to note that the meaning of M in M-theory, mentioned above, has been deferred until such time as any one of the presently possible string theories is accepted as the unifying theory!

Does science have all the answers?

All of the above is merely to present the notion that science is not without its doubts and is surely lacking, by its own admission, in the provision of *all* the answers, on the one hand, but does afford a very solid insight into the mechanisms of that which has been created on the other.

Francis Fukuyama, in his book *The End of History and the Last Man*, raises an interesting point about the motivation of scientists in their quest for scientific knowledge. He comments: 'Science itself does not tell us why men pursue science' and, more pertinently, goes on to add, 'Science as a social phenomenon unfolds not simply because men are curious about the universe, but because science permits them to gratify their desire for security.'

My own belief is that these scientific tenets do not absolve or relieve us from considering more deeply the reasons for, and the origins of, our nature and existence. We should not in any way rely on these scientific tenets, nor within ourselves find doubt in the existence of an omniscient entity or be complacent with these convenient, though inconclusive, scientific explanations.

Sir Isaac Newton and the Creator

In the realm of astronomy, Sir Isaac Newton in the seventeenth century unified the earthbound mechanics of Galileo with Kepler's laws. Kepler supplied the mathematical theory that confirmed planetary observations and Galileo supplied the observational evidence. This was an achievement comparable to solving the problems currently facing physicists, that of the unification of relativity and quantum mechanics.

The fact is well documented, and therefore will come as no surprise to many, that Isaac Newton was a devout Christian. He was an Arian, a doctrine that was derived from the teachings of the fourth-century

Isaac Newton 1643–1727.

theologian Arius, who lived and taught in Alexandria, Egypt. It held that Jesus and God were not of one substance and contradicted orthodox trinitarian christological positions and asserted that Christ, although divine, was created by God as the first creature.

In a seemingly well-researched book, *Isaac Newton: The Last Sorcerer* by Michael White, much information can be found on Isaac Newton, the 'man' himself. White states:

> He [Newton] reasoned that because God's work and God's word came from the same Creator, then Nature and Scripture were also one and the same. Scripture was a communicable manifestation or interpretation of Nature, and as such could be viewed as a blueprint for life – a key to all meaning. He also reached conclusions about the theological detail. He believed in the literal truth of the Creation story – that the world was made in seven days by a divine hand – but he qualified this with an ingenious addendum. Nowhere in the Scriptures, he reasoned, does it say that all seven days were of equal length: because during the first two days there was no Earth and therefore no twenty-four-hour day based upon planetary rotation, the length of a 'day' could be anything the Lord wished.
>
> *Isaac Newton: The Last Sorcerer*

Maynard Keynes, in his famous speech for the tercentenary celebrations of Newton's birth, also referred to Newton's belief, stating, 'He regarded the universe as a cryptogram set by the Almighty.'

What is perhaps not as readily recognised, however, is Newton's profound and lengthy involvement in alchemy. At the time of his death, his library contained 169 books on alchemy and chemistry (138 were considered 'pure alchemy', while 31 others are categorised as 'chemistry' texts), including works by some of the most important names in the history of the subject. It has been said that Newton possessed the finest and most extensive collection of alchemical texts ever accumulated up to his day – he left behind over a million words on the subject of alchemy. The late American scholar, Betty Jo Dobbs, produced a vast body of titles providing a detailed analysis of Newton's alchemical experiments in two academic titles, *The Foundations of Newton's Alchemy (1975)* and *The Janus Faces of Genius: The Role of*

Alchemy in Newton's Thought (1991). Others have begun to analyse his vast collection of writings on biblical prophecy and his ideas on a range of subjects from astrology to numerology.

As a further interesting comment on this, Michael White maintains that, 'it is also quite likely that the apple story was a later fabrication, or at least an exaggeration designed for a specific purpose – almost certainly to suppress the fact that much of the inspiration for the theory of gravity came from his subsequent alchemical work.'

Stephen Hawking on God

It is interesting to note that neither Stephen Hawking nor Albert Einstein found their theories and conclusions contrary to the concept of an omniscient entity, a God in other words. In Stephen Hawking's *A Briefer History of Time,* you can find many a reference to God (though openly he is rather ambiguous of what he exactly believes in or does not believe in):

> God may have originally decreed the laws of nature, but it appears that He has since left the universe to evolve according to them and does not now intervene in it.

> At the big bang and other singularities, all the laws would have broken down, so God would still have had complete freedom to choose what happened and how the universe began.

Stephen Hawking ends *A Briefer History of Time* beautifully when he speaks of a 'complete theory' and in so doing refers to God. He states:

> If we do discover a complete theory, it should in time be understandable in broad principle by everyone, not just the few scientists. Then we shall all, philosophers, scientists and just ordinary people, be able to take part in the discussion of the question of why it is that we and the universe exist. If we find the answer to that, it would be the ultimate triumph of human reason – for then we would know the mind of God.

A Briefer History of Time

Einstein, a student of philosophy including that of Kant and other metaphysicians, according to Hawking, once asked the pertinent question, 'How much choice did God have in constructing the universe?'

Einstein and God

One sound bite that is often trotted out is that Einstein believed in no personal God. However, like everything else, it needs to be taken in context. He was an exceptionally spiritual and contemplative person whose thoughts on such matters transcended the doctrines of religious systems.

Einstein summarised his own attitude to God and atheism by a distinction between organised religions and a God of 'cosmic harmony'. He stated:

> I have repeatedly said that in my opinion the idea of a personal God is a childlike one. You may call me agnostic, but I do not share the crusading spirit of the professional atheist whose fervour is mostly due to a painful act of liberation from the fetters of religious indoctrination received in youth.

He said that he believed in 'Spinoza's God', who reveals himself in the harmony of all that exists, but not in a God who concerns himself with the fate and actions of human beings. Instead, he embraced what he described as 'cosmic religion', a worship of the harmony and beauties of nature. He thought that it was very difficult to elucidate this feeling to anyone without it, and that the religious geniuses of all ages have been distinguished by this kind of feeling, which knows no dogma or God conceived in man's image; so that there can be no church whose central teachings are based on it. In this sense, Einstein advocated Buddhism, as based more on experience of natural and spiritual things, rather than on theology:

> Buddhism has the characteristics of what would be expected in a cosmic religion for the future; it transcends a personal God, avoids dogmas and theology; it covers both the natural and the spiritual, and

11

it is based on a religious sense aspiring from the experience of all things, natural and spiritual, as a meaningful unity.

According to the testimony of Prince Hubertus of Lowenstein, stated in his book *Towards a Further Shore* (and quoted in *Einstein: Life and Times* by Ronald W. Clarke), Einstein is also reported to have said, 'In view of such harmony in the cosmos which I, with my limited human mind, am able to recognise, there are yet people who say that there is no God. But what really angers me is that they quote me for the support of such view.' In this remark, Einstein dissociates himself entirely from atheism.

In his book, *The World As I See It*, Einstein emphasises his experience of the sense of mystery at the heart of true belief, something that cannot be penetrated:

> The fairest thing that we can experience is the mysterious. It is the fundamental emotion which stands at the cradle of true art and true science. He who knows it not and can no longer wonder, no longer feel amazement, is as good as dead, a snuffed out candle. It was the experience of mystery – even if mixed with fear – that engendered religion. A knowledge of the existence of something we cannot penetrate, of the manifestations of the profoundest reason and the most radiant beauty which are only accessible to our reason in their most elementary forms – it is this knowledge and emotion that constitute the truly religious attitude; in this sense, and in this alone, I am a deeply religious man. I cannot conceive of a God who rewards and punishes his creatures, or has a will of the type of which we are conscious in ourselves.
>
> *The World As I See It*

Einstein embraced what he described as a 'cosmic religion', which transcended a personal God and religious system but was not dismissive of an omniscient entity of God. Indeed, he stated that 'I cannot prove to you that there is no personal God, but if I were to speak of him, I would be a liar. I do not believe in a personal God of theology who rewards good and punishes evil. My God created laws that take care of that. His universe is not ruled by wishful thinking, but by immutable laws.' He also suggested that, 'The doctrine of a personal God interfering with natural events could never be refuted, in the real sense, by science, for this doctrine can always take refuge in those domains in which scientific knowledge has not yet been able to set foot.'

This lack of dismissal of an omniscient entity may be found in the following extracts from *The New Quotable Einstein* on various aspects of Einstein's personal beliefs:

Science and religion

Science without religion is lame, religion without science is blind.

Everyone who is seriously involved in the pursuit of science becomes convinced that a spirit is manifest in the laws of the universe, one that is partly superior to that of man ... In this way the pursuit of science leads to a religious feeling of a special sort, which is indeed quite different from the religiosity of someone more naïve.

God's creation

I can, if the worst comes to the worst, still realise that God may have created a world in which there are no natural laws. In short, chaos. But that there should be statistical laws with definite solutions, i.e., laws that compel God to throw the dice in each individual case, I find highly disagreeable.

In the beginning (if there was such a thing), God created Newton's laws of motion together with the necessary masses and forces. This is all; everything beyond this follows from the development of appropriate mathematical methods by means of deduction.

When I am judging a theory, I ask myself whether, if I were God, I would have arranged the world in such a way.

I want to know how God created this world. I am not interested in this or that phenomenon, in the spectrum of this or that element. I want to know his thoughts.

On his personal life

Strenuous intellectual work and the study of God's nature are the angels that will lead me through all the troubles of this life with consolation, strength, and uncompromising rigour.

My own career was undoubtedly determined not by my own will, but by various factors over which I have no control, primarily those mysterious glands in which nature prepares the very essence of life.

Belief and atheism

I cannot conceive of a personal God who would directly influence the actions of individuals ... My religiosity consists of a humble admiration of the infinitely superior spirit that reveals itself in the little that we can comprehend of the global world. That deeply emotional conviction of the presence of a superior reasoning power, which is revealed in the incomprehensible universe, forms my idea of God.

Everything is determined ... by forces over which we have no control. It is determined for the insect as well as for the star. Human beings,

Albert Einstein (1879–1955).

vegetables, or cosmic dust – we all dance to a mysterious tune, intoned in the distance by an invisible piper.

Mere unbelief in a personal God is no philosophy at all.

I am not an atheist. I do not know if I can define myself as a pantheist. The problem is far too vast for our limited minds.

On the Bible

I often read the Bible, but its original text has remained beyond my reach.

No one can read the Gospels without feeling the actual presence of Jesus. His personality pulsates in every word. No myth is filled with such life.

The New Quotable Einstein

Dawkins' delusion

One reason for introducing these extracts from Einstein (of which there are many others) is to illustrate the range of views he held about an omniscient entity and, in particular, to vehemently oppose the assertion made by Richard Dawkins in his book, *The God Delusion,* that 'Einstein was using "God" in a purely metaphorical, poetic sense.'

Richard Dawkins also accuses Stephen Hawking of slipping into the language of religious metaphor. The many examples presented above surely indicate otherwise. Einstein was a deeply contemplative individual, as can be seen from his *The World As I See It,* who had a firm grasp of his own spirituality, as well as a sense of and a belief in an omniscient entity. It is difficult to understand why Richard Dawkins, therefore, should assert so emphatically that Einstein did not believe in a God and that his references were purely 'metaphorical'.

Richard Dawkins is best known as a popular science writer, he is also the Charles Simonyi Professor for the Public Understanding of Science at Oxford University and a fellow of New College. He was catapulted into fame in 1976 with the publication of his book, *The Selfish*

Gene. Dawkins is an evolutionary biologist and has based his success on the emphatic adherence to this doctrine, and to the negation and dismissal of all other possibilities, especially that of creationism and the existence of an omniscient entity or God.

Richard Dawkins' recent *The God Delusion* (2006), quite apart from being often superficial, even arrogant in tone, at times does not at all make the point of a non-existent God. Instead his main thrust is to cling to the content of Darwin's *The Origin of Species* as the basis of his argument. This may be acceptable, but his frame of reference for such a text is narrow and, as is the case among some academics, his view is rather blinkered by the subject matter.

Most disconcerting, however, is that where following the theory of evolution and natural selection fails, he has conjured up his very own 'science' described as 'memes'. He coined the term 'meme' and it was publicised in 1976 in *The Selfish Gene*. The meme is defined as 'a unit of cultural transmission, or a unit of imitation'. This essentially contends that a cultural item is transmitted by repetition in a way similar to the biological transmission of genes, an extension of Darwinian principles to explain the spread of ideas and cultural phenomena, and that memes also evolve by natural selection. One of the difficulties with memes is what exactly constitutes one unit of cultural transmission. Dawkins apparently invented the name when he was seeking a monosyllabic word that sounded a bit like 'gene'. Particularly fascinating is that his theory is no more than the element of conjecture which he accuses religion, religious texts and the existence of a God of having!

This attitude manifests itself very early in the book when he asks us to take Einstein's references to God as merely metaphorical (as discussed above). If Einstein refers to his God, how can Dawkins suggest otherwise? Just to reiterate the extract from Einstein shown above: 'In view of such harmony in the cosmos which I, with my limited human mind, am able to recognise, there are yet people who say that there is no God. But what really angers me is that they quote me for the support of such view.' Why should Dawkins make his point that we should not believe in that which is, according to him, unsubstantiated but at the same time propose that we should take up his own arguments which, in my view, lack substance and convincing evidence and are often contradictory.

Nevertheless, in the book he does unintentionally help to point out the gaps in Darwin's theory and enable the location of more. So, whilst the book may be often laborious to read, it does emphasise the shakiness of Darwin's theory.

But the irony here is that Dawkins and his consistent following of Darwinism as the only possible solution is now revealed as nothing short of a 'faith' itself. It is, in fact, a belief in the *absence* of an omniscient entity - which has no empirical evidence to support it.

Stuck with Darwin's Evolution?

Charles Darwin's *The Origin of Species* appeared in 1859, some 30 years after he took his degree and embarked on a five-year voyage on HMS *Beagle* as a naturalist. The majority of his life was occupied with publishing his findings on the voyage and documenting his theory on the transmutation of species. The sum total of this research found its form in his book, which asserted that species evolved through natural selection. It seems nothing short of ironic that the theory of evolution, whilst it has been 'firmed up' by some disciplines, has not particularly evolved over the approximately 150 years since it was first published. What is particularly amazing is that it has become a definitive, factual assertion included in the traditional educational system of our formative years. There is absolutely no alternative or deviation from this course allowed.

All this is as a consequence of a man who was fraught with doubt and went to great lengths to describe his work as theory, in the most literal of terms. In his introduction to *The Origin of Species*, Darwin writes:

> After five years' of work I allowed myself to speculate on the subject ... My work is now nearly finished ... This abstract, which I now publish, must necessarily be imperfect ... No doubt errors will have crept in ... I can here give only the general conclusions.

On further reading there seems to be some confusion regarding species and varieties in nature, as evidenced in Chapter 2, *Variation under Nature*: 'No one definition has yet satisfied all naturalists; yet every naturalist knows vaguely what he means when he speaks of a species ... The term "variety" is almost equally difficult to define.'

Darwin, however, provides many of the doubts himself. There is an entire chapter dedicated to *'Difficulties on Theory'* – in *Organs of extreme perfection and complication,* for instance, he notes one such difficulty:

> To suppose that the eye, with all its inimitable contrivances for adjusting the focus to different distances, for admitting different amounts of light, and for the correction of spherical and chromatic aberration, could have been formed by natural selection, seems, I freely confess, absurd in the highest possible degree.

This individual and his work, which rocked the religious foundations of the time and continues to do so today, even refers to 'the Creator' concerning the eye.

> Have we any right to assume that the Creator works by intellectual powers like those of man? ... Further, we must suppose that there is a power always intently watching each slight accidental alteration in the transparent layers; and carefully selecting each alteration which, under varied circumstances, may in any way, or in any degree, tend to produce a distincter image ... and may we not believe that a living optical instrument might have been formed as superior to one of glass, as the works of the Creator to those of man?
>
> *The Origin of Species*

In *Summary of chapter* of the above extract, Darwin comments: 'We have in this chapter discussed some of the difficulties and objections which may be urged against my theory. Many of them are very grave.' And at the end of the following chapter titled *Instinct* he says, 'I do not pretend that the facts given in this chapter strengthened in any great degree my theory.'

Darwin's doubts within his own theory emphasise again the lack of certainty on the scientific accuracy of the Theory of Evolution, despite its being so widely accepted as the only scientific explanation of the development of life.

'On The Imperfection of the Geological Record' (Chapter 9)

These difficulties of Darwin's are further elaborated on in Chapter 9 – *On The Imperfection of the Geological Record*, which starts: 'I enumerated the chief objections which might be justly urged against the views maintained in this volume.'

Darwin despaired at the imperfection of the geological record and fossiliferous evidence to support his theory, as geological strata evidence did not confirm it. He goes on to say:

> But I do not pretend that I should ever have suspected how poor a record of the mutations of life, the best preserved geological section presented, had not the difficulty of our not discovering innumerable transitional links between the species which appeared at the commencement and close of each formation pressed so hardly on my theory' and also in the section *'On the sudden appearance of groups of Allied Species in the lowest known fossiliferous strata.* There is another and

Charles Robert Darwin (1809–1882).

allied difficulty, which is much graver...To the question why we do not find the records of these vast primordial periods, I can give no satisfactory answer.

In *Forbidden Archaeology: The Hidden History of the Human Race* by Michael A. Cremo and Richard L. Thompson, the point of the incompleteness of the fossil record is further advanced. The authors state that the standard idea is that the fossil record reveals a basic history, true in outline even though not known in every detail. But that this might not at all be the case. Can we really say with complete certainty that humans of the modern type did not exist in distant bygone ages? They suggest that, out of the 6 million years of human life, only 100,000 years may be represented by surviving strata. In the unrecorded 5.9 million years there is time for even an advanced civilisation to have come and gone, hardly leaving a trace. This line of thought is taken up further in chapters 2 and 3.

Cremo and Thompson go on to say that Darwin's appeal to the incompleteness of the fossil record served to explain the absence of evidence supporting his theory. That it was basically a weak argument. Admittedly, many key events in the history of life have probably gone unrecorded in the surviving strata of the Earth. But while these unrecorded events might support the theory of human evolution, they might also radically contradict it.

In Chapter 12 of Darwin's text on 'Geographical Distribution' we find further 'difficulty':

> The capacity of migrating across the sea is more distinctly limited in terrestrial mammals ... But if the same species can be produced at two separate points why do we not find a single mammal common to Europe and Australia or South America? ... Undoubtedly many cases occur, in which we cannot explain how the same species could have passed from one point to the other.
>
> *The Origin of Species*

This is particularly intriguing. Graham Hancock author of *Supernatural* claims that Australia was never populated by any other hominid species and was colonised by anatomically modern humans at an astonishingly early date, possibly as early as 60,000 years ago on some estimates, and perhaps (these 'extreme' dates are hotly contested) as far back as 75,000 years ago. As well as making the immense overland journey from their home in Africa, apparently over very few generations, and perhaps even within one generation, these pioneering humans were finally obliged to mount a feat of open-ocean sailing to reach Australia from South East Asia. The mystery deepens when we realise that the earliest evidence for the presence of modern humans in South East Asia (which straddles the overland route that migrants from Africa would have had to follow) dates back less than 40,000 years – i.e. at least 20,000 years after the arrival of modern humans in Australia.

Bill Bryson in his *A Short History of Nearly Everything* suggests that Homo erectus spread across the globe with breathtaking speed. He suggests, rather amusingly, that if you take fossil evidence literally it suggests that some members of the species reached Java at about the same time as, or even slightly before, they left Africa. (Bill Bryson won the Aventis Prize for best general science book in 2004 with *A Short History of Nearly Everything*. This is awarded by the Royal Society in the UK for science writing. This was followed in 2005 by the EU Descartes Prize for science communication. The Descartes Prize, the 'prize of prizes' is named in honour of the mathematician and philosopher René Descartes.)

On this subject of migration, there is contradiction among scientific theorists. There was, and still remains, the 'multi-regional hypothesis', proffered in the 1930s, versus the recent single-origin hypothesis or 'out of Africa' theory, which was initiated in the 1990s with the advent of archaeogenetics. Both hold true today depending on which paleoanthropologist one might speak to.

There is further contention regarding time-lines. As Cremo and Thompson explain in *Forbidden Archaeology*:

Even today there are many gaps in the presumed record of human descent. For example, there is an almost total absence of fossils linking the Miocene apes with the Pliocene ancestors of modern apes and ancestral humans, especially within the span of time between 4 and 8 million years ago. Perhaps it is true that fossils will someday be found that fill the gaps. Yet, and this is extremely important, there is no reason to suppose that the fossils that turn up will be supportive of evolutionary theory.

21

Another area in which Darwin's theory stumbles is that of the occurrence of homosexuality. As Richard Dawkins comments, 'Obviously there is no difficulty in explaining the Darwinian advantage of sexual behaviour. It is about making babies, even on those occasions where contraception or homosexuality seems to belie it.'

Although such simplicity is typical of Dawkins, he does, however, have a point. Darwin – natural selection, survival of the fittest for the purposes of procreation – how then are there a seemingly increased number of homosexuals and, if not increased, why do they exist at all today?

The missing links

In Darwin's last chapter, *Recapitulation and Conclusion,* he voices some of the doubts he had on the absence of links between the living and now extinct species and the lack of any scientific evidence of this in the fossilised geological formations:

> That many and grave objections may be advanced against the theory of descent with modification of the natural selection, I do not deny ... On this doctrine of the extermination of an infinitude of connecting links, between the living and extinct inhabitants of the world, and at each successive period between the extinct and still older species, why is not every geological formation charged with such links? Why does not every collection of fossil remains afford plain evidence of the gradation and mutation of the forms of life? We meet with no such evidence, and this is the most obvious and forcible of the many objections which may be urged against my theory. Why, again, whole groups of allied species appear, though certainly they often falsely appear, to have come in and suddenly on the several geological stages? ... For certainly on my theory such strata must somewhere have been deposited at these ancient and utterly unknown epochs in the world's history.

> I can answer these questions and grave objections only on the supposition that the geological record is far more imperfect than most geologists believe.

> *The Origin of Species*

New doubts on Darwin

Modern commentators have added to these doubts. Even the world renowned palaeoanthropologist, Louis B. Leakey, said in answer to a question about the missing link in 1967, 'There is no one link missing - there are hundreds of links missing.' Leakey unswervingly upheld Darwin's theory of evolution and was assiduous in his endeavour to prove that man originated in Africa. Despite this 'evolutionist' stance, Leakey was a religious man and a Christian who said, 'Nothing that I have ever found has contradicted the Bible. It's people with their finite minds who misread the Bible.'

An independent researcher and author, Alan Alford, has posed valid questions regarding this subject. On mankind's mutations over six million years, he is scathing in his comments:

> How do we explain the two percent, but significant, difference between man and chimpanzee, this split which occurred five–seven million years ago according to 'experts'. The same percentage difference exists between dog and wolf and the animals are very similar, there is more genetic difference between a zebra and a horse, a dolphin and a porpoise, how can our two percent account for so many 'value added' features in mankind.
>
> *Gods of the New Millennium*

> It is impossible to pinpoint a single example of a species (of which there are some 30 million on earth today) which has recently (within the last half a million years) improved by mutation or divided into two species. Yet mankind is supposed to have benefited from several macro mutations in the course of six million years.
>
> *(Ibid.)*

On the missing link in the theory of evolution, he points out further inconsistency in the disappearance of Homo erectus in other parts of the world:

> Approximately 1.5 million years ago, Homo erectus appeared on the scene with a larger cranium that its predecessors. Fossils indicate that Homo erectus left Africa and spread across China, Australasia and Europe between 1,000,000–700,000 years ago. However, they seemed

23

to have disappeared around 300,000–200,000 years ago. This should be from where Homo sapiens descended. Where is the missing link?

(Ibid.)

Mankind's use of tools is not seen as convincing evidence of the development of human intelligence:

Why did Homo sapiens develop intelligence and self-awareness while their ape cousins remained stagnant over the last 6 million years? The response is generally the use of tools. However, despite kangaroos, vultures, and some chimps employing tools, there is no sign of them developing to anywhere near the same degree.

(Ibid.)

Alan Alford also raises the question of why the human brain developed its capacity to such a high level of size and complexity.

Where is the competition to cause the human brain to evolve to such an extreme level of size and complexity? Perhaps Neanderthal man, however there is much evidence that Homo sapiens and Neanderthals co-existed in proximity and peacefully.

(Ibid.)

The appearance of Homo sapiens is not consistent with the understanding of evolution as a slow and gradual process: after millions of years of negligible progress with stone tools, Homo sapiens emerged 200,000 years ago with a 50% increase in cranial capacity, speech and modern anatomy. They continued to live primitively using stone tools for another 160,000 years. 40,000 years ago they changed to modern behaviour, expanded through the globe 13,000 years ago, after another 1,000 years discovered agriculture, 6,000 years later formed great civilisations with advanced astronomical knowledge and now 6,000 years later are exploring the solar system.

(Ibid.)

Other sources of scepticism on the lack of evidence from discovered human remains have come from other authorities and authors.

Bill Bryson mentions in his book his discussion with the curator of the American Museum of Natural History in New York on the shortage of evidence pertaining to the total world archive of hominid and early human bones. The problem appears to be that, since the beginning of time, several billion human or humanlike beings have lived, each contributing a genetic variability to the total human stock. Out of this vast number, the whole of our understanding of human history is based on the often fragmentary remains of perhaps 5,000 individuals.

The curator added informally that you could fit it all into the back of a pick-up truck if you didn't mind how you jumbled it all up.

Bryson goes on to say that all Homo erectus, if brought back to life, would not fill a bus and of Homo habilis there are just 2 partial skeletons and a number of isolated limb bones. There are hominid skulls in Georgia dated to 1.7 million years ago, then a gap of almost a million years before the next turns up in Spain, then another 300,000 years before Homo heidelbergensis in Germany and none of them look much like the other. It is from these kinds of fragmentary pieces of evidence that we are trying to work out the entire history of the species; some don't deserve to be regarded as a separate species at all.

In a similar way to the doubts expressed about the missing link, Darwin called the origin of flowering plants 'an abominable mystery'. The 'missing link' between these and the primitive non-flowering asexual plant has never been found, nor identified.

Despite the criticism of his theory, I find in Darwin, and from his comments given above, a man of doubt, modesty and honesty. He would surely have been, at very least, bemused at the notion that his theories, imperfect as they were, and by his own admission, now form an integral, uncompromising and definitive foundation of our education today with little advance on his theory and the same enduring initial objections raised against it.

DNA – friend or foe?

In interviewing a professor of Kings College, London, on this subject, he admitted that there were gaps in the Theory of Evolution but that science had since, to a degree, firmed up the theory. My response was,

'Perhaps, but it is the gaps that I am writing about.'

Francis Crick was a Nobel Laureate and co-discoverer of the structure of DNA. This discovery of DNA was confirmed in the 1980s, after some 25 years during which the model of DNA went from being plausible to being virtually correct according to Crick. While this book does not agree with the following theory, it is interesting to note that Crick did not relate DNA to evolution at all, but suggested the concept of 'panspermia', that the Earth was 'deliberately seeded with life by intelligent aliens'. Crick also asserted of DNA that the organised complexity found at the cellular level 'cannot have arisen by pure chance.'

Crick and his co-discoverer James Watson determined that the structure of DNA was a double-helix polymer in the shape of a spiral staircase or twisted rope ladder, consisting of two DNA strands wound around each other.

There is still much to learn about DNA, which carries the genetic information of a cell and consists of thousands of genes. However, some ninety-seven or ninety-eight per cent of our DNA consists of meaningless 'garble' without apparent function. These sections are

Representation of the DNA structure.

known as 'junk DNA' or 'non-coding DNA'. Along the strands of DNA are occasional sections that control and organise vital functions and these are called genes.

Genes are basically the instructions to make proteins which perform important tasks for cell functions or serve as building blocks for the cell. The combination of genes is known as the human genome, which is effectively an instruction manual for the human body. The configuration of the DNA molecule is highly stable and allows for it to replicate new DNA molecules. It does so by separating into two single strands, each of which serves as a template for a new strand.

However, it seems that the Theory of Evolution finds neither a friend nor support in the much heralded science of today, that of DNA. As Jeremy Narby writes in *The Cosmic Serpent*, 'DNA is self-duplicating and transmits its information to proteins, biologists concluded that information could not flow back from proteins to DNA; therefore, genetic variation could only be from *errors* in the duplication process.'

These mutations, a mistake during the replication process, seem to belie the intention of natural selection or an exact and progressive science of evolution. Narby goes on to quote the microbiologist James Shapiro:

> In fact there are no detailed accounts for the evolution of any fundamental biochemical or cellular system, only a variety of wishful speculations. It is remarkable that Darwinism is accepted as a satisfactory explanation for such a vast subject – evolution – with so little rigorous examination of how well its basic theses work in illuminating specific instances of biological adaptation or diversity.

DNA mutations are generally mistakes, failures of the DNA to accurately copy information. They are usually neutral or negative. It seems that it is not the primary mechanism that it needs to be – rather like the dynamic forces of natural selection in evolutionist theory.

Michael Behe, in his *Darwin's Black Box*, introduces the notion that many of the complex biochemical systems found in living organisms are irreducibly complex. The inference is that these systems are far too complex to have evolved from simpler or less complete precursors via natural selection. The contention is that they would have had to have been as fully functionally complex as they are now and could not have arisen from simpler beginnings. He suggests that Darwin realised that his theory of gradual evolution by natural selection carried a heavy burden. Darwin stated that, 'If it could be demonstrated that any complex organ existed which could not possibly have been formed by numerous, successive, slight modifications, my theory would absolutely break down.'

Behe uses the mousetrap to explain his concept. A mousetrap consists of several interacting pieces – the base, the catch, the spring, the hammer which would come down on the mouse. Behe's contention is that each of these parts is essential for the mousetrap to work, that no part can be effective on its own and that the removal of any one part makes the mousetrap entirely ineffective. This is analogous to biological systems which require multiple parts working together in order to function. The claim is that natural selection could not create, from scratch, those systems for which science is unable to find a viable evolutionary pathway of successive, slight modifications, because the selectable function is only present when all parts are fully assembled. Five phenomena, blood clotting, cilia, the human immune system, transport of materials within cells and the synthesis of nucleotides, are all systems that are so irreducibly complex that no gradual step-by-step Darwinian route could have led to their creation.

Bill Bryson has also written on this matter; he states that DNA is particularly unimpressive as evidence for the evolution of man. The amount of genetic material and how it is organised does not reflect the level of sophistication of the human species. We, as a species, have 46 chromosomes, but some ferns have 600. The lungfish, which is one of the least evolved of all complex animals, actually has 40 times as much DNA as we have. The Human Genome Project thought that we possessed some 100,000 genes however, it was very disappointing that the number is more like 35/40,000 genes, just about the same as grass.

Indeed, human DNA shows signs of having passed through an extremely long and peaceful evolution, which is inconsistent with an evolutionary split from the apes some 6 million years ago. Relating these comments on DNA to the complexity of the eye, Darwin himself was confounded by the fact that the intricate biochemistry must exist in a complete state and the complex biochemistry of vision cannot be reduced to its component parts.

It is not my intention here to refute Darwin's claims, nor the scientific tenets previously discussed. I think that they should be viewed as feasible and, in context relevant, but should certainly not taken as absolute. However, to hear some scientists speak, one could be led to believe that they are absolute fact. As Einstein suggested, one should rely on one's own knowledge: 'Let every man judge according to his own standards, by what he has himself read, not by what others tell him.' And that, of course, includes this book: there are enough sources cited that the reader can seek confirmation for themselves and to their own satisfaction.

Summary

In my view, science is less than convincing in terms of forming a world view that one can take to heart and, indeed, to mind. Whilst not dismissing the scientific tenets given here, I do not believe that we can firmly and solely rely on science or scientific explanation to settle any questions that we might have. These scientific tenets do not comfortably provide us with the understanding of the origins of our existence, nor satisfactorily explain our physical environment. Science seems to be lacking the conviction and absoluteness that it, on many occasions, professes to provide.

Concerning the divide between the evolutionists and the creationists it is clear that Einstein and particularly Newton were interested in metaphysics. Newton was, without doubt, a creationist and a 'deeply religious man'. Albert Einstein and Stephen Hawking, despite what constitutes their beliefs, have certainly often considered and referred to God. Even Darwin refers to 'the Creator'.

The Big Bang theory does not provide explanation of what existed *prior* to the Big Bang.

The Theory of Gravity is inconsistent with the Theory of General Relativity which in turn is inconsistent with quantum theory.

Quantum theory was derived from the Theory of Relativity which was initiated by Einstein; yet Einstein, despite winning a Nobel Prize for his contribution to quantum theory, could not embrace this theory.

In the endeavour to unify the Theory of Relativity with quantum theory, the answer may well be found in various string theories. However, this theory only really works out of the context and knowledge of our normal four dimensional existence and necessitates the consideration of many more dimensions and possibly the existence of additional universes.

It is clear that Darwin himself had doubts about the theory of evolution, raised because of the imperfection of the geological record and its lack of providing connecting links between 'living and extinct inhabitants of the world'.

The science of DNA also raises questions about the theory of evolution, considering the notion that biochemical systems are irreducibly complex – even Darwin was confounded by the complexity of the eye. In addition, replication of DNA is said to be due to random mutations, mistakes which are actually incongruent with the beneficial progressive steps that natural selection and evolution are supposed to take.

2

Anomalies in Ancient Histories

Only he who has travelled the road knows where the holes are deep.

Chinese proverb

As a further challenge to our preconceptions, this chapter will review a variety of geographical and archaeological issues which are not consistent with our traditional understanding of history. The first section deals with anomalies revealed by a study of ancient maps of continents of the world.

Who discovered America?

It is generally accepted today that Columbus's voyage in 1492 was not the first navigation across the Atlantic. The Viking Bjarni Herjolfsson discovered America by accident in approximately 985 CE. Whilst Herjolfsson did not land in America and returned to Greenland, Leif, the son of Erik the Red, did land and gave names to it such as Helluland, Markland and Vinland. The story of these and further voyages are recounted in the sagas of the Greenlanders and of Erik the Red.

There is also a controversial theory, supported by DNA evidence, that the Clovis, a prehistoric Native American culture dated approximately to 13,000 years ago, found their origins in an ancient European people called the Solutrean (dating from some 21,000–15,000 years ago). These Europeans are also linked to the Clovis by similar primitive technology, for instance, spearheads made of flint and shaped by the same method of working. The suggestion is that these Europeans

31

did not cross the Bering Strait and move southward through North America but, in fact, crossed the Atlantic. This was achieved by using survival skills, moving from ice floe to ice floe and using fishing for sustenance, in a similar way to that of the Inuit people or Eskimos.

Discovery of Antarctica 6,000 years ago?

What ancient world maps can tell us
On the subject of navigation there are some particularly ancient maps in existence, the most famous being the Piri Reis world map of 1513, presently housed in the library of the Topkapi Palace Museum in Istanbul. Piri Reis was an Admiral in the Turkish fleet who claimed that he benefited from 'about twenty maps and world maps' dating back to the fourth century BCE. He stated that, 'No one up to this day and age has made a similar kind of map.' The map referred to shows, not only the western coast of Europe and Africa, but also, surprisingly, the eastern coast of Central and South America and the northern coast of Antarctica.

Unfortunately I was unable to view the original, but the map clearly shows the Falkland Islands at their correct latitude, even though these islands were not 'officially' discovered until 1592. The most fascinating aspect of the map, however, centres on its depiction of Antarctica. It was an explorer called Fabian Bellingshausen who was the first person to sight the Antarctic continent on 27 January 1820. So the map of 1513 shows Antarctica some 300 years before this continent was officially discovered.

Even more interesting is that the lower part of the map portrays the Princess Martha Coast of Queen Maud Land, Antarctica, although the accuracy of the geographical detail can only be confirmed in our age by seismic survey technology. This shows that the coast was mapped in some way *prior* to the ice-cap, which is up to two miles deep in places today. Geographical evidence confirms that the last date that Queen Maud Land was ice free was 4,000 BCE and quite possibly earlier. Therefore the question must be asked, which cartographer existed some 6,000 years ago to provide a map of such amazing accuracy? Seismic technology and survey is a powerful tool, which detects what is below the earth's surface. It was first used in the 1920s and employs sound waves that reflect from underground rock layers, providing a vision into the earth. The recorded data then creates two-dimensional maps.

The Piri Reis map is not a hoax and, indeed, further maps exist to support this anomaly, such as the Oronteus Finnaeus map of 1531 which shows the entirety of Antarctica and depicts bays without ice and mountains that now lie under the ice-cap. There is also the 1737 map of Antarctica by Phillip Bauche, which shows the continent as two islands. Geologists maintain that it has been millions of years since the entire continent was free of ice; again it is only with the advent of seismology that, whilst we once thought of Antarctica as one continent, we now know that that it is made up of two land masses under a rather thick covering of ice. This impacts on Darwin's Theory of Evolution in that, if thousands of years ago we were supposedly an unevolved species, how then could the knowledge and ability to map at these times and with such accuracy have existed?

A full account of these and other such maps can be best found in Charles Hapgood's book, *Maps of the Ancient Sea Kings*, published in 1966. Charles Hapgood is also known for his work on earth crust displacement, which was endorsed by Einstein. This was a radical theory in its day and in an initial response to Hapgood's *Earth's Shifting Crust*, Einstein wrote, 'I find your arguments very impressive and have the impression that your hypothesis is correct. One can hardly doubt that significant shifts of the earth's crust have taken place repeatedly and within a short time.' Until the geological revolution of the 1960s – that of continental drift and plate tectonics – Hapgood's theory had not been taken seriously by the scientific fraternity. However, these two theories mentioned above are not entirely at variance with each other.

Einstein and Hapgood continued with their correspondence and met in 1955. Einstein wrote in the foreword to Hapgood's *Earth's Shifting Crust: A Key to Some Basic Problems of Earth Science*.

I frequently receive communications from people who wish to consult me concerning their unpublished ideas. It goes without saying that these ideas are very seldom possessed of scientific validity. The first communication, however, that I received from Mr. Hapgood electrified me. His idea is original, of great simplicity, and – if it continues to prove itself – of great importance to everything that is related to the history of the earth's surface ... I think that this rather astonishing, even fascinating, idea deserves the serious attention of anyone who concerns himself with the theory of the earth's development.

Unfortunately Hapgood lost a formidable champion for his work with the death of Einstein in 1955.

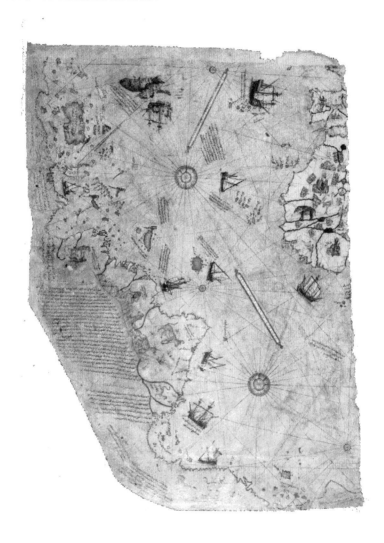

The Piri Reis Map of 1513.

Megalithic structures of antiquity

Megalithic, meaning made of or marked by large stones, features in many of the structures of cultures of antiquity around the globe. In many instances, it is quite remarkable that stones so large were used when smaller, more manageable ones would have sufficed.

The crane used for the lifting of heavy loads is known to have been invented by the Greeks in 6 BCE. However, information obtained at the Institute of Mechanical Engineers, London (and confirmed by many crane hire companies and two large construction companies in Dubai) shows that, while there are specialist cranes that are capable of lifting a greater weight, the average tower crane, as used on any building site and which builds our multi-storey buildings, can lift up to 19 tons. By contrast, the smallest ancient megaliths are at least an estimated 50 tons.

Sizes and weights of ancient megaliths around the world

All the ancient megaliths are of enormous size and in estimated weight vary from about 50 to over 1,000 tons, depending on the country and the site. Their forms range from massive building blocks, as in the Egyptian pyramids, to blocks for ancient external walls, as in the Temple of Solomon in Jerusalem, to gigantic statues, as in Easter Island.

Africa
In Axum in Ethiopia, there is a granite obelisk which stands upright and weighs 300 tons. It was a symbol of power of the Axumite (or Aksumite) kingdom established more than 2,000 years ago.

South America
In Peru a most impressive and beautiful site called Sacsayhuaman, the 'fortress' as it is referred to by some, is made up of many polygonal blocks which sit so precisely with their neighbours that the point of my penknife could not fit between them. The largest of the stone blocks making up the external wall is 28 ft in height and approximately 350 tons

Megaliths at Sacsayhuaman, Peru.

Megaliths at Ollantaytambo, Peru.

in weight. There are also impressively large stone blocks to be found at Machu Picchu. However, at another site, that of Ollantaytambo, you can find granite stone slabs weighing between 100 and 200 tons.

In Bolivia at Puma Punka, near the site of Tiahuanaco, which is thought to date back to 10,000 to 15,000 BCE, there exist two sandstone blocks estimated to weigh between 200 and 300 tons, and also a number of stones weighing from 100 to 150 tons, with one in particular weighing approximately 440 tons. There are also stones on this site that have extremely precise (though for unfathomable reasons) grooves and niches, in addition to tiny holes which can only be described as 'drilled'.

South Pacific

On Easter Island there are some 887 anthropomorphic Moai statues carved from volcanic rock, the largest being known as 'The Giant', which is 21.6 m high and weighs approximately 145–165 tons. The largest still in place is 9.8 m high and weighs approximately 82 tons. Moreover, there are several Moai statues, on top of which were placed crowns or top-knots, the largest being 1.8 m high and weighing approximately 11 tons.

Europe: UK

At Stonehenge in Wiltshire, which dates back to approximately 2,200 BCE, the linteled circle consists of sarsen stones some 20 ft tall and weighing up to 50 tons which were transported from 20 miles away. Another impressive site is at Avebury where, unlike Stonehenge, the local stones of the Avebury Circles (c. 2,600–2,100 BCE) are of natural unworked stone and weigh up to 20 tons and are 23ft or 7m long. And if you thought that Britain was devoid of pyramid-like structures you would be mistaken as there is Silbury Hill in Wiltshire, the largest man-made prehistoric mound in Europe. It is conical in shape and covers five acres, is 130 ft tall and 100 ft across its flat top and dates back to c. 2,660 BCE. It is much the same size as some of the smaller pyramids in Egypt.

India

In Orissa state, in the village of Konark, sits the Black Pagoda which has a capstone that weighs approximately 1,000 tons.

Megaliths of Stonehenge, Wiltshire, Britain.

Middle East

Within the Temple of Jerusalem (also known as the Temple of Solomon), dating back several centuries before Christ, of which only the western wall now remains, there are stone blocks ranging in weight from between 5 and 50 tons. The most spectacular of all, however, I accessed via the Western or Wailing Wall Tunnels where, at the base of the structure, there are huge stone blocks that are approximately 42 ft long, 11 ft high and 13 ft thick with a weight estimated at between 400 and 600 tons each.

In Egypt, the Great Pyramid at Giza is made up of over 2 million individual stones with a combined weight of approximately 6 million tons. Some of the stones are some 12 ft long and 6 ft thick with an estimated weight of approximately 200 tons. The pyramid rises to a height of over 450 ft and the conventional assertion that it took some twenty years to build would suggest that it required laying one block of stone every two minutes. Considering the complexity of the structure this defies belief. No description can do justice to the scale and immensity of it and it should be viewed with one's own eyes.

The Wailing (Western) Wall Tunnels, beneath the remaining Western Wall
in Jerusalem. This photograph shows a recreation of the Temple, behind is the
tunnel itself. In the lit area of the tunnel you see one of several large megaliths
below smaller rocks which constitute the original wall of the Temple.

It was on my third visit to Egypt that I went to see the Colossi of
Memnon, which consists of two large statues depicting the Pharaoh
Amenhotep III made out of one large stone that stands 65 ft high and
weighs approximately 1,000 tons. There are further examples in Egypt
which include the obelisk of Thutmosis I at Karnak, weighing
approximately 140 tons, and the Osireion at Abydos, which consists of
100 ton blocks.

In Lebanon, whilst visiting Phoenician and other sites, I went to a
location named Baalbeck where there is the Temple of Jupiter that dates
back approximately 5,000 years. Above several layers of carved stone
blocks and not at the base, which suggests elevation, there is what is
known as the 'Trilithon', three large stones weighing between 600 and
800 tons each. However, less than a mile away from the site is a fourth
megalith, for some reason unused, which is some 80 ft in length and
weighs around 1,100 tons. It is rather humbling to stand on the largest
hewn rock in the world.

As discussed at the beginning of the section, cranes today would
have great difficulty in moving such objects from a quarry to their

Sphinx with the Great Pyramid in the background.

present location and, in some instances, near impossible to transport such stones even using the technology available to us today. The traditional explanation for the ability to construct such edifices is man-power; however, many of the weights described here would have crushed wooden rollers and ruined dampened earth ramps. Indeed, there have been many televised programmes in recent years which have endeavoured to re-create such achievements; none of these efforts have been particularly successful albeit attempted on a much smaller scale.

Astronomical anomalies in ancient times

Many ancient sites such as Stonehenge are aligned with the solstices and may well have served a practical purpose in addition to a spiritual one, for example, assisting agriculture with the identification of seasonal change. The Maya employed astronomy to produce their calendar which, as Graham Hancock writes in his book, *Heaven's Mirror,*

Is a work of immense complexity, incorporating a more accurate calculation of the length of a solar year than the modern Gregorian

40

Author stands upon the largest hewn rock in antiquity. Baalbek, Lebanon.

calendar (that we use today), an exact calculation of the period of the moon's orbit around the earth, and an exact calculation for the synodical revolution of Venus.

The start date of their long count calendar is 3,114 BCE. Officially the approximate date for the inception of these peoples is 400 BCE.

In Egypt, the three pyramids at Giza and the Nile mirror the three stars in Orion's belt, with the Nile corresponding to the Milky Way. However, as cited in *The Orion Mystery*, by Robert Bauval and Adrian Gilbert, it was at a time, due to the precession of equinoxes, dated as 10,500 BCE. The official dating of the pyramids is 2,500 BCE. The Earth goes through one complete precession cycle in a period of approximately 25,800 years, during which the positions of the stars will slowly change. The Egyptians surely, with their precision in building, would have built the structures accordingly and without 'mistake' to reflect 2,500 BCE. The Sphinx is aligned to the constellation of Leo as it rises above the

Representation of the Orion Correlation Theory.

horizon but here, again, due to the precession of equinoxes as it would have appeared over the horizon in 10,500 BCE. The precession of equinoxes is the motion of the equinoxes (the time or date, twice a year, at which the sun crosses the celestial equator) along the ecliptic (the plane of the Earth's orbit caused by the cyclic precession of the Earth's axis of rotation). As there is no evidence that the Egyptians had any knowledge of precession, what then is the significance of this date, some 8,000 years prior to the official dating of this civilisation?

This theory, known as the 'Orion Correlation Theory' (OTC), has been a recurring theme in the works of Graham Hancock and Robert Bauval, in individual works and also in the collaborative effort *Keeper of Genesis*. Above is a representation of the 'Orion Correlation Theory', where the pyramids at Giza are superimposed over a photograph of the stars in Orion's belt.

There is another point of interest relating to Sirius or the 'Dog Star', which is the brightest star in our galaxy and is found to the south east of Orion's belt. Sirius B, its neighbour, is blotted from our vision due to the brightness of A and the minute size of B. Sirius B burnt out some 30 million years ago and is known as the White Dwarf. Dwarf stars are made of dense material, Sirius B weighs about one metric ton and it was not discovered until 1926 by western astronomers. The Dogon tribe, who are located in Mali in West Africa, knew of this star some time prior to the discovery, at least hundreds of years before, the information having been passed down from generation to generation. This was initially reported by two French anthropologists, Marcel Griaule and Germaine Dieterlen, who spent 25 years with the Dogon from 1931 to 1956 and were initiated into the tribe. The two anthropologists also reported that the Dogon appeared to know of the rings of Saturn and the moons of Jupiter, which were not discovered until after the invention of the telescope in the seventeenth century.

Anomalies at other ancient sites

Mexico
Whilst the stone heads of the Olmecs at La Venta did not make it into the megalithic section of this chapter, they are worthy of note. The Olmecs were a tribe that preceded the Maya, their official existence dating from approximately 1,200 BCE to 400 BCE. What is left of their culture can best be seen at La Venta in the state of Tabasco, Mexico. The large stone heads, of which 17 have been found, are up to 9 ft tall, 22 ft in diameter and the largest weighs more than 20 tons.

In addition to the remarkable feat that it would have taken to move these stones into place, some sixty miles through jungle and swamps, the most incongruous aspect are the facial features of these heads. Their appearances are all African or Negroid in origin. Let us not forget that they were a tribe that existed prior to the Maya and significantly prior to the arrival of Columbus et al. in the New World. There is equality here, however, in that whilst no heads were found, there were a number of stelae which depict bearded men of Caucasian origin at Olmec sites.

In the *Popol Vuh*, the sacred book of the Maya, it says, 'There were then, in great number, the black men and the white men of many classes,

Two views of an Olmec head at La Venta in Tabasco, Mexico.

men of many tongues, that it was wonderful to hear them.' This merely adds to the confusion since, according to our traditional understanding, there should have been no black or white men in Central America at any point BCE or indeed prior to Columbus and Europeans in the New World, yet these images clearly point to their existence.

Did the Olmecs come from Africa?
When I was in Zimbabwe visiting the sites of antiquity there I had a quasi-epiphanic moment. I was sitting alone at a high point at Great Zimbabwe, one of their more visited locations, at the top of what is called Sorcerer's Rock, letting my mind wander as I often do at these places, and remembering previous sites visited and their similarities. Great Zimbabwe is situated in the Matopo Hills, granite country, and it dawned on me that this was perhaps a connection. Perhaps the Olmecs had originated in Africa; why else would they have traversed miles of jungle and swamp to find volcanic rock from which to sculpt their monuments. It is also interesting to note that Matopo is also spelt 'Matobo', meaning 'bald heads', and indeed I have not seen an Olmec stone head which depicted hair. Later that evening back at my hotel, I spoke to their in-house guide and produced a book which I had taken with me, *The Lost Realms* by Zecharia Sitchin, which illustrated a number of the heads and their individual features. The guide was taken

aback by what I showed him and ascribed nationalities to the heads according to their features, so convinced was he that they were African in origin. It is all a tad tenuous, I admit; however, I have yet to hear of a better possible link or explanation.

There have been a number of rather bigoted archaeologists who refuse to acknowledge the Negroid features of these heads; this is not dissimilar an attitude to that regarding the Black Pharaohs of Egypt. In a recent article on this subject in *National Geographic* magazine, February 2008, the author points out:

> The ancient world was devoid of racism ... artwork from ancient Egypt, Greece and Rome shows a clear awareness of racial features and skin tone, but there is little evidence that the darker skin was a sign of inferiority. Only after the European powers colonized Africa in the 19th century did western scholars pay attention to the colour of the Nubians' skin, to uncharitable effect.

The article goes on to say that it is only recently that archaeological thought has moved away from the declaration that 'black Africans could not have possibly constructed the monuments'. These monuments referred to are the pyramids in modern day Sudan which are 'greater in number than all of Egypt'.

Mayan Crystal skulls
Crystal Skulls of varying sizes have been found in South America and linked to the Maya. Tests on one in 1970 at Hewlett Packard's crystal laboratories in Santa Clara show it to have been made from pure and natural quartz. This particular skull would have been made from an unusually large piece of quartz; despite the cranium being detached from the jaw-bone it was proved that both pieces were made from the same piece of quartz. The anomaly is that quartz is only marginally softer than diamond, which makes it incredibly difficult to carve; in addition to which, it is brittle and has a tendency to shatter. In their book, *The Mystery of the Crystal Skulls* by Chris Morton and Ceri Louise Thomas, they point out that: 'The workmanship on the skull was so exquisite the [investigating] team estimated that even if the carvers had used today's electrically powered tools with diamond tips, it would

have taken at least a year to carve such an incredible object.' Moreover, it would have been impossible to use such a power tool on the skull since the resultant vibration would have shattered the skull. The skull showed no signs of tool markings and therefore it had to be made by hand – this would have been a slow process taking an estimated 300 years. The carvers would have had to start with a crystal three times as large as the finished skull and if they had made a mistake at any time along the way they would have had to start all over again.

A crystal skull is on display at the British Museum. Behind the glass, it appears to be the product of amazing craftsmanship: however, it is officially described as a hoax, not of great antiquity and of more modern European manufacture. In an article in the *Daily Mail*, 17 May 2008, this has since been contradicted by American experts who claim that there was evidence that ancient civilisations had also used grinding wheels for carving.

Peru: the Nazca Lines

Peru is full of sites of antiquity belonging to a series of tribes and cultures, the last of which were the Incas. In addition to the sites mentioned earlier, the Nazca Lines, some 2,000 years old, are a site to behold. On a desert plain stretching over 50 kilometres from north to south and 5 to 7 kilometres wide there are hundreds of carved straight lines, two of which are 9 kilometres long and absolutely straight (see illustration).There are also geometric patterns, such as a quadrangle some 1,600 metres long and gigantic figures including the Humming Bird, the Spider, the Condor, the Monkey and the Whale to name a few. There is one which is particularly curious called the Astronaut. This, however, does not have the same feel as the others and one wonders whether it may be 'graffiti' by someone of much more recent times. Nevertheless, my guide assured me that it was as old and by the same people as the other grand drawings.

Many experts think that there is a direct correlation between these figures and various constellations. The features on this plain, however, can only be seen in their individual entirety from the air by taking one of the tours in a small aeroplane. The scale is truly remarkable and one wonders why the Nazcans went to such lengths to produce such images on the ground when they could not see them. It should be noted that

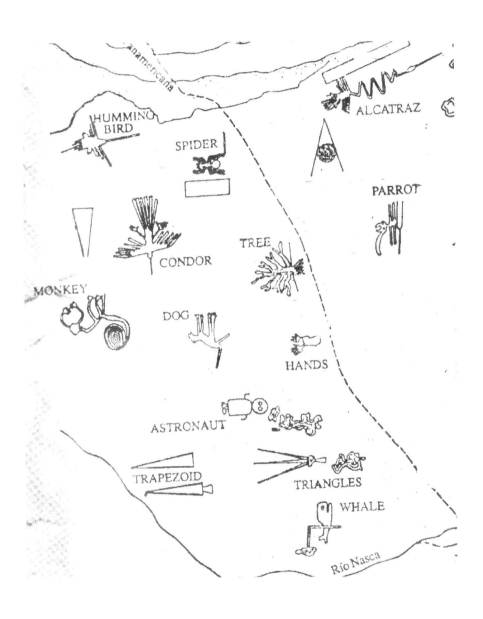

Nazca Lines, Peru.

there is no high ground in the vicinity on which one might be able to appreciate this work of such magnitude.

Lines at Malta and Gozo
There is another instance of lines or tracks, which I have also seen myself. It was on my trip to the islands of Malta and Gozo to see the officially most ancient temple sites on the globe which date from 4,000–2,500 BCE. These cart tracks are by no means as spectacular as those at Nazca, but they are strangely bizarre since they seem to go from nowhere to nowhere. Whilst they are found elsewhere in Malta, it is near the Dingli Cliffs that they are most impressive; they are nicknamed Clapham Junction due to the similarity with the busy London railway station of that name. These complex networks of tracks are several inches deep and their age and purpose are still an unsolved mystery, with explanations of erosion by ancient cart wheels or sledges or by the weather being hotly contested.

Giza, Egypt: How old is the Sphinx?
The Sphinx at Giza, mentioned previously, has one further anomaly. The structure is officially dated and attributed to the Pharaoh Khafre who ruled between 2,520 and 2,494 BCE, despite no inscription ever being found to link the two. John Anthony West and Dr Robert Schoch, a faculty member of Boston University, a Ph.D. in Geology from Yale University and also an expert on the weathering of limestone of which the Sphinx is made, disagree vehemently. The reason for this is that the Sphinx is eroded, as evidenced by vertical and horizontal fissures which are exclusively due to heavy rain over thousands of years. The difficulty revolves around the fact that Giza was as arid a land in 2,500 BCE as it is today; therefore, how can one explain such erosion? It is fact that the last time it rained sufficiently to erode the Sphinx to the extent that it has been was between 7,000 and 5,000 BCE. Author of *Serpent in the Sky*, John Anthony West, however, feels that the date could be even earlier at 10,000 or perhaps 15,000 BCE.

What did the ancient Egyptians use for illumination?
At the temple site of Dendera, where one can find the Dendera calendar, there are reliefs and transcriptions on the walls that seem to depict an

electric bulb. There can be no proof that this is the case and, indeed, the official explanation is that it is a dream representation of a lotus flower. It is interesting to note, however, that today one sees the ceilings of other temples blackened by the fires of exiled Christians who used them as temporary dwellings. In temples not used by them or in which there were no fires, however, there are no such blackened ceilings. If the Egyptians used fire such as tallow torches in the depths of the temples, why is there no longer any evidence of this?

The Dendera calendar

On Dendera I feel compelled to mention this amazing temple with its extraordinary calendar. To view the calendar, you have to walk along a number of corridors, at the end of each is a 90 degree turn taking you along another corridor and so on. Each corridor is dimly lit by a narrow window at the end allowing in a thin shaft of light, enough to see that the walls and ceiling are covered with hieroglyphs which have a strangely mesmerising effect on you. Finally, you arrive and can see the Dendera calendar carved on the uppermost platform. As I exited the room and went onto the roof of the temple into the sunlight, it came as a great surprise to me that I was several storeys high. It is as if one has been transported to that height, such was the lack of energy used to get there, due to the slightly inclined and 'hypnotic' corridors.

Ancient 'airships'?

Eric von Daniken was a proponent of extraterrestrial technology being the reason behind many of these ancient achievements. Personally, I do not support a theory whereby the technology for the remarkable feats attained by these ancient peoples were inherited from 'green men' from Mars or anywhere else extraterrestrial for that matter. However, much has been written about Unidentified Flying Objects since the Roswell UFO incident in July 1947, when mysterious wreckage was discovered in Roswell, New Mexico. The US military claimed that it was the remains of a top-secret research balloon that had crashed, whereas believers in UFOs continue to maintain that it was the wreckage of an alien spaceship.

It is interesting to note that within the Vedas, the sacred texts of the Hindu religion, written in the second century BCE, it describes 'airships' called 'vimana' at some length. The *Mahabharata*, a sacred text, describes the vimana as 'an aerial chariot with sides of iron and clad with wings'. The *Ramayana*, another sacred text, describes the vimana as a double-decked, circular aircraft with portholes and a dome which flew with the 'speed of the wind' and gave forth a 'melodious sound', a description referred to by David Childress in *Technology of the Gods*. Childress goes on to say that, in 1875, the *Vaimanika Sastra*, a fourth century BCE text written by Maharshi Bhardwaj, was rediscovered in a temple in India. The book dealt with the operation of ancient vimanas and included information on steering, precautions for long flights, protection of the airships from storms and lightning and how to switch the drive to solar energy. Vimanas were said to take off vertically and were capable of hovering in the sky.

There are further examples of this aerial activity in ancient times; King Solomon, who built the temple in Jerusalem to house the Ark of the Covenant, is written about in the *Kebra Negast*, the sacred book of the Ethiopians. King Solomon had a son with the Queen of Sheba, Menelik ancestor to Haile Selassie, who returned with his mother to Ethiopia. King Solomon would visit mother and son by flying in a 'heavenly car', asserts Childress. 'The king ... and all who obeyed his word, flew on the wagon without pain and suffering, and without sweat or exhaustion, and travelled in one day a distance which took three months to traverse.'

The Hopi people of North America spoke of the turmoil of the Third World and how:

> Some of them made a *patuwvota* [shield made of hide] and with their creative powers made it fly through the air. On this many people flew to a big city and attacked it ... soon many people of many cities and countries were making *patuwvotas* and flying on them to attack one another.
>
> *Book of the Hopi*

In Chinese mythology, the Eight Immortals, mentioned later, used 'celestial locomotion'. Finally, we come across what look very much like aeroplane models: the first instance of which, found in Colombia, were small delta-winged gold jets thought to be 1,000 years old. They have been described as bees or flying fish, to provide a couple of explanations;

however, unlike any known animal, they possess both vertical and horizontal tailfins. The second example was found in a tomb at Saqquara, Egypt in 1898. It has been dated to approximately 200 BCE and was labelled 'wooden bird model' – however, 'the bird' not only had straight wings but also a vertical tailfin.

The Bahamas: a man-made 'giant pavement'?
Off the Island of Bimini, there is approximately half a mile of limestone blocks of rectangular and polygonal shapes, many 10 to 15 ft in length, which form 'a pavement'. While some believe this to be a naturally occurring geological feature, there are those who believe that there is little doubt that the 'Bimini Road', as it is sometimes referred to, is a man-made construction, due to the proximity and arrangement of the stones and their individual shape. I have snorkelled over this site on two separate visits years apart and, to my untrained eye, I remain convinced that it is a man-made construction. There really does seem to be a human element to the location of the stones and the pattern in which they are laid out.

Similarities of mythologies in different ancient cultures

There is a great deal of similarity between the mythologies of many ancient cultures and this is discussed in greater depth in Chapter 4. In this section, we discuss how these cultures first came into being. In many ancient cultures there seems to have been a rather sudden start to their civilisations, that is to say these peoples lived or rather existed quite comfortably, close to and dependent upon nature, concerning themselves with hunting and agriculture, a way of life enhanced by the use of fire and eased by an application of knowledge of the seasons. Across the world and within most of these societies, shortly after the end of the ice-age, there seems to have been a 'spurt', when they suddenly started believing in a God or omniscient entity and felt the impulse to build large structures made up from incredibly large stones.

There are many legendary or mythological accounts where a migration of people from other countries beyond the native shores are associated with the building of these large structures on these sites.

This seems to lead to a similarity of structures in sites, sometimes thousands of miles apart, where there could have been no apparent previous communication. In certain ancient texts, accounts of these migrations often refer to the 'flood' that destroyed their own countries and where only a handful of survivors escaped.

Cambodia

With the Khmer people of Cambodia, there are many beautiful temples to be found today, for example, Angkor Wat, Angkor Thom and Bayon. It must be noted here that standing in front of a number of the Cambodian temples one could easily imagine standing in front of any one of a number of Mayan temples, such are some of the similarities in structure between these cultures who, by our traditional understanding, had no contact with each other. This sudden temple building in Cambodia was started in the ninth century CE and was continued for approximately 420 years by a succession of leaders named Jayavarman, the first of which came 'from across the sea'.

South Pacific

Nan Modal is an ancient site on the island of Pohnpei, the capital of the Federated States of Micronesia. It consists of 92 man-made islands covering 150 acres made out of basalt. The hexagonal stone logs of the major constructions are up to 25 ft in length, 25 ft high, weigh approximately 50 tons each and remain an archaeological mystery. Recent discoveries below the tidal level show that the site was occupied as early as 200 BCE. The origin of the basalt stones is unknown and the hexagonal shape is natural and not man-made. According to Graham Hancock in his book, *Heaven's Mirror*, the people of Pohnpei recount a legend that the canals separating their temples were originally dredged by a 'dragon' which offered its assistance to Olosopa and Olosipa, the two mythical founders of the city. These two were said to be 'Ani-Aramach', primordial god-kings who arrived in boats 'from a land to the West' bringing with them a 'sacred ceremony'.

On Easter Island, on which the Moai statues previously described are sited, a potent supernatural being by the name of Uoke came from a place called Hiva, a mysterious island of enormous size which had suffered a great cataclysm and was submerged below the sea. A group of some 300 survivors from Hiva then set sail to seek out the island (Easter Island). It is said in one account that a reconnaissance voyage had previously been made by seven sages to prepare the island for settlement.

Egypt

Egypt too had 'Seven Sages', depicted in the Temple of Edfu which dates back to 2,500 BCE, who allegedly fled from a far-off land, an island home of the primeval ones that had been destroyed by the flood. The task of these sages was to construct sacred mounds at key locations within Egypt. Perhaps one and the same were the Shemshu Hor, the followers of Horus, semi-divine beings who settled in the Nile Valley in the remote past, 'the early primeval age'.

From the Egyptian *Book of the Dead*, there is a reference to the 'primeval fathers and mothers' who arose from the 'Celestial Waters':

Under the influence of Thoth, or that form of divine intelligence which created the world by a word, eight elements, four male and four female, arose out of the primeval Nu [Celestial Waters]; collectively they were called 'Khemenu' or the 'Eight' and they were considered as primeval fathers and mothers.

Book of the Dead

Mexico

In Mexico there is the legend of Quetzalcoatl, as named by the Aztecs, or Kulkulcan, as described by the Maya. One should understand that the Aztecs lifted their belief system wholesale from the Maya, including the Mayan calendar, much like the Romans inherited their mythology from the Greeks.

Kulkulcan is depicted as a plumed or feathered serpent and can be found on many of the Mayan and Aztec temple sites. In this culture we also find seven individuals, as can be identified by figures found at the remote site of Dzibilchaltun and as reliefs at the temple site of EkBalam. Indeed, in the sacred book of the Maya, the *Popol Vuh*, it speaks of peoples coming from the east:

It is not quite clear, however, how they crossed the sea; they crossed to this side, as if there was no sea; they crossed on stones, placed in a row over the sand. For this reason they were called Stones in a Row, Sand under the Sea, names given to them when they crossed the sea, the waters having parted when they passed.

Popol Vuh

Might the stones referred to here be similar to the Bimini Road described previously? The text goes on to refer to the disappearance and end of 'the first men who came there from the other side of the sea, where the sun rises'.

In the *Chilam Balam*, a collection of Mayan texts, it speaks of the first inhabitants of the Yucatan, known as the Chanes, or 'people of the serpent', also having come across the water from the east in boats with their leader Zamna, also known as Itzamna, 'Serpent of the East', a healer who could cure by the laying on of hands.

The *Popol Vuh* also refers to the flood: 'Truly, they are clear examples of those people who were drowned, and their nature is that of supernatural beings.' And, as Bishop Las Casas says in his commentary on the *Popol Vuh*, 'They [the Maya] believed that certain persons who escaped the flood populated their lands, and they were called the great father and the great mother.'

North America
From the Hopi tribe of North America, the Kachina people came into the Fourth World. They were not people but spirits, having taken the form of people to give help and guidance to the other clans. The Hopi believe that the Third World was also brought to conclusion by flood. It was said in the book of the Hopi that 'waters were loosed upon the earth' and that 'waves higher than mountains rolled in upon the land. Continents broke asunder and sank beneath the seas.'

China
In Chinese culture, there are the Mythical and Legendary Kings, the first of which, Fu Hi (2953 to 2838 BCE) settled in Shensi. According to *Myths and Legends of China* this mythical cultural hero 'was the offspring of a miraculous conception, and had dealings with dragons'. Like the Babylonian Ea, a Mesopotamian deity (also known as Enki in Sumerian mythology), he instructed people how to live civilised lives. Before Fu

Hi came, 'They lived like animals ... they kept records by knotted cords, and he instructed them in the mysteries of lineal figures, which had a mystic significance ... [He] also instructed the people to worship spirits.' In some accounts of an earlier period, Fu Hi is succeeded by his sister Nu Kwa, the heroine of the flood.

Within the Taoist religion there are descriptions of the Eight Immortals (Pa Hsien), one of the most popular representations in China (their portraits are to be seen everywhere, on porcelain vases, teapots, fans, scrolls and embroidery to name only a few instances). There were initially seven however; they (the Eight Immortals) occupied seven of the eight grottos of the Upper Spheres and wished to see the eight occupied so nominated Ts'ao Kuo-chiu because 'his disposition resembled that of a genie'.

E.T.C. Werner in his book *Myths and Legends of China* discusses the *Hsiu hsiang Pa Hsien tung yu chi*, an illustrated account of the Eight Immortals' Mission to the East. Werner writes that the phrase Pa Hsien kuo hai refers to 'the Eight Immortals crossing the sea', and that 'the usual mode of celestial locomotion – by taking a seat on a cloud [reminiscent of vimanas of Indian mythology?] – was discarded by Lü Yen who recommended that they should show the infinite variety of their talents by placing things on the surface of the sea and stepping on them' (not dissimilar to the account by the Maya in the *Popol Vuh*).

Peru

In Peru, and of the Incas, there is the venerated Viracocha, meaning 'lake of creation' and also referred to as Illa or 'light', a bearded man, universal creator and master of all. He made humankind, first by creating a generation of giants, whom he turned into stone when they displeased him; the remainder were dispatched by a great flood that inundated the world.

Mesopotamia

Within Mesopotamian mythology, Atra-hasis (meaning 'extremely wise'), who also appears in the Gilgamesh epic where he is referred to as Utnapishti ('he who found life'), is named on a list of Sumerian Kings showing those who ruled before the flood and those who ruled afterwards (antediluvian and postdiluvian). He, like Noah, was chosen to survive a deluge and to build a ship and to fill it with pairs of animals.

India

In India there are the seven sages or the seven Rishis, who are the authors of the Vedas, from the Sanskrit word 'veda', meaning 'knowledge' or 'wisdom', one of the sacred books of the Hindus from the fifth century BCE.

According to legend, the Rishis were men of extraordinary creativity and magical powers, and much of Sanskrit literature is devoted to accounts of their supernatural powers including, for example, flying.

Rishi literally means seer, a Hindu saint or sage; of these the saptarshi, the seven seers, are particularly prominent.

The day of the Brahma or Hindu cycle/era of existence lasts some 306,720,000 years according to *Encyclopaedia Britannica*. Each is divided into fourteen manvantaras over which presides a Manu, or teacher. Each manvantara is followed by a deluge, a flood which destroys existing continents and swallows up all living things, except for a few who are preserved for the repopulation of the earth.

Ancient Greece

In Greek mythology there is the account of Deucalion and Pyrrha, who survived a great deluge, having been forewarned by Prometheus, in a ship that was well provided with food and came to rest on the peak of Mount Parnassus.

In addition to all of these there are further examples of such similarities and overlapping of myth by ancient cultures, between which there should have been no transmission of information. These include serpents or dragons as in Chinese mythology, the underworld and cycles or eras of civilisation and existence. Of the latter, previous eras or cycles were renewed and this point was marked by a calamity. An example of this is in the parallel between the Greek five successive ages of man and the Maya with their five worlds.

The Greek version is to be found in Hesiod's second surviving poem *Works and Days*, where he tells the creation story and the lineage of man through five successive ages from the Golden Age to the Iron Age. The Maya have five periods and believed that each of the previous worlds had been destroyed; the fifth and present era is to be brought to conclusion in 2012 by catastrophic earthquakes. In Indian mythology, by comparison, we are in the seventh Manu cycle.

On a recent trip to Greece, I visited the National Archaeological Museum in Athens. I was reminded of a further instance of overlap between cultures when I viewed a vase on which was the swastika design. Better known for being used by the Nazi movement in Germany this was several centuries BCE and from the Sanctuary of Zeus on Mount Hymettos. I had previously seen this symbol on various Mayan Temples in Latin America and Buddhist temples in Singapore and Hong Kong. There is archaeological evidence that the swastika dates back to the Neolithic period and is employed by other religions such as Hinduism, Jainism and several Native American cultures.

How did ancient civilisations start?
As mentioned previously, in many cultures of antiquity there seems to have been a rather sudden start to their civilisations. However, across the world and within most of these societies, sometime just after the end of the ice-age, there seems to be a dramatic shift in their being when they suddenly started believing in a God or omniscient entity and adopted a spiritualness. This was abundantly more than mere cave paintings exemplifying their daily rituals and environment, or shamans depicting the results of tapping into their subconscious, due possibly to hallucinogens. They also rather abruptly felt the need to build incredibly large structures consisting of particularly large stones.

To put it into perspective, *Forbidden History* by J. Douglas Kenyon asks us to take Egypt as an example. From 5,000 BCE, the end of Epipaleolithic years (the period of transition between the Palaeolithic and Predynastic eras, between the hunter-gatherers and village dwelling cultures after 5,500 BCE) to 2,500 BCE, this agrarian society progressed from stone axes, flint arrowheads and pottery, to quarrying, moving and placing 200 ton stones as the foundation of a 480 ft high pyramid approximately the height of a 50 storey building, including 70 ton rocks hoisted to a level of 175 ft. Moreover, there seems to be no precedent, no discernible stages of development that led to this ultimate physical achievement.

In addition to this, a pyramid inch is .001 inch larger than a British inch, there are 25 pyramid inches in a cubit, there are 365.24 cubits in the square base of the Great Pyramid and there are 365.24 days in the calendar and one pyramid inch is 1/500 millionth of the earth's axis of rotation. Perhaps these could all be coincidences, or maybe they suggest that these builders, of an age thousands of years before Christ, had extensive knowledge about the dimensions of the planet.

These cultures all seem to recount the time when these changes took place by pointing to influential figures that were affected by a flood and arrived on their shores. We might be able to find immediate and comfortable explanation should such an event occur solely between Mesopotamia and Greece, for instance, where, due to their geographical proximity, there could have been communication of this knowledge. This, however, is absolutely not the case; we find a diffusion of particularly similar knowledge between cultures which were in existence and location remote from each other and which, by our traditional understanding, would have had no interaction.

Summary

World maps which were particularly accurate existed prior to Columbus's voyage west in 1492. Indeed, such maps were so precise and accurate as to map Antarctica in 4,000 BCE, which suggests that there existed the ability to map more accurately than in the 1900s or that those individuals possessed seismic survey technology.

A great many structures of great antiquity consist of blocks of stone that would, at very least, challenge, if not make impossible their re-creation, even with our 'advanced' technology of today.

Despite the official dating of the pyramids at Giza being 2,500 BCE, they mirror the constellation of Orion and, due to the precession of equinoxes, the resultant date is very much earlier at 10,500 BCE.

Past generations of the Dogon tribe of West Africa knew of Sirius B while our astronomers only discovered them in 1926.

The Olmec, a tribe which preceded the Maya and are officially dated as existing from 1,200 BCE to 400 BCE, carved their images in stone which possess definite Negroid features. Stelae also exists depicting individuals of Caucasian origin. The Olmec existed prior to Columbus and others who followed, who introduced both Africans and Caucasians to the New World.

A great deal of ancient mythology speaks of 'airborne' vehicles and appears to indicate literal meaning and seems to surpass metaphor.

There is a wealth of mythology which suggests that there was a flood in ancient times. As these mythologies derive from all parts of the globe which, from our traditional understanding, would have had no contact with each other, then there is good reason to believe that the phenomenon of the flood was spread across the world at that time.

3
Evidence of an Unknown Antediluvian Civilisation?

It is beyond our powers to know or tell about the birth of the other gods; we must rely on those who have told the story before, who claimed to be the children of the gods, and presumably know about their own ancestors.

Plato (428/427 BCE–348/347 BCE) *Timaeus*

I shall leave the reader to decide whether a civilisation existed prior to the flood. However, there does seem to be a preponderance of evidence that makes this a possibility worthy of some consideration. In *The Scientific Fraternity, Forbidden Archaeology* by Cremo and Thompson stated that out of 6 million years, only 100,000 may be represented by surviving strata. In the unrecorded 5.9 million years there is time for even an advanced civilisation to have come and gone, leaving hardly a trace.

The last chapter cited evidence of ancient technology that created enormous megalithic structures of various kinds which would be extremely difficult, if at all possible, to re-create today, even with our own advanced technology. Also cited were the numerous similarities of mythologies from a variety of cultures of antiquity. Mythology today possesses the connotation of a false or fictitious narrative; however, these 'stories' have been passed down from the earliest of times, generation after generation. Many of these have survived from centuries before Christ and have been imprinted upon our psyche and formed, at least in part, our religious systems of today. Can we, therefore, freely wave them aside and dismiss them as inconsequential and fictitious?

Among the mythologies discussed in Chapter 2 were global accounts of a great flood where a number of people, in particular from an island, survived and arrived on the shores of inhabited nations, before influencing them in spiritual matters and assisting in the development of culture, the erection of large structures, and enhancing agriculture.

The flood is, of course, best known from the biblical story of Noah in the Book of Genesis. But it is interesting to note that it is also included in the mythology of as wide a group of nations as the Sumerians, Babylonians, Chinese, Indians, Indonesians, Australians, Greeks, Germans, Irish, Finnish, Maya, Aztec and Hopi to name but a few. Yet the flood is officially scientifically unproven and remains unacknowledged by the scientific fraternity. It probably occurred at the end of the last ice age, approximately 10,500 BCE or thereabouts. This may be why, as mentioned in the last chapter, the positioning of both the Sphinx and the pyramids at Giza mirror that date – a message perhaps that we should focus our attention on it.

Evidence of Noah's flood?

Possible evidence for a global flood, sometimes attributed to Noah's flood, is the Black Sea which is located at the south eastern extremity of Europe. It is connected to the distant Atlantic Ocean by the Bosporus, via the Sea of Marmara, the Aegean Sea and the Mediterranean Sea. It is contended that the Black Sea was originally a fresh water lake which eight thousand years ago, was abruptly transformed into a salt water sea, increasing its size by some thirty percent due to a prehistoric flood. This cataclysmic event replaced some 60,000 square miles (twice the size of Ireland) of populated land and raised the water level by some 500 ft. This was due to the earth becoming warmer after the end of the Ice Age and the ice over the northern hemisphere melting as a result. Oceans and seas consequentially increased in volume resulting in the Mediterranean Sea swelling and its saline waters pushing through the Bosporus with two hundred times the force of Niagara Falls. The human settlements on the banks would have been flooded and the displaced and terrified survivors would have recounted the tale of this great flood.

61

The evidence for this contention was derived from core samples taken from the once lake bed, which showed evidence of an abrupt change from fresh water molluscs to a salt water variety. There was also sonar evidence which showed plant life, indicating that the area was previously exposed to the air, and also of a more ancient shoreline. There was evidence of human habitation in the form of cut rock, samples of wood which, unlike rock, can be carbon dated. Unfortunately these only revealed more recent litter rather than corroborate an ancient flood. Research and expeditions to find signs of human occupation continues.

Those who disagree with the theory suggest that, over millennia, salt water has trickled into the Black Sea from the Mediterranean Sea. However, erosion at the entry point of the Black Sea from such an explanation would produce a channel of erosion which curved to the right due to the rotation of the earth. Sonar images have provided unambiguous evidence of erosion inclined to left; such a force against the earth's rotation would indicate a much more catastrophic event.

Archaeological evidence of a global flood?

Author Bill Bryson, in *A Short History of Nearly Everything*, writes about the extreme changes in the earth's temperature from hot to cold in approximately 10,000 BCE creating the conditions for a great flood. He suggests that, towards the end of the last big glaciation some twelve thousand years ago, the Earth began to warm quite rapidly but then abruptly plunged back into bitter cold for a thousand years or so in an event known to science as the 'Younger Dryas'. At the end of this thousand year onslaught, average temperatures increased again by as much as 4 degrees Celsius, which is equivalent to changing the climate of Scandinavia to that of the Mediterranean in just two decades. What is particularly disconcerting is that we have no idea whatsoever what natural phenomena could so dramatically and swiftly affect the Earth's temperature.

It is feasible then that a great flood could have occurred due to these extremes. Bryson goes on to say that the next phase of our history could see us melting a lot of ice rather than making it. If all the sheets melted, sea levels would rise by almost 200 ft (the height of a twenty storey building) and every coastal city in the world would be flooded. Perhaps this possible future scenario occurred in much the same way, or even to a greater degree, some twelve thousand years ago.

Whilst it is contended that the dynamics of glaciation, the movement of glaciers themselves, explains the fact that boulders have been found in places from which they obviously had not originated, such as, for example, granite boulders high on the limestone flanks of the Jura Mountains (a small mountain range located north of the Alps), it is also feasible that the effect could have been due to massive flood waters scoring away the sides of mountains. J. Douglas Kenyon, in *Forbidden History*, describes this further:

> A picture emerging of a planet scarred by massive movements of water, generally from the northwest to the southeast, over its surface. The northwestern sides of whole mountains were scored as if they had been subjected to fast-moving waters containing gravel and boulders. Floodwater was unmistakably the source of the scoring because science could see the same effect from fast-moving rivers. Furthermore, those same sides of the mountains were also home to massive buildups of drift materials, detritus presumably left behind by receding waters. Again, this was an effect that mimicked natural actions in the real world. These drift deposits even contained the remains of animals, including the woolly mammoth.
>
> More horrifying to nineteenth-century scientists than the evidence of water damage and silting were the gigantic boulders exposed to public view all over the European countryside in places where they did not belong. These oversized rocks, many weighing thousands of tons, could have been moved only by massive flood waters carrying them along and then depositing them when the waters receded. The movement of these rocks by the floodwaters would have been, in part, responsible for the aforementioned mountainside scouring.
>
> *Forbidden History*

Kenyon goes on to suggest that, 'The glacier theory did not explain why giant boulders ... were found in desert regions where no glacier could possibly go.' In addition to which, he says, 'Glaciers are flows of ice that, like rivers, respond to gravity. Glaciers do not climb hills and do not travel across level land.'

Found with the woolly mammoth deposits were the remains of exotic animals, insects, birds and vegetation, which could never have been local to where the glacial drifts were found, suggesting that all had been caught up in whirlpools, mixed together and deposited wherever the water settled. There has also been such a mix of bones and plant life found deep in caves, a process that could have only occurred if they had been carried into these crevices by the recession of massive floodwaters.

If recent finds, large submerged structures, off Japan's Yonaguni Island and India's Bay of Cambay are proved to be man-made sites, sunken cities, the fact that these sites lie below the existing water level would go to supporting, even proving, the occurrence of a flood and that potentially advanced societies existed before it, 'antediluvian' civilisations in fact.

Plato's 'Atlantis'

Whilst ancient cultures across the globe spoke of an island submerged by a deluge from which the survivors escaped to new shores, it was the Greek philosopher Plato, student of Socrates, who in the context of western philosophy first discussed such an island. This island he named as 'Atlantis' and it is written of in his dialogues, *Timaeus* and *Critias*.

Many of Plato's twenty plus philosophical discourses are largely hypothetical, such as his work *The Republic*, but *Timaeus* and *Critias* seem to be a factual accounts of the world in which we live. This includes the story of Atlantis, which occurs in a conversation between Critias and Socrates. This was a story that was recounted by Solon to Critias, being of the same name and the grandfather to the Critias in the book, and was related to him by Solon when he was an old man.

> Critias: Listen then Socrates. This story is a strange one, but Solon, the wisest of the seven wise men, once vouched safe its truth ... Solon came there [Egypt] on his travels and was highly honoured by them [Egyptian high priests], and in the course of making inquiries from

64

those priests who were most knowledgeable on the subject found that both he and all his countrymen were almost entirely ignorant about antiquity. And wishing to lead them on to talk about early times, he embarked on an account of the earliest events known here, telling them about Phoroneus, said to be the first man, and Niobe, and how Deucalion and Pyrrha survived the flood and who were their descendants ... Our records tell how your city [Athens] checked a great power which arrogantly advanced from its base in the Atlantic ocean to attack the cities of Europe and Asia. For in those days the Atlantic was navigable. There was an island opposite the strait which you call the Pillars of Heracles (Hercules) [The Strait of Gibraltar], an island larger than Libya and Asia combined; from it travellers could in those days reach the other islands ... On this island of *Atlantis* had risen a powerful and remarkable dynasty of kings, who ruled the whole island and many other islands as well and parts of the continent.

Plato: Timaeus

Socrates later comments: '... and it is a great point in its [the account of Atlantis] favour that it is not a fiction but a true history.' The book and the account go on to describe the island of Atlantis in great detail.

Other writing on Atlantis

A great deal has been written of Atlantis and a lost civilisation over the years. There are many theories on where Atlantis is to be found, ranging from the heights of Peru in South America, to Santorini in the Mediterranean, to beneath the Antarctic ice-cap due to earth crust displacement. Wherever it is to be found, if it is ever to be found, there does seem be compelling inference that it did in fact exist at some point in the past.

Might there be evidence to be found of Plato's account of this island being in the Atlantic Ocean in the similarities of the temples on either side of the island from which the inhabitants fled? Certainly the Maya described in the *Popol Vuh* how these people came from the east; might the arrival of the individuals in Egypt mentioned earlier have been from the west? Surely it cannot be a coincidence that the Pyramid of the Sun at Teotihuacan in Mexico and the Great Pyramid of Giza in Egypt possess the same base measurements, nor mere chance that the same 43.5 degree angle was adopted by two pyramids, one at Teotihuacan and one at Giza. This angle is an adaptation of *pi*, as in the theorem attributed to Pythagoras, but some 2,000 years before his birth between 580 and 572 BCE.

A modern day prediction
Edgar Cayce (1877-1945), also known as the 'sleeping prophet', would self-induce a sleep state within which he was able to commune with all space and time. He did much with his clairvoyance, but of particular interest here was that he forecast the rising of Atlantis again in 1968 or 1969. Whilst this was not to be in the most literal of terms, it was within this time frame that the 'Bimini Road', described in the last chapter, was located. The 'Bimini Road' is also referred to as the 'Atlantis Wall'. Cayce also believed that the submergence of this island occurred in approximately 10,600 BCE. He also suggested that there was a 'Hall of Records' to be found beneath the Sphinx. Thanks to seismic survey technology, we now know that there is indeed a cavity below the Sphinx but there have been no excavations to date.

Some modern texts on Atlantis
There are a great many texts on the subject including: *Atlantis: The Antediluvian World* by Ignatius Donnelly, *Atlantis to the Latter Days* and *The History of Atlantis* by Lewis Spence and *The Legends of Atlantis and Lost Lemuria* by W. Scott-Elliot. However, in this day and age, few have researched the subject more widely and intensely than Graham Hancock, who brought the concept within the grasp of the average person.

If such a civilisation did exist and was destroyed by a deluge with its survivors fleeing to foreign shores, as described by many ancient cultures, then let us take an evolutionist stand for a moment and consider the overlapping of the different stages of the development of man; for instance, that Homo sapiens coexisted with Neanderthal people. Erik Trinkaus, of Washington University in St Louis, announced that a skeleton of a child who died 24,500 years ago found in Portugal in 1999 was a hybrid and proof that modern humans and Neanderthals interbred. Might we, Homo sapiens, then have overlapped with the

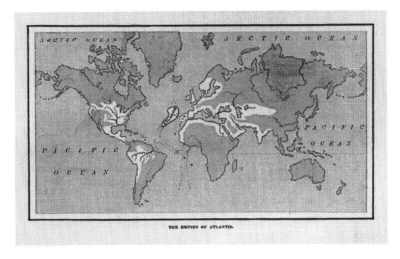

Map showing the extent of the Atlantean Empire as suggested by Ignatius Donnelly in his book Atlantis: The Antediluvian World.

Atlanteans had they existed? There are certainly descriptions of this in Greek mythology, as found within Hesiod's *Theogony*. Hesiod lived in the eighth century BCE and the *Theogony* is the earlier of his two surviving poems and contains a systematic genealogy of 'the Gods' from the beginning of the world. It speaks of mortal man interacting with the Gods and, in particular, bedding with mortals and bearing 'children resembling the Gods'.

Another account is given in *Mythology*, edited by C. Scott Littleton which refers to the giant invaders of ancient times in Peru:

> The peoples of coastal Peru inherited legends of ancient invaders. These were giants, where the heads of ordinary men would come up to their knees and their eyes were the size of plates. The giants were loathed because they forced the native and human population to submit to them sexually.
>
> *Mythology*

Biblical accounts

There is another reference to this subjection by giants in the Bible in Genesis 6:1:

> And it came to pass, when men began to multiply on the face of the earth, and daughters were born unto them,
> That the sons of God saw the daughters of men that they were fair; and they took them wives of all which they chose ...
> There were giants (the Nefilim) in the earth
> in those days; and also after that,
> when the sons of God came in unto
> the daughters of men, and they bare
> children to them, the same became
> mighty men which were of old, men
> of renown (fame, prominence, eminence).

Shortly thereafter, and related also in the Book of Genesis, the flood occurred.

Within *The Book of Enoch*, it asserts:

> And when the angels, the sons of heaven, beheld them, they became enamoured of them, saying to each other, Come, let us select for ourselves wives from the progeny of men, and let us beget children ...
> Then they took wives, each choosing for himself; whom they began to approach, and with whom they cohabited; teaching them sorcery, incantations, and the dividing of roots and trees.

And in a later chapter it states, 'In those days shall the elect and holy race descend from the upper heavens, and their seed shall then be with the sons of men.' (Richard Laurence: *The Book of Enoch*)

The Zohar

In the *Zohar*, a book that lies at the heart of Kabbalah study and which is discussed in Chapter 5, we find this account:

When Uzza and Azael fell from the abode of their sanctity above, they saw the daughters of mankind and sinned with them and begat children. These were the Nefilim (giants), of whom it is said , *the Nefilim were in the earth* ... The descendants of Cain were 'the sons of God'. For Cain was born from Samuel and his aspect was not like that of other human beings, and all who came from his stock were called 'sons of God' and the Nefilim were called so also.

The Zohar

Other ancient accounts

Returning to Plato's *Timaeus* in the context of this overlap, we find the Egyptian high priests speaking to Solon, 'You [Athenians] remember only one deluge ... you and your fellow citizens are descended from the few survivors that remained, but you know nothing about it because so many succeeding generations left no record in writing.'

Indeed, within the Egyptian *Book of the Dead* it mentions that, 'The priests of Ra [the highest of Egyptian deities] claimed to have the veritable blood of Ra, and they asserted that their high priests were the offspring of Ra by human mothers ... The belief that Ra came down from heaven and was united by mortal woman.' I stated in the previous chapter that, from the same book, collectively they were called 'Khemenu' or the 'Eight' and they were considered as primeval fathers and mothers.

A further source also mentioned in the previous chapter, Bishop Las Casas in his commentary on the *Popol Vuh*, writes: 'They [the Maya] believed that certain persons who escaped the flood populated their lands, and they were called the great father and the great mother.'

If it was the case that modern humans interbred with these refugees, the 'Gods', as described often by ancient cultures, these displaced foreigners who arrived on their shores, then perhaps their contribution to our species as we exist today is 'consciousness', a most human characteristic which cannot be derived by natural selection and indeed cannot be devolved. It seems to me that consciousness, much like altruism, belies the fundamentals of Darwin's Theory of Evolution.

Evidence of Atlantis from ancient maps

Charles Hapgood and ancient maps also give further evidence. In the last chapter of *The Maps of the Ancient Sea Kings: A Civilization that Vanished,*

Hapgood comments:

> When I began this work [the book] I was aware of no definite evidence
> of an ancient advanced world civilization, though I was aware that
> others believed it had existed. Now I have found in the maps, evidence
> that I accept as decisive in answering this question in the affirmative.

Hapgood goes on to mention that several myths were brought from
legend into reality, such as Babylon of Mesopotamian mythology in
1811 by Claudius Rich, Champollion solving the problem of Egyptian
hieroglyphics returned Egypt to the forefront of historical study, and
Troy, discovered by Schliemann, which was previously thought not to
have existed, gave substance to the myths of Crete. He goes on to ask,
'But is this all? Is the process at an end? Are there no more lost
civilizations waiting to be discovered? It would be contrary to history
itself if this were the case.'

He maintains that the ancient maps appear to suggest the existence
in remote times of a true civilisation of a comparatively advanced sort
some 20,000 or more years ago, while Paleolithic peoples were living in
Europe, and that we have inherited a part of what they once possessed,
passed down through generations. He further suggests that the idea of
the simple linear development of society, from the Paleolithic (Old
Stone Age) through the successive stages of the Neolithic (New Stone
Age), Bronze, and Iron Ages, must be given up. Today we find primitive
cultures co-existing with advanced modern society on all continents
such as the Bushmen of Australia and South Africa and truly primitive
peoples in South America and New Guinea.

It is not only the inference of the maps (due to the sophisticated
mapping described in Chapter 2) that denotes an advanced knowledge
and civilisation, but there is also the Kircher map of 1665. Athanasius
Kircher (1601–1680), a German Jesuit sometimes described as the last
Renaissance man, important for his prodigious disseminating of
knowledge and, on occasion, compared to Leonardo da Vinci,
published *Mundus Subterraneus*, which included a map of Atlantis
placing Atlantis between Africa and North America. The map was
taken from Egypt by the Romans, probably in 30 BCE, and on this map
is inscribed in Latin: 'Site of Atlantis not beneath the sea according to

The Athanasius Kircher Map of 1665.

the beliefs of the Egyptians and the description of Plato.'

The reader will notice that the map shows Africa and America on the wrong side of the Island of Atlantis; this is because to the Egyptians north is south, that is, Lower Egypt is northern Egypt and Upper Egypt is in the south. This, therefore, lends to the veracity of the map.

Lewis Spence, in his *The History of Atlantis,* points out that absence of documentary proof is not an argument for not accepting Plato's original description of Atlantis:

> The bare idea of Atlantis as described by Plato has been met with derision by generations of archaeologists, simply because no direct documentary evidence relating to its existence survived. But can one reasonably expect direct documentary evidence of a civilization which totally disappeared more than eleven thousand years ago? It is manifest that another kind of proof than documentary must be drawn upon to justify the existence of such a culture.

My personal view is that there is compelling inference, based on cultural diffusion, mythology of antiquity and geological anomalies, that points to a great flood or deluge and also the existence of an antediluvian civilisation. Whilst there are solid sources, to my mind, there is no proof and this is outside the parameters of my intent to be consistent with the provision of the facts and evidence available.

Summary

There is some physical and archaeological evidence to suggest that there was indeed a flood, despite the fact that the scientific fraternity does not officially recognise the existence of such an event.

The philosopher Plato was the first in the West to suggest an island which was destroyed by flood and referred to it as 'Atlantis'. He seems to be describing the existence of a factual event and civilisation.

There is also widespread evidence from ancient cultures of not only a flood occurring but also of survivors from it populating their lands and becoming intimately involved with the population.

In the seventeenth century Athanasius Kirchner published an ancient map depicting the island of Atlantis in the Atlantic (the original dating back to Roman times).

4

Esoteric Spiritual Texts

On hearing the way, the best of men
Will earnestly explore its length,
The mediocre person learns of it
and takes it up and sets it down
But vulgar people, when they hear the news
Will laugh out loud and if they did not laugh,
it would not be the way.

Lao-Tzu (sixth century BCE), founder of Taoism

In this chapter we follow on from the discussion on the validity of mythologies in the last two chapters to explore the ancient religious and spiritual texts available to us.

There is a fine line that can be drawn between mythology and religion, and some commentators choose not to differentiate between them at all and bundle the two together as though there were no difference. However, as previously mentioned, one has to ask the question: why should these ancient stories be dismissed when they have been imprinted upon our psyche for so long? Why should their contents be rejected when they continue to provide the very foundations of our laws and moral standards?

The philosopher William James, whose work I will discuss shortly, suggests that there is the 'moral argument' and that moral law presupposes a lawgiver. He states that, 'The argument *ex consensus gentium* is that the belief in God [or an omniscient entity] is so widespread as to be grounded in the rational nature of man, and should therefore carry authority with it.'

It may be interesting to note here that a poll of religious adherents in 2005 suggested that, of the world population, 85.73% were religious or 'believed' as opposed to 14.27% who were non-religious or atheists.

Conflicts between world religions

It can be accepted that religion over the centuries has gathered a bad reputation for itself in many quarters as being responsible for many wars, and often full of corruption. However, it is not the texts themselves that are corrupt but man who has corrupted them and used them for his own gain. What is it that drives leaders of religions to insist, on many occasions with force, that their religious beliefs are the better ones and therefore are to be imposed on others? This seems particularly inapposite when, for example, it is considered that of three of the main religions, Judaism, Christianity and Islam, all derive from Abraham.

The Aztecs, apart from the violence imposed on them by the Spaniards, found no fault with the Christian religion in that, inherently, they considered it much the same as their own. On my first trip to Mexico in 1998, I visited the villages of Zinacantan and Chamula in the state of Chiapas. There, one can see symbols of Christian worship and effigies in churches, intermingled with those from Mayan traditions. One local anthropologist even suggested that traditions as ancient as the Olmec were reflected in the services. Moreover, in the Far East, I have seen on the temples of Cambodia the two religions of Buddhism and Hinduism at peace with one another, with sacred Hindu parables etched on Buddhist temples. Furthermore, the *Qur'an* (5:69) speaks of Abraham, Moses and Jesus and states, 'Those who believe [in the *Qur'an*], and the Jews and the Sabi'in, and the Christians, who believe in God and the Last Day and do good, there is no fear for them, nor shall they grieve.' This tolerance of differing faiths clearly exists and yet today we find violent divisions exacerbated by Islamic fundamentalists.

Imposition of and conflict within Christianity and Islam
Christianity has, for many centuries, had periods of imposing its religion upon various foreign nations, such as the Crusades and the European invasion of the New World. It could be argued that it is now

not surprising that Islam should be as desirous of a similar dominance. What gives the West a special right to deny them their day? Islam as a religion is the newest of all the mainstream ones as it was initiated by Muhammad, who was born over 500 years after Christ. Christianity has had time to work on its global impositions and has also made itself particularly wealthy in the process. Islam is a younger religious system going through a similar developmental stage and possessing all the righteousness that originally obsessed Christianity. The situation is not unlike that of the West enjoying its historical economic booms, but, now that there is the 'green movement', going on to find fault with the ecological ramifications of the economic booms of China and India. Again, it could be asked, who are we in the West to deny these nations their economic prosperity? This is all in principle of course since surely, as self-described and allegedly intelligent human beings, we should have learnt from our mistakes and stupidities of the past.

On the current matter of the Islamic fundamentalists and today's violence, however, few would dispute that these extremes and extremists are altogether inexcusable and truly abhorrent.

Even more ridiculous than the conflict that exists between religions, and between the religious and non-religious, are those internal conflicts between sub-systems within the *same* religion. Examples of this are Catholics and Protestants within the Christian faith and Sunnites and Shi'ites from the Islamic world. One has to ask: for how long are we to perpetuate this ridiculous vicious and violent downward spiral? Have we not learnt anything from the past?

While the religious systems may be corrupted, it is not the texts of any mainstream religion that make it corrupt, but the so-called teachers and interpreters of today and yesteryear who are to blame. It is essential to glean from these texts an individual understanding of the message that they offer. Indeed, it would be beneficial for the individual to read a variety, or as many texts as possible, in order to get to some one truth or original source and to see the glaring similarities between the texts. In this way, to read a number of the spiritual texts of a variety of cultures and compare the testimony of each would serve to supplement, strengthen and throw further light upon the content of the others.

Mainstream and derivative texts
Whilst we will look at the mainstream texts, it is not primarily these 'bibles', such as the *Tanakh* (Bible used in Judaism), the *New Testament* and the *Qur'an* that I intend to explore in this chapter. Instead I will focus on what particularly might be gleaned from derivative texts and spiritual books which contain profound esoteric matter. The benefit of these texts is that they have been less tampered with than some mainstream texts, in some instances having been hidden for many hundreds of years. This comment applies primarily to the New Testament Bible which, though success has been achieved in providing an authoritative version, has suffered initially from non-precise copies being made by scribes and translators. The *New Testament* consists of twenty-seven books; however, there were many more originally and it was Athanasius, Bishop of Alexandria, who advised that these twenty-seven books should be read as scripture in churches, excluding all others. Even after this decision, the debates continued on which books should be considered and it was not for hundreds of years after they had been written that they were collated into one canon.

A 'spiritual experience' in esoteric texts
It is my belief that these spiritual texts also bear witness to, and provide evidence of, a specific 'spiritual experience'. On this point there is again evidence of a glaring overlap within cultures which, having been established well before the Common Era, should realistically have had no communication with each other. It is clear that, if this significant overlap and unifying element has not previously been overlooked, it certainly has not been embraced. This is unfortunate, since I feel that the identification of such could, and should, provide a basis upon which a cessation of conflict between religious thought could begin.

What emerges from these esoteric texts is a common focus on three main elements: seeking truth, gaining knowledge and achieving wisdom. Added to these is a profound sense of contemplation, introspection and meditation; and what particularly fascinated me initially was the constant similar references across cultures and in all cases to an association with 'light'. Consistently, 'light' is associated by context with the idea of unity and communication with the divine, which manifests itself in a particular physical experience.

This chapter will take a focused and unconventional view of religions and will present a preponderant amount of evidence from scriptures across the globe which provides evidence of this experience and its association with 'light'. The forerunners of these religions and spiritual thought themselves had such an en*light*ening experience, but on these messiahs, prophets, and transformational figures I will elaborate in Chapter 6 when discussing the experience itself.

William James: The 'mystic' experience

William James (1842–1910) discusses this very same experience in his book *The Varieties of Religious Experience: A Study in Human Nature* (*Varieties*). The author and this particular work were suggested to me by Dr Raymond Moody, whose work will be discussed in Chapter 7.

William James was an original thinker in and between the disciplines of physiology, psychology and philosophy, who imparted such ideas as 'the stream of thought'.

In *Varieties*, James' interest is not in religious institutions, ritual, or even

William James (1842–1910).

religious ideas particularly, but in 'the feelings, acts, and experiences of individual men in their solitude, so far as they apprehend themselves to stand in relation to whatever they may consider the divine.' It is an empirical enquiry into the natural history of human consciousness, replete with case studies and examples of individuals who have had such an 'experience' and its association with 'light'. James suggests that 'every religious phenomenon has its history and its derivation from natural antecedents', and poses the question, 'Under what biographic conditions did the sacred writers bring forth their various contributions to the holy volume? And what had they exactly in their several individual minds, when they delivered their utterances?' James cites Judaism, Christianity, Islam, Hinduism and Buddhism and suggests that spiritual texts were not composed out of whim but must have possessed some original foundation and instance to their compositions. He also suggests that this experience corroborates 'incompatible theological doctrines.'

The experience articulated in and of the forerunners of religion and spiritual thought and texts James also associates with 'light' in some volume. James describes this experience as a 'mystical' one, which astonishes its subjects by its suddenness, and which manifests itself in individuals who 'even in the absence of any acute feeling, the higher condition, having reached the due degree of energy, bursts through all barriers and sweeps in like a sudden flood.' He differentiates this experience from that of an individual of religious faith who is taken by the spirit in some flurry of religious ecstasy. This, James describes as 'a pre-appointed type by instruction, appeal and example' and suggests of this type of individual that their religion has been made for them by others and communicated to them by tradition, determined to fixed forms by imitation, and retained by habit. Of the 'experience' and these latter types, he states that it would not be beneficial to study these second-hand/removed religious lives and experiences, and with this I agree.

James points out that the experience is of a private nature when he states that, 'The religious experience we are studying is that which lives itself out within the private breast.' In addition to the association with light, which is mirrored by the evidence in the spiritual texts we will now consider, he proposes that it is also associated with the union of the Self and the divine. This will be corroborated by Dr Richard Bucke and others in Chapter 5 and 6.

Spiritual texts from the Middle East:

With spiritual texts originating from the Middle East, the emphasis is more on spiritual texts or derivative books (often related to religious sects) than mainstream texts for the reasons mentioned above, that of a greater emphasis on spirituality.

The spiritual texts to be looked at are:

The *Dead Sea Scrolls* (Essenes)
The *Nag Hammadi Library* (Gnostic)
The *Zohar* (Kabbalah or Jewish mysticism)
The *Tanakh* (Judaism)
The *New Testament* Bible (Christianity)
Christian mysticism
The *Qur'an* (Islam)
Islamic mysticism

In each case I will review the discovery, heritage or origin of these texts and then provide specific extracts from the texts showing the common emphasis on the elements of 'truth', 'knowledge' and 'wisdom' and, in particular, the consistent references to 'light' as an association with the divine.

The *Dead Sea Scrolls*: Essenes

Discovery in 1947
In 1947, a young Bedouin shepherd, Muhammad edh-Dhib, was in search of his lost goat and accidentally found the first of the lost Hebrew scrolls (known today as the *Dead Sea Scrolls*) in a cave in Qumran in the Judean desert in Israel. Today, they can be found in the Rockefeller Museum in Jerusalem, which I would highly recommend anyone to see; some of the written text is so impossibly miniscule that it is worthy of marvel. The scrolls were secreted in caves and remained undisturbed for almost 2,000 years; they reveal the history of the Second Temple

period (520–70 BCE) and between 1951 and 1956 there was much activity to find additional manuscripts in further caves.

In an eight kilometre strip of cliffs, eleven caves yielded manuscripts; five were discovered by Bedouins and six by archaeologists. A habitation site was also discovered, a complex of stone structures, which was neither military nor private in character, but made up communal quarters.

This site was established and occupied by a sect known as the Essenes, probably from the second century BCE. Their name is taken to mean 'holy ones' and there are further suggestions of 'silent ones', 'healers' or 'pious ones'. The Essenes and their leader 'the Teacher of Righteousness', an anonymous priest who was the spiritual leader of the community, were a separatist group who, according to Flavius Josephus (a first century Jewish historian), were one of three groups who formed a division of the Jews of the Second Temple period. It is not known who this founder of the Essenes was, nor from whence he came nor when he died.

The Essenes were an ascetic (the practice of severe self-discipline for religious and/or spiritual reasons) monastic community that retreated into the wilderness of the desert for profound contemplation and 'to separate themselves from the congregation of perverse men'. These 'perverse men' were probably Jonathan and/or Simon Maccabaeus, controversial High Priests in Jerusalem at the time that might have displaced their Teacher of Righteousness as High Priest.

An interesting feature of the Essene sect is their calendar, which differed from the Jewish calendar in possessing 364 days and fifty-two weeks unlike the latter which had 354 days. The Essene calendar began on a Wednesday, the day on which God created the 'luminaries', a description which becomes increasingly relevant. The existence of this sect lasted through two centuries with them occupying themselves with study and a communal way of life that included worship, prayer, meditation and work. There were also many Essenes who resided in towns and villages outside of the Qumran area.

In the *Community Rule*, a chapter within the *Dead Sea Scrolls*, the text refers to the sect as the 'men of holiness' and the men of 'perfect holiness', who were exclusively devoted to contemplation and spirituality. The extracts which follow are from *The Complete Dead Sea Scrolls in English*, translated by Geza Vermes.

In the introduction by Geza Vermes it states of the Essenes:

> They were expected to become proficient in the *knowledge* of the 'two spirits' in which men walk and how to recognise a 'son of light' from a 'son of darkness' belonging to the lot of Belial (Satan).

> The elect as they were known or the Essenes were guided by the spirit of *truth* in the ways of *light*.

> The Master shall instruct all the sons of *light* and shall teach them the nature of all things.

> From the God of *Knowledge* comes all that is and shall be ... and has appointed to him two spirits in which to walk ... those born of *truth* spring from a fountain of *light*.

The Essenes stressed constantly that God's assistance was necessary to remain faithful to his Law and that the very knowledge of that Law was a gift from heaven:

> From the source of His Righteousness
> is my justification,
> and from His marvellous mysteries
> is the *light* in my heart.
> My eyes have gazed on that which is eternal,
> on *wisdom* concealed from men,
> on *knowledge* and wise design
> (hidden) from the sons of men ...
> God has given them to His chosen ones
> As an everlasting possession
> And has caused them to inherit
> The lot of the Holy Ones.
>
> *The Lot of the Holy Ones*

These illustrate the many instances of this reference to the seeking of truth, knowledge and wisdom through profound contemplation and introspection and their consistent association with the 'light'. I believe that this reference to 'light' surpasses mere metaphor and find a basis in reality. As I will show, this is not only applicable to the Essenes but also to a great number of spiritual individuals and groups over a variety of cultures in various geographic regions.

The aim of the holy life of the Essenes was to penetrate the secrets of heaven in this world and to strive for mystical knowledge through study, contemplation and meditation. Their esoteric teachings were recorded in secret books. There are schools of thought that assert that Jesus, if not an Essene himself, at least had interaction with this sect. This meditation, knowledge and wisdom, when mentioned in the *Dead Sea Scrolls,* is consistently associated with the word 'light', as we will see throughout this and other chapters of this book.

The *Dead Sea Scrolls* were found in fragments as shown in the illustration below. The square brackets in the extracts below indicate missing words which have been inserted by restorers and translators such as Geza Vermes.

These short extracts are fragments selected from various chapters to further illustrate the emphasis on the elements of spirituality discussed above.

Hymns and Poems:

[G]lory is the perfect *light* of *knowledge.*

The Triumph of Righteousness or Mysteries:

...nor do they understand the things of the past ... wickedness shall be banished by righteousness as darkness is banished by the *light* ... *knowledge* shall fill the world and folly shall exist no longer.

Wisdom Literature:

Happy is the man to whom it (*Wisdom*) has been given thus ...
Seek her and find her, grasp her and possesses her ...
... in the approaching mystery search its beginnings ...
You are a poor man. Do not say:
Since I am poor, I will not seek knowledge
Shoulder every discipline and with every ... refine
your heart,
And your thoughts with a multitude of understanding.
Search the approaching mystery
and consider all ways of *truth* ...
Then you will know what is bitter for a man
and what is sweet for a human being ...
[day and] night he *meditates* on the approaching mystery
Then you will know *truth* and injustice,
wisdom [and folly] ...
For the God of *knowledge* is the foundation of *truth*
And through the approaching mystery ...
And you will understand the beginning of your reward ...
And this is the vision issuing from the *meditation* ...
And you son, look...at the approaching mystery
And know the heritage of all the living.
And you, elect of *truth*
And pursuers of [righteousness and] jud[gement]
... guardians of all *knowledge*
How will you say:

We labour for understanding
and keep awake to pursue *knowledge* ...
We have laboured in the works of *truth*
And we exhausted ourselves in all ages.
Will they not walk in eternal *light*
[and inherit g]lory and great splendour ...
For God has assigned a heritage to all the [living]
And all those wise in heart will understand.

Songs of the Sage:

For God has caused the *knowledge* of understanding to *shine* in my heart.

The Testament of Amram:

[For all the Sons of Light] ... and by all their *knowledge* they will ... and
the Sons of Darkness will be burnt ... For all folly and wicked[ness are
dar]k, and all peace and *truth* are *brigh*[t]. For all the Sons of the Light
[g]o towards the *light,* towards [eternal] jo[y and rej]oicin[g].

The Book of Enoch:

The bulk of the fragments from the *Dead Sea Scrolls* are too small for
translation and the following excerpts are taken from *The Book of Enoch*
translated by R. H. Charles. (*The Book of Enoch* is also referred Chapter 6.)

And after all that all the secrets of the *lights* and *lightning* were shown
to me, and they *lighten* for blessing and for satisfying.

In the concluding section of the book:

XCII. I. The book written by Enoch - [Enoch indeed wrote this
complete doctrine of *wisdom*] ... for all my children who shall dwell on
earth; and for the future generations who shall observe uprightness
and peace.
2. Let not your spirit be grieved on account of the times; for the holy,
the Great One, has prescribed a time to all.

It continues:

> Let the righteous man arise from slumber; let him arise and proceed in the path of righteousness in all its paths; and let him advance in goodness and eternal clemency. M ... shall walk in eternal *light* ... from my heavenly vision and from the voice of angels have I acquired *knowledge*; and from the tablet of heaven have I acquired *understanding*.

Here we have seen the consistent reference to truth, knowledge, wisdom and 'light' from this ancient text hidden in caves and left untampered with for almost 2,000 years, without any subsequent amendments, as is the case with other biblical texts. The communication of spirituality, therefore, seems more immediate.

It is also worth noting that, as with the Book of Genesis in the *Old Testament*, The *Dead Sea Scrolls* mention the flood. 'All the windows of heaven opened, and all the abyss[es] overflowed [with] mighty waters.' There is also reference to the intimate interaction of angels, the 'sons of heaven', in taking wives from the daughters of men (mentioned in the previous chapter).

The *Nag Hammadi Library*: Gnostic texts

The Nag Hammadi Library (*The Library*), also known as the Gnostic Gospels, is another text which remains untampered with, having also been hidden for hundreds of years. It forms a collection of religious texts, Gnostic esoteric 'mystic' scriptures translated from Greek into Coptic, the language in use when it was originally buried around 400 CE. Like The *Dead Sea Scrolls*, they too were found accidentally, but a little earlier in 1945 in the Nag Hammadi region of Upper Egypt, and they are now exhibited in the Coptic Museum in Cairo.

The word 'Gnostics' is derived from the Greek word 'gnosis', translated as 'knowledge'. Gnosis, however, is meant to mean more than just rational knowledge. In this context it can be translated as 'insight' or esoteric spiritual knowledge, since gnosis involves an intuitive process of knowing oneself. The Gnostics were of the firm belief that the only answers were to be found within themselves and by embarking on an intensely private and spiritual inward journey. The individual who then 'experienced' their own nature would become enlightened.

The collectors and authors of *The Library* were essentially Christians and many of the essays were originally composed by Christian authors. However, much of their work and that of Gnosticism was later declared as heresy, a betrayal of the original Christian position and, as a result of this, they were hidden. Much like the Essenes prior to the discovery of The *Dead Sea Scrolls*, Gnosticism was also a movement about which little was known until the Nag Hammadi texts were found. One of the texts, also like The *Dead Sea Scrolls*, refers to a Zoroastrian heritage.

Again, *The Library*, in a similar way to The *Dead Sea Scrolls*, concerns itself with the search for the same elements of truth and derived wisdom and the association with the 'light'.

This can be seen below in these excerpts taken from the various chapters in The *Nag Hammadi Library* (ed. James M. Robinson).

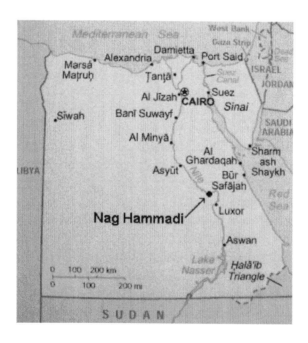

Map showing region in Egypt where the *Nag Hammadi Library* was found.

The Apocalypse of Peter:

> I am the intellectual Spirit filled with radiant *light*. He whom saw you coming to me is our intellectual Pleroma, which unites the perfect *light* with my Holy Spirit.

The 'Pleroma' generally refers to the totality of divine powers. However, the Pleroma is often referred to as the light that exists above our world. This word is also particularly relevant to the spiritual experience as are the following selected from other chapters in the *Nag Hammadi Library*.

The Gospel of Truth:

> It is within Unity that each one will attain himself; within *knowledge* he will purify himself from the multiplicity into Unity, consuming matter within himself like *fire*, and darkness by *light*.

> They are the ones who appear in *truth*, since they exist in true and eternal life and speak of the *light* which is perfect and filled with the seed of the Father, and which is in his heart and in the Pleroma, while his Spirit rejoices in it and glorifies the one in whom it existed.

The Gospel of Philip:

> *Knowledge* then, is the *light* through *light*.

The Gospel of the Egyptians:

> … the *light* of the word and the *truth* …

The following extracts from other chapters refer specifically to the spiritual experience of named individuals.

Allogenes:

> …the eternal *Light* of *Knowledge* that saw the *light* that surrounded me and the Good that was in me, I became divine.

Zostrianos:

The truth with truth and knowledge and eternal *light* …
I pondered these things to understand them … I did not cease seeking.
But when souls are illuminated by the *light* in them
… the perfect mind of the *light*, so that immortal souls might receive
knowledge for themselves.
There stood before me the angel of the knowledge of eternal *light*.
His knowledge dwells, it dwells with the one who examines himself
The knowledge of the knowledge is there together with a setting up of
ignorance. Chaos is there and a perfect place for all of them, and they
are strange. True *light* is there.

Trimorphic Protennoia:

And I am inviting you into the exalted, perfect *Light*. Moreover (as for)
this (*Light*), when you enter it you will be glorified by those [who] give
glory, and those who enthrone will enthrone you. You will accept robes
from those who give robes and the Baptists will baptise you and you will
become gloriously glorious, the way you first were when you were *Light*.

The Library is full of references to introspection in this way and
acknowledges a distinct form of knowing obtained by experience
or perception. This is gained from inward personal and absolute
knowledge of the authentic truths of existence. Gnosticism asserts that
'direct personal and absolute knowledge' and the attainment of such
knowledge is the supreme achievement of individual knowledge,
rooted in the self, and this knowledge leads to spiritual freedom.

It will come as no surprise that here too, within these texts, the flood
is mentioned, together with the angels and their intimate interaction
with the 'daughters of men'.

The Zohar: Kabbalah or Jewish mysticism

Jewish mysticism has long existed, initiated primarily to unravel the
mysteries of the biblical texts of Judaism. Is still exists today in the form

of Kabbalah, which has gained great popularity and a celebrity following over recent years. It should be noted, however, that the Kabbalists were preceded by the ma'aseh merkabah mystics. This group is among the very earliest movements in Jewish mysticism and based this mysticism on a vision of Ezekiel, as recounted in the Book of Ezekiel. The ma'aseh merkabah mystics meditated on the very same image as in Ezekiel's vision to develop a fuller understanding of God. Although ma'aseh merkabah precedes Kabbalah, they possess several practices and theories in common.

The *Zohar* is the premier text of Jewish mysticism and is considered as the foremost Kabalistic. As Professor Rufus Jones is quoted in the introduction to The *Zohar* 'Mysticism is religion in its most acute, intense, and living stage.' According to Jewish tradition, it is not advisable to read The *Zohar* before the age of forty because of the profundity and mysticism of these volumes. The title itself is Hebrew for 'splendour' or 'radiance' and here, again, we find the connection to light.

This group of books, The *Zohar*, is a commentary on the *Torah*, written in both Aramaic and Hebrew and of great antiquity, and is an accumulation of treatises, texts, extracts or fragments of texts belonging to different periods but all parallel in their mystical interpretation of the *Torah* and of Jewish and non-Jewish mystical thought. It is thought that these teachings of the Kabbalah were transmitted from teacher to teacher until its redaction by Simeon ben Yohai. Some scholars see a great deal of the background of The *Zohar* in the religion of Zoroastrianism, of which the philosopher Nietzsche was a great advocate.

According to tradition, when an individual studies the writings of this Kabalistic canon, they gain knowledge of what was previously hidden from them. It is only after acquiring a heightened spiritual sense through study that they begin to feel and see what was previously unrevealed.

Every individual has a natural ability to develop this heightened spiritual being, and it is for this reason that The *Zohar* transmits the knowledge of the structure of the upper spiritual world. When an individual is exposed to these writings, they may not initially grasp what they are reading. However, if they want to understand, and employ effort in the correct way, they invoke what is called the Surrounding Light, a light which descends from above and the light which corrects them; and they are shown spiritual reality. The terms 'to correct' and 'correction' are used in Kabbalah to describe a change in the desire to receive and to acquire the qualities of the spiritual world and of an omniscient entity or Creator.

The *Zohar* gives the reader the conviction of this inner, unseen, spiritual universe. It asserts that the 'upper universe' mirrors the 'lower universe' and both find their unity in God. Earth is a copy of heaven and not unlike the ancient Egyptian declaration 'as above so below', there is no duality but an absolute unity, or *Atman* in the context of Buddhism. It goes on to say that, 'The Lord is near unto all them that call upon him, to all that call upon him in truth.'

The fundamental doctrine of The *Zohar* is that, with a gradation of emanations, the human mind may recognise in each the supreme mark and thus ascend to the cause of all causes.

This ascension can only be made, however, after the mind has attained four stages of knowledge:

1. The knowledge of the exterior aspect of things, or, as in The *Zohar* 'The vision of all through the mirror that projects an indirect light.'

2. The knowledge of the essence of things, or 'the vision through the mirror that projects a direct light.'

3. The knowledge through intuitive representation.

4. The knowledge through love, since the Law 'reveals its secrets only to those who love it'. After the knowledge through love comes the ecstatic state, which is applied to holy visions. To enter the state of ecstasy, one has to remain motionless, with the head between the legs, absorbed in contemplation and murmuring prayer and hymns, a meditative technique if you wish.

There are seven ecstatic stages, each of which is marked by a vision of a different colour. It is maintained that The *Zohar* is written solely for those who have achieved spiritual competence and contains all the spiritual states that people experience as their souls evolve to conclusion, which the Kabbalists refer to as 'the end of correction', the highest level of spiritual wholeness or enlightenment. One who has ascended through these seven stages becomes 'one who knows' and who no longer reincarnates or transmigrates.

There is much too much esotericism within The *Zohar* to expound on within this chapter. However, it is important to note that there is reference to reincarnation and numerous references to wisdom and knowledge, as well as communion with the infinite, and all of these are associated with the instance of light.

Like The *Dead Sea Scrolls* and The *Nag Hammadi Library* texts, The *Zohar* mentions the flood of biblical times. Similarly, it also mentions the angels who intermingled with the daughters of mankind; beings from 'The abode of their sanctity above, they saw the daughters of mankind and sinned with them and begat children.'

The *Tanakh*: Judaism

The *Tanakh* is the Hebrew bible and is an acronym for the three divisions of the Hebrew canon: *Torah* (instruction or Law and also known as the *Chumash* or the *Pentateuch* in Greek), *Nevi'im* (prophets) and *Ketuvim* (writings). In its entirety, the *Tanakh* consists of twenty-four books. Tradition holds that much of the compilation of this Hebrew canon was completed in 450 BCE. However, other sources contend that it was finalised later between 200 BCE and 200 CE.

The *Torah* of Judaism literally means doctrine, instruction or teaching and is sometimes referred to as the *Law*. According to Orthodox Judaism, within this text are the revealed words of God to Moses on Mount Sinai (Torah min Hashamayim) and are considered the substance of divine revelation to mankind. Other branches of Judaism, however, such as the Liberal / Reform / Progressive groups, consider the *Torah* to be the work of humans who were divinely inspired, and this work is a human attempt to understand divine will. It is a text comprising five books which also constitute the first five books of the *Old Testament*, and is revered not only by Jews but also by the Samaritans and Christians. Jewish, Roman Catholic, Eastern Orthodox and Protestant canons all agree on their order: Genesis, Exodus, Leviticus, Numbers and Deuteronomy.

Much of Islam also draws heavily from The *Torah* for its concepts, teaching and history of the world. Abraham is the first of the Hebrew patriarchs and the Arabs are thought to be descended from Abraham's son Ishmael, the half-brother of Isaac. Isaac was then the father of Jacob, who was renamed Israel and thus, biblically, Arabs and Jews are cousins.

In addition to The *Torah*, the Hebrew text has the two further divisions. Firstly, the *Nevi'im* or *Prophets*, which is subdivided into the 'Former Prophets', with anecdotes about major Hebrew persons in the books of Joshua, Judges, Samuel, and Kings, and stories of the 'Latter Prophets' exhorting Israel to return to God in Isaiah, Jeremiah, Ezekiel, and the Twelve Minor Prophets. And secondly, the *Ketuvim* or *Writings*, with poetry and theology to be found in Psalms, Proverbs, Job, Song of Songs, Ruth, Lamentations, Ecclesiastes, Esther, Daniel, Ezra-Nehemiah, and Chronicles.

The theme of 'light' in the Torah ·

In Deuteronomy, God is described as a 'consuming fire' and in the Book of Wisdom it is stated that, 'She [wisdom] is a reflection of the eternal *light*' and we find further instances in the books of Daniel and Psalms,

> There is a man in thy kingdom, in whom is the spirit of the holy gods; and in the days of thy father *light* and understanding and wisdom, like the wisdom of the gods, was found in him; and the king Nebuchadnezzar thy father, the king, I say, thy father, made him master of the magicians, Chaldeans, and astrologers. (Daniel 5:11)

> O send out Thy *light* and Thy truth; let them lead me; let them bring me unto Thy holy mountain, and to Thy dwelling places. (Psalms 43:3)

> He revealeth the deep and secret things; he knoweth what is in the darkness and the *light* dwelleth with him. (Daniel 2:22)

The *New Testament Bible*: Christianity

The *New Testament* is a collection of twenty-seven books that underpin the Christian faith. These books were collated over centuries, with the *New Testament* taking the form that we know today near the beginning of the fourth century, some three hundred years after the death of Christ. In fact, the first surviving instance of anyone affirming the set of twenty-seven books in the *New Testament* is a letter by a powerful bishop of Alexandria named Athanasius written in 367 CE. Up to this time, Christianity was a small, minority religion in the Roman Empire, often opposed and persecuted by the authorities. It was not until the Roman Emperor Constantine converted to the Christian faith in 312 CE that professional scribes were used to copy and collate the books of the Bible and churches built, giving this religion the momentum to become the largest and one of the most influential powers in history.

The theme of 'light' in the New Testament
In the *New Testament*, 1 John 1:5 it states that God is *light* and Jesus is described as the true *light*.

As in The *Torah*, there are numerous instances of 'light' being mentioned but here it is mainly in relation to St John or Jesus Christ.

> There was sent a man from God, whose name was John. The same came for a witness, to bear witness of the *Light* that all men through him shall believe. (John 1:6)

> But he that doeth truth cometh to the *light*. (John 3:21)

> In whom the God of this world hath blinded the minds of them which believe not, lest the *light* of the glorious gospel of Christ , who is the image of God should shine unto them. (2 Corinthians 4:4)

> For God, who commanded the *light* to shine out of darkness, hath shined in our hearts, to give the *light* of knowledge of the glory of God in the face of Jesus Christ. (2 Corinthians 4:6)

The eyes of your understanding being *enlightened*; that ye may know what is the hope of his calling. (Ephesians 1:18)

This then is the message which we have heard of him, and declare unto you, that God is *light*. (1 John 1:5)

For one is given by the Spirit the word of wisdom, to another the word of knowledge by the same Spirit. (1 Corinthians 12:8)

Whereby, when ye read, ye may understand my knowledge in the mystery of Christ. (Ephesians 1:17)

Christian mysticism

In addition to the aforementioned examples, there is also Christian mysticism to briefly take into account. James in *Varieties* discusses Christian mysticism and states that the experiences of these have been treated as precedents, and that a codified system of mystical theology has been based upon them, in which everything legitimate finds its place.

The basis of the system is 'orison' or meditation, the methodical elevation of the soul towards God. Through the practice of orison, the higher levels of mystical experience may be attained and there are manuals which exist to attain this. He further states that sensorial images such as an imaginary figure of Christ are usually employed as part of the meditative technique and play a vital part in Christian mysticism. However, in certain cases the imagery may disappear and in the highest raptures this is the norm. The individual's state of consciousness then becomes insusceptible to any verbal description. Mystical teachers are unanimous in this and Saint John of the Cross declares that this state is reached by 'dark contemplation'. Saint Teresa describes this experience as 'Orison of union' and much like other spiritual texts in this chapter describes this as 'When God raises a soul to union with himself.' There is a similar condition and experience which is called 'raptus' by theologians. Raptus is the Latin for 'seized', from 'rapere' 'to seize', which, as will be seen in further chapters, is included in the description used by many with regards this experience.

St John of the Cross was born in 1542 and died in 1591. As a Carmelite friar, he was an enthusiastic supporter of a movement to restore original and strict rule. However, his untiring work resulted in him being imprisoned, during which time he wrote his first poem. He was canonised in 1726 and declared a Doctor of the Church in 1926. In the beautifully worded book *The Mystical Doctrine of St John of the Cross*, he too stresses the importance of meditation and knowledge. He refers to the 'experience' as 'luminous' – *lighting* the soul in which it is found in a way of which it can never, even to itself, give a satisfactory account. The result is only a deeper impression of obscurity. This ineffability, he states, is:

> Because this spiritual light is so clear, pure, and diffused, neither confined to, not specially related to, any particular matter of understanding, natural or divine ...

We will see much more commentary on this inability to sufficiently describe the profound impact of this unique 'experience'.

The *Qur'an*: Islam

This is the book at the foundation of Islam and which is the infallible word of Allah (God) that was revealed to the Prophet Muhammad by the Angel Gabriel. Except for a few opening passages where the Prophet or the Angel speaks in the first person, the speaker throughout is Allah. Muhammad was born in Mecca in 570 CE and would retire to a cave to give himself up to solitary prayer and meditation. According to tradition, in approximately 610 CE it was at such a time when he was asleep or in a trance that the Angel Gabriel came to him.

Of the mainstream religions today, Islam is the only one that laid down a broad basis of faith in all the prophets of the world, and the recognition of truth in all religions is a distinctive characteristic. As a religion, it requires not only belief in divine revelation to the Prophet Muhammad, but also belief in divine revelation to the whole of humanity and to all nations of the world.

A Muslim is one who believes in all the prophets of God sent to any nation, whether mentioned in the *Qur'an* or not. In 40:78 it is stated that 'There are some that We have mentioned to thee, and there are others whom We have not mentioned to thee.' The *Qur'an* relates how God has always been known to man through divine revelation and that revelation is a universal fact. In 35:24/25 it says, 'Every community has been sent a warner ... messengers came to them with clear signs, scriptures, and *enlightening* revelation.'

The theme of 'light' in the Qur'an

> 3.184 And if they deny thee, then they deny messengers who were before thee, who came with miracles and with the Psalms and Scriptures giving *light*.

> 4.174 O mankind! Now hath a proof from your Lord come unto you, and We have sent down unto you a clear *light*.

> 5.044 Lo! We did reveal the Torah, wherein there is guidance and *light*.

> 22.008 And among mankind is he who disputeth concerning Allah without knowledge or guidance or a scripture giving *light*.

> 57.019 And those who believe in Allah and His messengers, they are loyal ... ; they have their reward and their *light*.

> 64.008 So believe in His messenger and the *Light* which we have revealed.

In the chapter titled 'Light' in the *Qur'an*, it states that there has been advice given to those who are contemplative of God and that 'God is the *Light* of the heavens and earth' and that 'God guides whoever He will to his *Light*.' This light is compared to a lamp whose oil gives light even when no fire touches it, a *'light* upon *light'*, suggesting more than metaphor and pertains to a particular instance.

Islamic mysticism
Islam also has its own brand of mysticism known as Sufism. Islamic mysticism is properly known as Tasawwuf, but has been referred to as Sufism in the West since the early nineteenth century. This is the mystical Islamic belief and practice in which Muslims seek to find the

truth of divine love and knowledge through a direct and personal experience of an omniscient entity. It was originally thought that the roots of this Islamic mysticism were formed from non-Islamic sources in ancient Europe or India. However, it is now generally accepted that it was founded out of early Islamic asceticism.

Though still with the absolute belief that Islam is the highest manifestation of the divine, the Sufi mystics thought that intuitive knowledge was essential in acquiring *illumination* of the mind and the unification of one's being with the divine, to which reason had no access. This direct 'tasting' of the experience was essential to the Sufis and was known as dhawq. These mystics were also known as awliya, denoting the Muslim mystic who had attained a proximity to God and were ones who are, 'friends of God who have no fear nor are they sad'. The path to this 'illumination' imperatively includes meditation and interior knowledge or knowledge of the Self.

This experience and the idea of the manifestation of divine wisdom were also connected with the prophet Muhammad, who was described as 'light from light' and on whom I will elaborate in Chapter 6.

The last great figure in the line of classical Sufism is Abu Hamid al-Ghazali who died in 1111 and is mentioned along with Sufism in James' *Varieties*. Al-Ghazali's book *al-Munqidh min al Dalal*, 'Deliverance from Error', is described as a 'spiritual biography' and would rate as an Islamic classic. It provides a mode of interpretation and guidance for the life of a Muslim who wishes to penetrate to deeper levels of the Muslim spirituality. Suffice it to say that al-Ghazali's book contains many references to 'light' and states of his personal experience that it was an 'effect of *light* which the God Most High cast into his breast. And that *light* is the key to most knowledge.'

In all these texts from the Middle East there is constant reference to light as a manifestation, associated with seeking knowledge, wisdom and truth and employing contemplation. We can now look at the ancient texts of the Far East and find the very same combination within the esoteric spiritual texts of Eastern philosophy and religions.

Spiritual texts from the Far East

In India, and of Hinduism, the most ancient of sacred literature are the *Vedas*, a Sanskrit word meaning 'knowledge', which is a large corpus of texts that form the sacred texts of Hinduism. But, as in the previous section, we will again focus on the derivative spiritual texts, in this case of Hinduism, of profound meaning within which there is an abundance of evidence.

The two Hindu texts are:

The *Upanishads*
The *Bhagavad Gita*

We will also look at other Eastern sacred texts in:

Taoism
Buddhism
Jainism

The *Upanishads*: Hinduism

This title literally means 'sitting near the feet of the teacher' and is a philosophical work exposing a secret doctrine. The name itself refers to the secret knowledge acquired by sitting near the master. It is an accumulation of spiritual treatises, the oldest of which were composed between 1,000 and 600 BCE. The philosopher Schopenhauer said of the *Upanishads*: '[their reading] has been the consolation of my life, and will be of my death'. The composers were teachers and sages and, in an introduction, the translator Juan Mascaró states:

> These compositions are as much above the mere archaeological curiosity of some scholars as light is above its definition. Scholarship is necessary to bring us fruits of ancient wisdom, but only an elevation of thought and emotion can help us enjoy them and transform them into life.

Later Mascaró continues:

> The *light* of Truth is the End of the [spiritual] Journey. The path of the
> Upanishads is essentially the path of light, the consciousness of the
> Brahman (the holy spirit) which is far beyond all mental consciousness.
>
> Juan Mascaró: Introduction to *The Upanishads*

The *Upanishads* represent the last stage of the *Vedas* and the teaching of
it is called Vedanta, the meaning in Sanskrit being the conclusion of the
Veda. As a work they are more inspirational than defined instruction
and develop the concept of union with the Supreme Being.
Fundamental to all Hindu thought of is the equation of *Atman* (the Self)
with Brahman (ultimate reality, eternal, irreducible, omnipresent).

The theme of 'light'
In these derivative Hindu texts there are similar examples of
knowledge, spirituality and the use of 'light':

> He is known in the ecstasy of an awakening which opens the door of
> life eternal … For a man who has known him, the *light* of truth shines.

> He is seen in Nature in the wonder of a flash of *lightning*. He comes to
> the soul in the wonder of a *flash* of vision.

> I know Nachiketas, that sacred *fire* which leads to heaven. That *fire*
> which is the means of attaining the infinite worlds.

> When he is perceived as 'He is', then *shines* forth the revelation of
> his essence.

> One hundred and one subtle ways come from the heart. One of them
> rises to the crown of the head. (This is reflected in Chapter 6.)

> All things find their final peace in their inner most Self, the Spirit …
> the sense of 'I', thought, inner *light*. OM, or AUM, has three sounds.
> He who rests on the first his meditation is *illumined* thereby.

The *Bhagavad Gita*: Hinduism

The *Bhagavad Gita* (The *Gita*) is an equally important spiritual text of Hinduism included within the *Mahabharata*, one of two Sanskrit epics, the *Ramayana* being the other, of ancient India, probably written prior to 500 BCE. Like The *Upanishads* it was originally written in Sanskrit, a language from which not only Persian, Greek and Latin but also Celtic, Germanic and Slavonic languages were derived from a primitive unwritten language called Aryan.

In an introduction also by Juan Mascaró to The *Bhagavad Gita* he writes:

> There is a prayer in the Vedas which for over 3,000 years has been every morning on the lips of millions of Indians. It is the famous Gayatri, which when translated means 'Let our meditation be on the glorious *light* of Savitri. May this *light* illumine our minds. The poet of the Vedas who chanted these words saw into the future; the mind of India has never tired in search for the *Light*.

Mascaró goes on to say that within the *Vedas* we have the beginning of philosophical inquiry: the poets of the *Vedas* saw that for the progress of the mind man requires doubt and faith and that in the Vedas we have the dawn of spiritual insight, in The *Upanishads* we have the splendour of inner vision. The *Gita* is in the form of allegory and is a poem of the great spiritual struggle of the human soul.

Mascaró suggests that, 'Initially there is the impending battle for inner victory and the soul ready to give up the struggle, the soul is afraid of death and the cessation of all physical experience and wonders if death is the end of all. There then is the voice of the Eternal in man which discusses our immortality. After which there are sounds of serenity and peacefulness, a peace from passions, and peace from fears and lower desires. Then the call to action, the music becomes more urgent. Sweet human melodies are heard which is the descent of Eternity into time and the incarnation of the divine, the music becomes more majestic, it is the vision of all things and of the whole universe in God. In this theme there is wonder and fear. The music finally descends to softer melodies and is the vision of God as man, as the friend of the struggling soul.'

The *Bhagavad Gita*.

There are several themes within The *Gita* such as Yoga which also means 'Samadhi', a state of inner communion with the object of contemplation which when turned towards the source of all creation, we have light, which again is reflected in Chapter 6. Spiritual vision, above all scriptures pre and post *Gita*, focuses on the spiritual experience. It states:

> When thy mind leaves behind its dark forest of delusion, thou shalt go beyond the scriptures of times past and still to come. When thy mind, that may be wavering in the contradiction of many scriptures, shall rest in divine contemplation, then the goal of Yoga is thine.

The *Gita* places the man of Jnana, the man of 'light', above all men; he is in God. It is the highest theme in The *Gita*: 'The man of vision and I are one', 7.18 says Krishna in the vision of Arjuna in The *Gita*:

101

If the *light* of a thousand suns suddenly arose in the sky, that splendour might be compared to the radiance of the Supreme Spirit.

And Arjuna saw in that radiance the whole universe in its variety, standing in a vast unity in the body of the God of gods.

Mascaró states that the spiritual visions of man confirm and illumine each other in The *Bhagavad Gita* and, within this work, we have faith, a faith based on spiritual vision and in this vision we have 'light'.

We find within all Sanskrit literature, including the *Vedas*, the *Mahabharata* and derivative but esoteric texts, this continuing instance of introspection, contemplation, visions and an experience closely aligned to 'light.'

In India we find further instance in Sikhism, which means 'learner' in Punjabi. Its founder, Nanak, was raised a Hindu but, much like other prophets / messiahs, made several solitary journeys seeking knowledge. He stated that one must meditate to progress towards enlightenment and, indeed, Sikhs describe one's individual 'light' as being derived from God's Supreme Light.

Taoism

Of the Texts of Taoism, the *Tao Te Ching*, was written or compiled by the Chinese sage named Lao Tzu or 'Old Master', who was born in approximately 601 BCE. Taoists venerate Lao Tzu as 'Daotsu', one of the eight immortals mentioned previously in Chapter 2, in relation to Chinese creation mythology. Though he was some fifty years older than Confucius, they were contemporaries, the two men meeting more than once. There are references to earlier sages whose words the author copied to 'sentence makers', whose maxims he introduced to illustrate his own sentiments. Tao literally means 'way', 'path' or 'course' but was extended to mean 'path ahead' or 'way forward' or 'the way'. Te means 'virtue', in the sense of personal character or inner strength; the semantics of this Chinese word resemble the English 'virtue', developed from (a now archaic) sense of inner potency or divine power. Ching finds meaning in rule, plan, scripture or classic.

The *Tao Te Ching* praises self-knowledge, 'knowing the self is enlightenment' and then adds that 'mastering the self requires strength'. There are also further examples of 'light' mentioned in the text:

Who uses well his *light*,
Reverting to its source so bright,
Will from his body ward all blight
And hides the unchanging from men's sight.

James Legge: *The Texts of Taosim*

They may in the *light* of the Tao all be reduced to the same category. It was the separation that led to completion; from completion ensued dissolution. But all things, without regard to their completion and dissolution; may again be comprehended in their unity. (Ibid.)

Representation of Lao Tzu.

Therefore the scintillations of *light* from the midst of confusion and perplexity are indeed valued by the sagely man. (Ibid.)

He whose mind is grandly fixed emits a Heavenly *light*. In him who emits this heavenly *light*, men see the (True) man. When a man has cultivated himself (up to this point), thenceforth he remains constant in himself. When he is thus constant in himself the human element will leave him but Heaven will help him. (Ibid.)

Buddhism

There are few other texts which so greatly emphasise self-knowledge and introspection, attaining wisdom (the ability to perfectly understand and to patiently accept the Fourfold Noble Truth) and meditation (practising concentration of the mind) as the texts of Buddhism. James in *Varieties* describes this philosophy 'in strictness' as a system which is 'atheistic' in that 'popularly, of course, Buddha himself stands in the place of a God'.

They are perhaps the least tampered with of all of the texts discussed in this book to show the unadulterated way to 'enlightenment'. As Albert Einstein suggests of this philosophy,

> The religion of the future will be a cosmic religion. It should transcend a personal God and avoid dogma and theology. Covering both the natural and the spiritual, it should be based on a religious sense arising from the experience of all things natural and spiritual as a meaningful unity. Buddhism answers this description. If there is any religion that could cope with modern scientific needs it would be Buddhism.

Gautama Buddha, or Siddhartha, abandoned his home and became a mendicant, a beggar, in the middle of the fifth century BCE. Though a prince, he was greatly depressed by the suffering of his father's subjects. He employed meditation for forty-nine days, which resulted in his gaining enlightenment at the age of thirty-five under a Bodhi tree. He spent the rest of life teaching his insights, wisdom and compassion.

Within *The Teaching of Buddha* there is a constant reference to 'light' as a way to self realisation:

Following the Noble Path is like entering a dark room with a light in the hand; the darkness will all be cleared away and the room filled with *light*.

Make of your self a *light*. Rely upon yourself; do not depend upon anyone else. Make my teachings your *light*. Rely upon them; do not depend upon any other teaching.

Jainism

Much the same can be attributed to the ancient religious and philosophic system of Jainism, the follower of which is called a Jina or 'spiritual victor'. The *Tattvartha Sutra* is, by common consent, the book of books in the Jaina tradition, acclaimed as an authentic and systematic compendium of the essence of Jainism, as taught by Lord Mahavira (sixth century BCE). It is based on the premise that the goal of human life is liberation, which is defined as perfect knowledge, perfect intuition and eternal bliss, and describes the path to liberation as an enlightened world-view, which is enlightened knowledge and enlightened conduct. It states that each individual has his or her unique perception of the world, which is a mixture of truth and ignorance; all perceptions are valid but incomplete. It provides the gateways of investigation as a means for broadening one's knowledge and understanding.

Jainism does not fall under the umbrella of Vedic (Hindu) traditions as described earlier. It is a non-theistic religion with its own sacred texts and Jinas, or Spiritual Victors, whose teachings are neither derived through divine revelation, nor manifested through some inherent magical power. It is the individual human soul which, aided by earlier teachings, comes to know the truth.

Latin and South America: The Maya and the Inca

For religious cultures in South America such as the Maya and Inca, which have been referred to in previous chapters, the spiritual texts unfortunately no longer exist as they were mostly destroyed by the Spanish centuries ago. If they were not destroyed, then any surviving text and the association with light were corrupted, as Hunbatz Men writes in *Secrets of Mayan Science/Religion*:

> The Mayan word for illumination or enlightenment is *cizin*. Unfortunately its significance was distorted by the Spanish friars, as well as by the laws of the Inquisition. *Cizin* means radiating energy. But today, in the Yucatan, the word is associated with the devil because of the friars' distortions. Over time, Mayan spiritual refinement has been brutalized by Catholic ideas.

Suffice to say that such spiritual thought was not lost or missed by the Maya or the Inca, as will be discussed later in this book.

An overall view

A summarisation of the different types of spiritual texts in different regions of the world cannot be better described than in Mascaró's introduction to The *Bhagavad Gita* as the various spiritual visions of man all coming together in 'One Light':

> The spiritual visions of man confirm and illumine each other. We have the cosmic greatness of Hinduism, the moral issues of Zoroaster, the joy in Truth of Buddha, the spiritual victory of Jainism, the simple love of Tao, the wisdom of Confucius, the poetry of Shinto, the One God of Israel, the redeeming radiance of Christianity, the glory of God of Islam, the harmony of the Sikhs. Great poems in different languages but they are all poetry, the spiritual visions of man all from One Light. In them we have Lamps of Fire that burn to the glory of God. If we read the scriptures and books of wisdom of the world, if we consider the many spiritual experiences recorded in the writings of the

past, we find one spiritual faith, and this faith is based on a vision of Truth. Not indeed the truth of the laws of nature gradually discovered by the human mind; but the Truth of our Being.

In the Bhagavad-Gita we have faith, a faith based on spiritual vision. In this vision we have *Light*. Shall we see? This Song calls us to Love and Life. Shall we hear?

Every moment of our life can be the beginning of great things.
Juan Mascaró: Introduction to The Bhagavad Gita

As Heraclitus, a Greek philosopher, said, 'For wisdom, listen not to me but to the Word, and know that all are one.' And it was Jesus who said 'man know thyself'; in other words, meditation and the search for knowledge of oneself and the seeking of wisdom and truth.

This chapter accounts for and provides some history and context to the religions of the world in addition to esoteric spiritual texts. It is not merely to show the anomaly of the number of glaring overlaps of these global sacred texts, as in previous chapters, but moreover to cite a specific occurrence of a physical nature, a tangible instance of a spiritual event which is in connection with God or an omniscient entity and is solidly and consistently associated with the combination of knowledge of the Self, internal and external, contemplation and meditation and this continuous instance of 'light'. As we will see later on, it is not only global scripture that highlights the instance of light, but also that the forerunners and originators of these religions and spiritual thought had *enlightening* experiences, in the most literal of terms.

It is my conviction that this use of 'light' as a specific instance is more than mere metaphor and finds a basis in reality, which I will expand upon in Chapter 6. This experience will be elaborated upon in detail after presenting further evidence of this phenomenon from historically more recent sources. The following chapter will look at some of the great thinkers from the last six centuries who, intentionally or not, followed the suggestion and advice cited in this chapter. They contemplated widely and profoundly, resulting in their experiencing this 'light'.

Summary

We should at least consider and preferably embrace the overlap and unity of messages from these sources as a basis for a process initiating the cessation of conflicts between the religions and spiritual philosophies. We can use this unifying element as a means to potentially wave aside all of our existing prejudices. On this matter, William James suggested that there be 'an impartial science of religionswhich might sift out from the midst of their discrepancies a common body of doctrine which she might also formulate in terms to which physical science need not object.'

It is clear that ancient spiritual texts across the world all teach the utmost importance of knowledge, truth and wisdom.

This is to be found through study of the self and matters profound and spiritual. The employment of meditation is crucial in this endeavour. At the end of the process there is identification, if not union, with 'the divine'.

There seems to be a direct correlation with carrying out this study and endeavour, culminating in the consistent instance of 'light', which possesses a literal connotation and surpasses the use of metaphor.

5

The Spiritual Philosophers

Those who love wisdom must investigate many things.

Heraclitus (Greek philosopher 535–475 BCE)

This chapter is so titled for reasons similar to those given in the chapter *The Scientific Fraternity*, that is, it is not intended here to summarise the works of all the many philosophers who have existed and their particular and various genres of thought, but instead to concentrate on certain specific individuals.

Reference was made to Kant and Hegel in the Introduction and this chapter will also discuss Goethe, Dante, Nietzsche, Jung and Plato. In the eighteenth and nineteenth centuries, scientists took over from philosophers, whose domain originally included science though this is no longer the case; a division into two separate and distinctly different disciplines occurred. Today we would perhaps benefit from the reconnection or, at very least, a closer alliance of the two.

There are a great many philosophers who have lived over the past centuries, from Plato to Aristotle, through Kant and Hume to Wittgenstein and Satre and, as with *The Scientific Fraternity*, it is not my intention to belittle their contributions by not including them. In the context of this chapter, it is not relevant that all those not mentioned and their work should be written of at length, or at all, though they may well be explored in a future work.

The spiritual experience and association with 'light'
As discussed in the previous chapter, it is my assertion that, associated with 'light', as is mentioned in a wide variety of traditional and

esoteric texts, is a specific and tangible experience. I intend to provide further evidence of this spiritual experience and its specific association with light. It is my contention that the men of profound contemplation, the philosophers discussed in this chapter, had such an experience, the very same as alluded to in spiritual texts, and that they were 'illumined' by this instance. This moment of enlightenment, in its most literal of meanings, had a dramatic impact upon them and was a great influence on their subsequent lives, work and outlook.

The spiritual experiences of some 'contemplative' writers and philosophers
This takes into account profoundly contemplative individuals who focused on self-knowledge and profound introspection and, as in the case of Carl Gustav Jung, combined this with lateral, global academic study, deriving deeply personal experiences from such an approach. This experience, in addition to the case of Jung, can be found in Goethe's *Faust* and in the life and writings of Nietzsche. This is as opposed to the philosophers who were observers and investigators of various aspects of life and of the human being, concerned with the analysis of such but perhaps not delving as deeply into the origin and nature of the soul and of esoteric spiritual matters. Of some of these latter philosophers and their writings, conclusions are derived with the same blinkered, though comfortable and reconciliatory, optimism that can be found in Voltaire's *Candide*.

Voltaire and his satire Candide
Candide or *Optimism* was written by Voltaire in 1758 at the age of 64, and whilst one might find *Candide* an amusing read, it is worth noting that Voltaire was a great satirist, not dissimilar to Jonathan Swift, who was greatly affected by the earthquakes which had occurred in Lima (1746) and Lisbon (1755), killing many. This work was a contemptuous attack on the rather 'optimistic' philosophers of the day, such as Leibniz, who would assert that all was for the best and that such tragedies were for the sake of the general good; some positive could always be found.

The story of the hero, Candide, is one fraught with trial and tribulation, verily a roller-coaster ride of good fortune merely to set up a great plummet into misfortune. Despite all these events, and for the entirety of the text, Candide remains 'optimistic' and faithful to the philosophy, as agreed with his mentor Pangloss, that he is living in the best of all possible worlds. The book concludes with Candide reconciled with his lot and without desire to pursue what might have been, having been disappointed on so many occasions.

Candide's more physical and challenging journey, however, pales in comparison to Goethe's *Faust* and his rather more challenging spiritual one. Whilst many have written of Faust, it remains unclear as to whether he was a character of fiction or indeed based on several potential factual persons.

1 Johann Wolfgang Von Goethe: *Faust*

The original work, *Historia von D. Johann Fausten*, was anonymous and circulated in Germany in 1587. It has since been retold by many, including the Elizabethan dramatist Christopher Marlowe and, was also made into an opera by Charles Gounod in the nineteenth century and others who have been fascinated by and have taken up the story.

Goethe read the 1725 *Faust* chapbook (a pocket-sized booklet, popular from the sixteenth through the nineteenth century) and it preoccupied him for much of his life. Goethe's *Faust*, his *magnum opus*, is written in two parts and was commenced in his twenties. The first part was concluded in his fifties, whilst Part Two was not completed until Goethe was in his early eighties.

The story of Goethe's verse play
At the beginning, the Lord makes a wager with Mephistopheles in relation to Faust, who, as a devout servant of God 'hankers after heaven's loftiest orbs', wisdom and knowledge, to the point of 'madness, half suspected on his [Faust's] part'.

> Philosophy have I digested,
> The whole of Law and Medicine,
> From each its secrets I have wrested,
> Theology, alas, thrown in ...
> Can voice or power of spirits start,

To do me service and reveal
The things of Nature's secret seal ...
Then shall I see, with a vision clear,
How the secret elements cohere,
And what the universe engirds
And give up huckstering with words.

God intends to reward Faust for his assiduous and consistent endeavour; however, Mephistopheles (Satan) suggests that he can lead Faust from 'his true source' by 'guiding him in paths that I [Mephistopheles] choose for him'. God gives his permission, confident that though a 'man must strive, and striving he must err', and that a 'good man in his dark, bewildered course, will not forget the way of righteousness'.

Despite Faust having acquired much knowledge, he is full of malcontent and a deep sense of incompleteness and turns 'to the abyss of necromancy'. Necromancy here means divination, the seeking of spirits of divination for a variety of reasons from spiritual protection to wisdom. Mephistopheles interacts with Faust and so begins his

Johann von Goethe (1749–1832).

embarking on a spiritual journey fraught with visions, 'now we wend our way, it seems into witchery and dreams,' and as Mephistopheles says, 'So here we are, at the uttermost bounds of understanding – that is to say, where the wit of man breaks down.'

It is in Part Two that we see the bulk of Faust's spiritual experiences and, in this context, his change and growth. He awakes in a 'Pleasing Landscape', 'The mystery closer seeing, In mirrored hues we have our life and being.'

Faust eventually dies and Mephistopheles stands over the body awaiting his prize, Faust's soul. However, a host of angels from Heaven descend and rise again, 'bearing away with them the immortal part of Faust' and leaving Mephistopheles looking around himself indignant, wondering to whom he should complain for the stealing of the 'soul pledged mine'.

> ANGELS (*hovering in the higher atmosphere, bearing all that is immortal of Faust*)
> Saved is our spirit-peer, in peace,
> Preserved from evil scheming:
> 'For he whose strivings never cease
> Is ours for his redeeming.'
> If, touched by the celestial love,
> His soul has sacred leaven,
> There comes to greet him, from above,
> The company of heaven.

Use of 'light' in Faust

Toward the end, Faust, having wandered through the underworld interacting with a variety of spiritual entities, now walks 'with wisdom's deeper heed', and here we find several instances and use of 'light'.

For instance, there is Faust's speech near the end of Part Two:

> FAUST (*blinded*)
> Deep falls the night, in the gloom precipitate;
> What then? Clear light within my mind shines still;
> Only the master's word gives action weight,
> And what I framed in thought I will fulfil.

113

Ho, you my people, quickly come from rest:
Let the world see the fruit of bold behest.

And later when the host of angels appear 'with venomous light' in the passage of the chorus of the angels:

Turn, flames of love, once more
Pure *light* reveal.
Those who their lives deplore
Truth yet shall heal;
Rescued, no more the thrall
Of evil cares,
Soon with the All-in-All
Bliss shall be theirs.

Did Goethe have a similar experience himself?
It does not seem to me that Goethe's *Faust* can be appreciated fully from a purely academic standpoint. It is an allegory of the combination of academic study and learnedness into matters deeply spiritual and esoteric and, combined with meditation, a spiritual journey can be undertaken with its resulting spiritual experience associated with light, contentedness and even reward. This will be discussed more fully in Chapter 6 but can be seen in the following explorations of the writings of Nietzsche and Jung who actually lived through similar experiences themselves, as opposed to this fictional portrayal. However, it should be at least worth considering whether the passion and detail within the writing of *Faust* does not suggest that Goethe may also have gone through such an experience himself. Frank McLynn's biography of Jung maintains that Rudolph Steiner, like Jung, asserted 'that Mephistopheles was simply an aspect of Faust'. Perhaps Faust was an aspect of Goethe.

Indeed, much like Faust, Goethe refers to himself in one of his poems. While travelling he wrote:

Keine Ferne macht dich schwierig,
Kommst geflogen und gebannt,
Und zuletzt, des Lichts begierig,
Bist du Schmetterling verbrannt.

An etching of Faust by Rembrandt (1606–1669) located at the Rijksmuseum in Amsterdam. This print has mystified experts for centuries; it depicts Faust, pen in hand, leaning on a table with a writing-slope and books on it. There is an interesting interplay of light from both real and imagined sources. A bright radiating disk has appeared at the window of his study, from which the glare to the left makes contact with Faust. Within this disk is written an anagram which reads INRI ADAM TE DAGERAM AMRTET ALGAR ALGASTNA; what this means remains unclear. In 1791, Goethe used this etching on his title page for his publication of *Faust*. I would rather like to think that Rembrandt has captured the moment of Faust's 'experience' and included, most appropriately, this associated instance of 'light'.

(Aware of neither toil nor distance, as thou fliest on, decoyed, till yielding to the flame's instance, butterfly, thou art destroyed.)

Not to know of this 'death and re-birth,'Goethe claimed, was to 'be but a mournful guest on this somber earth.' Richard Friedenthal: *Goethe: His Life and Times)*

Goethe, like the character of Faust and the other individuals discussed in this chapter, was a varied and well-studied man. Among his studies was that of alchemy, which provided the foundation from which *Faust* originated. The transmutations of his alchemy were frequently distorted and scarcely recognisable in his poetry. He was fascinated and read as much as he could on the Orient, reading not only the *Bible* and the *Qur'an* but also listening to recitals of the Suras from the latter at Islamic services in Weimar, Germany. In addition, he was fascinated by Egyptian hieroglyphics after stumbling across an abandoned obelisk in Rome, and also read widely about the languages and wisdom of India.

It was Goethe's conviction that people who followed him would reap knowledge beyond their imagination. Few people realise that Goethe also produced a sizeable body of scientific work that focused on such diverse topics as plants, colour, clouds, weather, morphology and geology.

In particular, his intense fascination with light went to such a degree that he was sceptical of Newton's work on the matter and competed bitterly with Newton for decades on the definition of light. His writings on this research can be found in *The Theory of Colour (Zur Farbenlehre)* published in 1810. It is fascinating to note that Goethe's last words in life were not an appeal to God for eternal rest but, 'More light'!

In the *Book of Enoch* (among the *Dead Sea Scrolls*), Enoch's journey holds amazing similarities to that of Goethe's Faust character in that he, too, journeys through other-worldly realms, a narrative that is also full of the mention of 'light' and is reviewed in Chapter 6.

Christopher Marlowe's play: The Tragical History of Dr Faustus
Christopher Marlowe's verse play of the Faust story is far less involved and shorter in length than Goethe's version. Marlowe's account is simplistic and less spiritual in its narration of Faust, who here appears

as a scholar and black magician, and who promises his soul to the Devil and his agent Mephistopheles in return for wisdom and experience. In Marlowe's narrative, as opposed to that of Goethe's, Faust's learning is trivialised and one can see Faust as a fool, significantly different from his spiritual journey in Goethe's play.

Marlowe produced two works, with the publication of the A-text in 1604 and the B-text in 1616. In both, good and bad angels vie for his soul and, at the conclusion, Faust experiences an excruciating demise for having made the wrong choice: 'We'll give his mangled limbs due burial.' This narration is merely a tale of morality, that of good versus evil with dire penalty for choosing the latter path, as is written in the epilogue of the A and B-text:

CHORUS:
Cut is the branch [Faust] that might have grown full straight,
And burned is Apollo's laurel bough
That sometime grew within this learned man.
Faustus is gone. Regard his hellish fall,
Whose fiendful fortune may exhort the wise
Only to wonder at unlawful things,
Whose deepness doth entice such forward wits
To practise more than heavenly power permits.

I have also read the 1592 edition of *The History of the damnable life and deserved death of Doctor John Faustus* (anonymous and translated into English by P.F. Gent) and you can clearly see from where Marlowe's story originates. This original is marginally more complex than Marlowe's rendition, but is also essentially a moral and Christian tale of good and evil paths and penalty for taking the path of evil. This can be seen in the title of the penultimate Chapter LXII: *Here followeth the miserable and lamentable end of Doctor Faustus, by which all Christians may take an example and warning.* In fact, in this original work, the account of Faust's end could have been taken from a modern day horror film:

They found no Faustus, but all the hall lay besprinkled with blood, his brains cleaving to the wall: for the Devil had beaten him from one wall against another, in one corner lay his eyes, in another his teeth, a pitiful

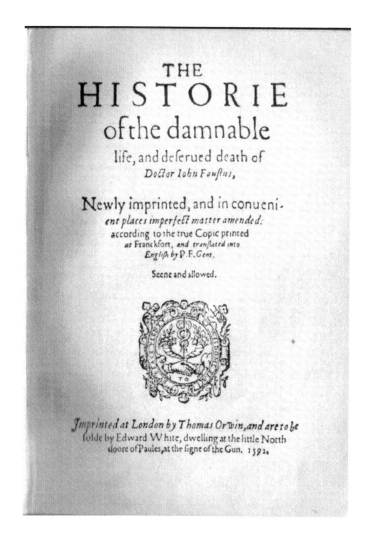

THE
HISTORIE
of the damnable
life, and deſerued death of
Doctor Iohn Fauſtus,

Newly imprinted, and in conueni-
ent places imperfect matter amended:
according to the true Copie printed
at Franckfort, and tranſlated into
Engliſh by P.F.Gent.

Seene and allowed.

Imprinted at London by Thomas Orwin, and are to be
ſolde by Edward White, dwelling at the little North
doore of Paules, at the ſigne of the Gun. 1592.

A facsimile of the title page of the 1592 edition of The History of the damnable life
and deserved death of Doctor John Faustus. It is interesting to note the caduceus
symbol in the middle of the emblem.

and fearful sight to behold ... they found his body lying on the horse dung, most monstrously torn, and fearful to behold, for his head and all his joints dashed in pieces.

While the original is a very good narrative, it lacks the volume, complexity, passion and 'spirituality' of Goethe's rendition. It is clear that Goethe retold the Faust story in his own very personal way.

2 Dante Alighieri: *The Divine Comedy*

There are several tales that possess an enduring quality by cutting so close to the heart and mind of man as to necessitate their recounting by a variety of media over the centuries by many writers and artists alike. As with Faust, Dante's *The Divine Comedy* is another such tale.

Further parallels can be drawn from Dante's *The Divine Comedy* (*Commedia*) translation and commentary provided by Robin Kirkpatrick. Whilst Dante (1265–1321) is thought of as a poet, he was certainly a great student of theology and philosophy, visiting the great schools of philosophy at the Sorbonne. Philosophy, Dante argued, was literally philo-sophia or 'love of wisdom' and he immersed himself in the study of books to the point where he nearly destroyed his eyesight. Dante is quoted as saying, 'The love of her [philosophy] banished and destroyed every other thought.' Philosophy was extremely important to Dante in all its forms, scientific, theological, logical and literary. In the *Convivio*, a work which preceded the *Commedia*, Dante begins with a quote from Aristotle: 'All human beings by nature desire to know.'

The *Commedia* is an intellectual synthesis which suggests that all things in the universe can be fully understood and explained. This work was probably started in 1307 and concluded only a few months before Dante's death in 1321. It has been illustrated by Sandro Botticelli, Gustave Doré, Salvador Dalí and William Blake. It is wonderful to see Blake's unique artistic representation bring much of the *Commedia* to the eye.

The narrative is largely of a spiritual struggle and a quest for truth, though interspersed with the politics of the day that affected him. The poem is divided into three volumes, or cantica, Inferno (Hell), Purgatorio (Purgatory) and Paradiso (Paradise/Heaven). Dante is

119

guided principally by Virgil, author of the *Aeneid*, whose work Dante studied in great depth and who was regarded in the Middle Ages principally as a seer. Their first meeting is an account of both a spiritual and literary reawakening. In the latter part of Paradiso, Dante is guided by Beatrice, a woman whom he was deeply in love with for the entirety of his life. He remained so even after her death and it was after her demise that Dante immersed himself in intense study. It is thought that the use of Beatrice, as opposed to Virgil, in the latter half of Paradiso was intended to reflect the beauty and profound feeling of love associated with his 'experience'.

References to 'light' in The Divine Comedy
Beneath this work lies much historical reference and this account of spiritual warfare refers constantly to the Old and New Testaments, as well as the ancient Greek narratives. The similarities are to be found in the traversing of these other-worldly realms and the meeting of a variety of spirits. However, it is not until Purgatorio (the condition or place of spiritual cleansing), the second realm, that we start to see the full extent and numerous instances of light, this imagery evoking the phenomena of change, process and regeneration until the return to earthly existence in Paradiso.

Canto 2 opens with a sudden display of supernatural illumination.

> a light came so swift across the sea
> that nothing else in flight could equal it.
> And, having briefly drawn my eyes away
> To ask my leader (Virgil) what this *light* could be,
> I saw it now grown greater and more bright.
> And then, around it, all appeared to me
> a something of I-did-not-know pure white,
> and, bit by bit, another under that.
>
> *Purgatorio: Canto 2: 17–24*

Virgil then declares that Dante, henceforth, must accustom himself to such moments of revelation, as in these later instances:

> And then it seemed that, wheeling slightly round,
> as terrible as *lightning*, down it struck

Dante Alighieri (1265–1321), by Sandro Botticelli.

and tore me upwards to the sphere of fire.
And there the eagle and I, it seemed, both blazed.
And this imagined fire so scorched and seared
that, yielding, dreaming sleep just had to break.

Purgatorio: Canto 9: 28–33

Virgil explains that Dante, having arrived at the steps that lead to the gate of Purgatory, was lifted there not by an eagle but by a Christian Saint, St. Lucia, whose name means 'light', and the heat that he experienced in his dream was, in fact, the light of revelation.

The second half of Canto 9 moves inward to a region of ecstatic vision in which, beyond any scientific or rational explanation, the mind is enraptured and informed by powers beyond itself.

The conclusion of Purgatorio is the nearing of the end of Dante's spiritual journey and his entry into Earthly Paradise and a new level of thought. He declares that his purpose must be to write for the benefit of mankind and, having received the visions, return to the world and, for its benefit, reveal the perspectives of divine truth. He associates himself with seers and prophets of the Old and New Testaments, particularly with Ezeziel and with St. John of the Apocalypse. Dante's progress has depended not upon heroic effort or intellectual discrimination but upon a descent into unconsciousness.

In Paradiso, perhaps the most deeply personal of all three cantica, we hear him describe his spiritual journey and experience:

> Glory, from Him who moves all things that are,
> Penetrates the universe and then shines back,
> Reflected more in one part, less elsewhere.
> High in that sphere which takes from Him most *light*
> I was – I was! – and saw things there that no one
> Who descends knows how or ever can repeat.
>
> *Paradiso: Canto 1: 1–6*

The *Commedia* is not a work of fantasy and Dante himself describes it as a 'sacred' work, making him 'over many years grow gaunt.' He also modestly suggests that this work is a little flame that might ignite a great bonfire.

In Paradiso, Dante is guided through the nine celestial spheres of heaven and in the entirety of this cantica there are numerous references to 'light'. One can hardly turn a page without viewing numerous examples. He again meets many souls, several of whom, as in Canto 21, are fellow contemplatives, each spinning in a concentrated circle of light. Here, Dante speaks of the penetration of God's light into the soul and, simultaneously, of the enwombing of the soul in the light of God. These contemplatives are Christian philosophers who, like Dante, devoted their lives to wisdom and the investigation of the created cosmos.

As a result of his experience, Dante states that he 'saw now better than [he] had before'. His guide later in Paradiso describes the light as the power that overcomes sight and 'is one from which no shelter can be sought. Here is all wisdom, and the strength that cleared the

Dante and his guide Beatrice before the 'divine light' in Paradiso, Canto 31.
By Gustave Doré.

William Blake
English 1757–1827
*Illustration to Dante's **Divine Comedy** 1824-27*
1. Dante at the Moment of Entering the Fire
pen, ink and watercolour over black chalk and pencil
52.8 x 36.9 cm
National Gallery of Victoria, Melbourne, Australia
Felton Bequest, 1920 (1018-3)

Illustration 1 is from Purgatorio (the cleansing of the soul). Virgil, his guide at this time, has just entered the flames and awaits the fearful Dante's entry. The angel who invited Dante into the flame in a previous painting hovers above. The colours are now richer than in the earlier depictions of Purgatorio. As with Doré's depiction, Blake's representations are filled with a superfluity of light which is an accurate reflection of Dante's writing.

William Blake
English 1757–1827
Illustration to Dante's **Divine Comedy** 1824-27
2. Dante Adoring Christ
pen, ink and watercolour over pencil and black chalk
52.7 x 37.2 cm
National Gallery of Victoria, Melbourne, Australia
Felton Bequest, 1920 (1020-3)

Illustration 2 is from Paradiso, Dante describes the crucified Christ entirely in terms of
heavenly light. It may be significant that his guide at this time, Beatrice, does not share
the vision, indicating the individual nature of Dante's powerful spiritual experience.

125

open road that runs from Heaven to earth,' which was for so long Dante's desire. This destination is described in Paradiso as where 'Our human nature is at one with God,' where 'What we hold in faith, not argued through but known for what it is, as the primal truth that all believe.'

It is my belief that the *Commedia* is a book of revelation which, as the commentator Kirkpatrick asserts, resists the imposition of any final answer and even questions the desirability of any final answer. Kirkpatrick suggests that the rhetoric of the last canto in Paradiso repeatedly emphasises the inadequacy of Dante's words in recording any ultimate experience of divinity. In my view, as I will elaborate in the next chapter, this 'experience' is a particularly difficult one to articulate, define and elucidate.

It is entirely possible that William Blake himself was a subject of this very same spiritual experience, which we will touch on briefly in the next chapter.

3 The philosopher Friedrich Nietzsche and his 'experience'

Nietzsche was certainly one of the greatest philosophers within the spiritual realm, who drove himself to extremes in matters of great profundity and, I believe, encountered the very same experience as that of Dante. It has been suggested that Nietzsche is perhaps not the best of examples to use, mainly due to his insanity and also due to his presentation of the idea of 'Superman', which was later distorted by the Nazis. Again it is all about context and a fuller understanding, rather than embracing unfounded preconceptions. Although the concept of 'Superman' was later usurped by the loathsome Nazi movement, Nietzsche had nothing to do with this as he lived in the nineteenth century, well before the emergence of the Nazi party in Germany. His insanity highlights a potential aspect of the experience in that, whilst it is a beatific experience and of light, if the individual does not manage it well it can lead to delusions of grandeur and perhaps even insanity. Therefore, if the reader is not sympathetic to Nietzsche he or she should at least read this commentary with an open mind.

Friedrich Nietzsche was born in 1844 and he wrote a number of books, including *The Birth of Tragedy* (1872), *Human, All Too Human* (1878), *Thus Spoke Zarathustra* (1883), and *Twilight of The Idols* (1889). His final work, *Ecce Homo*, is perhaps the most spiritually all-encompassing of his works. He felt that, at this point, he had reached some conclusion which justified a retrospective. Indeed, in *Ecce Homo*, he provides commentary on all his prior publications, himself and his spiritual journey and experience. Unfortunately he never saw this work published as he died in 1900.

Nietzsche is not the easiest of reads. However, much as with *Faust*, I persisted as I was familiar with his subject matter and what he was alluding to. Whilst in this text he refers to, and asserts many of, the points that I myself maintain, the style of writing is rather unfortunate in that it is particularly arrogant and egotistical in delivery and articulation. If one cannot bypass or overlook this, it can detract from the otherwise solid insights into his spiritual journey and resultant experience.

Friedrich Nietzsche (1844–1900).

127

Insight into Nietzsche's 'experience'
In the following selection of excerpts from his writings, there is clear insight into the thoughts, state of mind and the 'experience' of the man.

Ecce Homo - How One Becomes What One Is, which is very much a retrospective, on occasion is arrogantly presented, but particularly insightful to his spiritual journey and his experience. Nietzsche states his intentions in the Foreword when he writes:

> Seeing that I must shortly approach mankind with the heaviest demand that has ever been made on it, it seems to be indispensable to *say who I am* ... the last thing *I* would promise would be to 'improve' mankind ... *to overthrow idols* (my words for 'ideals') – that is rather my business.

Of his writing and how demanding it is he states:

> He who knows how to breathe the air of my writings knows that it is an air of heights, a *robust* air. One has to be made for it, otherwise there is no small danger one will catch cold. The ice is near, the solitude is terrible – but how peacefully all things lie in the *light*! how freely one breathes! how much one feels beneath one! ... Philosophy, as I have hitherto understood and lived it, is a voluntary living in ice and high mountains – a seeking after everything strange and questionable in existence, all that has hitherto been excommunicated by morality. From the lengthy experience afforded by such a wandering in the *forbidden* I learned to view the origin of moralising and idealising very differently from what might be desirable.

In terms of seeking this knowledge he says of himself:

> How much truth can a spirit *bear*, how much truth can a spirit *dare* ... Every acquisition, every step forward in knowledge is the *result* of courage, of severity towards oneself, of cleanliness with respect to oneself.

This unfortunate overindulgent confidence is continued when he writes of his work *Thus Spoke Zarathustra,* which is widely acknowledged as perhaps Nietzsche's best literary work and described by himself as the 'deepest ever written'. Zarathustra, also known as Zoroaster whose 'experience' will be explained later, is sometimes referred to as 'the first prophet'. He is the founder and prophet of the ancient Persian religion Zoroastrianism, the bible for which is the *Zend-Avesta.*

In this example of similar self-confident tone, Nietzsche declares how privileged the reader is to access his 'exalted' works:

> I have with this book given mankind the greatest gift that has ever been given it. With a voice that speaks across millennia ... It is also the *profoundest*, born out of the innermost abundance of truth, an inexhaustible well into which no bucket descends without coming up filled with gold and goodness ... Here speaks no fanatic, here there is no 'preaching', here *'faith'* is not demanded: of an infinite abundance of *light* ... Such things as this reach only the most select; it is an incomparable privilege to be a listener here.

Nietzsche asserts in *Ecce Homo* that he who reads his works will experience ecstasies of learning from his books: 'For I come from heights no bird has ever soared to, I know the abysses into which no foot has ever yet strayed' and he describes any of his readers as 'a monster of courage and curiosity, also something supple, cunning, cautious, a born adventurer and discoverer.'

References to 'light' in Thus Spoke Zarathustra
In *Thus Spoke Zarathustra* Buddha is also discussed and again there are numerous references to 'light' and to knowledge, which appear in a variety of his texts, but especially within this one.

> Where is the *lightning* to lick you with its tongue? Where is the madness, with which you should be cleansed?

> Behold, I teach you the Superman: he is this *lightning*, he is this madness!

> I love him who lives for knowledge and who wants knowledge that one day the Superman may live.

Nietzsche compares himself to Zarathustra and describes himself as 'a prophet of the *lightning* and a heavy drop from the cloud'; but this *lightning* is called Superman and he desires to 'Teach men the meaning of their existence: which is the Superman, the *lightning* from the dark cloud.'

It should be explained here that Superman, sometimes translated as 'overman' from the German, *Übermensch*, and used by Nietzsche, was also used by Goethe. In philosophy, it means a superior man who justifies the existence of the human race and would not be the product of long evolution but would emerge when any man with superior potentiality completely masters himself and dispenses with 'herd mentality' to create his own values, which are rooted in life on this earth.

On the matter of knowledge and his independent drive for it, Nietzsche feels that 'Truly, it is more when one's own teaching comes out of one's own burning!', and says of himself in *Ecce Homo - Twilight of the Idols*:

As if in me a *second consciousness* had grown, as if in me 'the will' had turned on a *light* for itself over the *oblique* path on which it had hitherto been *descending* ... The *oblique* path – it was called the 'path to truth'... And, in all seriousness, no one before me has known the right path, the *ascending* the path: only after me are there again hopes, tasks, prescribable paths of culture - I *am the bringer of the good tidings of these* ... Precisely therewith am I a destiny.

Nietzsche's 'inspiration' in Twilight of the Idols
Twilight of the Idols is perhaps one of the more synoptic of his books. It was formed from thoughts gleaned from previous writings and, in a letter to his friend Carl Fuchs, he described how he had felt 'most uncommonly inspired': 'I would get up (or rather jump up) at two in the morning, "driven by the spirit"'.

Furthermore, in the chapter titled 'What I Owe the Ancients', he refers to his selective taste in ancient books in obtaining knowledge:

In conclusion, a word about the world which I sought to approach, and to which I perhaps found a new approach – the ancient world. Here again my taste, which may be the opposite of a tolerant taste, is far from saying yes indiscriminately: it is very loathe to say yes, and prefers to say no, likes best of all to say absolutely nothing ... This is true for whole cultures; it is true for books – it is also true of locations and landscapes. Basically there are a very small number of ancient books that count for anything in my life; the most famous are not among them.

A 'free spirit' in Human All Too Human

Human All Too Human states that a freed spirit should be understood in no other sense; a spirit that has *become free*, that has again seized possession of itself.

He compares himself to Voltaire who 'is above all a grandseigneur of the spirit: precisely what I am too. - The name of Voltaire on a writing by me-that was really progress – *towards myself.*' He again provides comments on his self-imposed learning and seeking 'the truth' in preparing himself and resulting in his 'experience'.

> A downright thirst seized hold of me: thenceforward I pursued in fact nothing other than physiology, medicine and natural science – I returned to actual historical studies openly when the *task* imperiously compelled me to. It was then too that I first divined the connection between an activity chosen contrary to one's instincts, a so-called 'calling' to which one is called *least of all.*

> My task, to prepare a moment of supreme coming-to-oneself on the part of mankind.

Additional commentary on his preparation (in retrospect) and just prior to the 'experience' can also be found within *Human, All Too Human*, which consists of a series of 638 aphorisms:

> 292 *Onwards.* And so onwards along the path of wisdom, with a hearty tread, a hearty confidence! However you may be, be your own source of experience! Throw off your discontent about your nature; forgive yourself your own self ... Likewise, you must be familiar with history and the delicate game with the two scales: "on the one hand – on the other hand." Stroll backwards, treading in the footprints in which humanity made its great and sorrowful passage through the desert of

131

the past; then you have been instructed most surely about the places where all later humanity cannot or may not go again ... You have it in your power to merge everything you have lived through – attempts, false starts, errors, delusions, passions, your love and your hope – into your goal ... Do you think this kind of life with this kind of goal is too arduous, too bereft of all conflicts? Then you have not yet learned that no honey is sweeter than that of knowledge ... The same life that comes to a peak in old age also comes to a peak in wisdom, in that gentle sunshine of continual spiritual joyfulness; ... Towards the light – your last movement; the joyful shout of knowledge – your last sound.

633 And in fact, the fervor about having the truth counts very little today in relation to that other fervor, more gentle and silent, to be sure, for seeking the truth, a search that does not tire of learning afresh and testing anew.

634 Incidentally, the methodical search for truth itself results from those times when convictions were feuding among themselves. If the individual had not cared about *his* 'truth', that is, about his being right in the end, no method of enquiry would exist at all.

Nietzsche's own experience in Thus Spoke Zarathustra
It is in *Ecce Homo - Thus Spoke Zarathustra* that I believe the best evidence for Nietzsche having had his 'experience' can be found. The commentaries of others who have had the 'experience' in the following chapter will show how Nietzsche writes with similar striking imagery of the 'concept of revelation', 'an ecstasy', a 'superfluity of light' and 'a tempest of a feeling of freedom ... of divinity'.

The great seriousness first arises, the real question-mark is the first step up, the destiny of the soul veers round, the clock-hand moves on, the tragedy *begins* ... one is merely incarnation, merely mouthpiece, merely medium of overwhelming forces. The concept of revelation, in the sense that something suddenly, with unspeakable certainty and subtlety, becomes *visible*, audible, something that shakes and overturns one to the depths, simply describes the fact ... a thought flashes up like *lightning* ...

I never had any choice. An ecstasy whose tremendous tension sometimes discharges itself in a flood of tears while one's steps now involuntarily rush along, now involuntarily lag; a complete being outside of oneself with the distinct consciousness of a multitude of subtle shudders and trickles down to one's toes ... a superfluity of *light* ... Everything is in the highest degree involuntary but takes place as in a tempest of a feeling of freedom, of absoluteness, of power, of divinity ...

The confidence and knowing due to this 'experience' can be found in his commentary in *Ecce Homo - The Birth of Tragedy* and *The Untimely Essays*. Nietzsche refers to his search for truth and knowledge and having attained insight, finding himself eventually 'no longer speaking with words but with lightning-bolts' as a result of the courage of his conviction.

The insight that is strictly confirmed and maintained by truth and knowledge ... To grasp that this requires *courage* and, as a condition of this, a superfluity of *strength*: for precisely as far as courage *may* dare to go forward, precisely by this measure of the strength does one approach truth.

What I am today, *where* I am today – at a height at which I no longer speak with words but with *lightning-bolts* – oh how far away I was from it in those days! But I *saw* the land – I did not deceive myself for a moment as to the way, see, danger *and* success! ... it is my sagacity to have been many things and in many places so as to be able to become *one* person – so as to be able to attain *one thing*. For a time I *had* also to be a scholar.

In fact Nietzsche feels that he is one of the very few who has had such 'experience' and of this he states:

This reflects my own experience of inspiration; I do not doubt that one has to go back thousands of years to find anyone who could say to me 'it is mine also'.

Nietzsche's arrogance?

Nietzsche perceives that he is the only one to have had such an experience and only in greatest antiquity might there have been others. He therefore sees his works and insights as a great legacy to mankind and this is shown in his typically overindulgent manner in *Ecce Homo - Why I am a Destiny*, the final chapter, when he proclaims 'I am not a man, I am dynamite' and 'I was the first to discover the truth':

> I know my fate. One day there will be associated with my name a recollection of something frightful – of a crisis like no other before on earth, of the profoundest collision of conscience, of a decision evoked *against* everything that until then had been believed in, demanded, sanctified. I am not a man, I am dynamite. And with all that there is nothing in me of a founder of a religion ... I have a terrible fear I shall one day be pronounced *holy* ... *Revaluation of all values*: this is my formula for an act of supreme coming-to-oneself on the part of mankind which in me has become flesh and genius. It is my fate to have to be the first *decent* human being, to know myself in opposition to the mendaciousness of millennia ... I was the first to *discover* the truth.

Nietzsche feels that the result of this 'light' and 'experience' was a great improvement on systemised religion. Of this he states that:

> The *lightning*-bolt of truth struck precisely that which formally stood highest: he who grasps *what* was then destroyed had better see whether he has anything at all left in his hands. Everything hitherto called 'truth' is recognized as the most harmful, malicious, most subterranean form of the lie; the holy pretext of 'improving' mankind as the cunning to *suck out* life itself and to make it anaemic.

Here we can see the unfolding of Nietzsche's spiritual journey to the point of conclusion; this profound 'experience' will be explored in the next chapter. It is, however, debatable whether, due to his rather abrasive articulation and philosophic narcissism, it can be described as a full 'experience'. The reader will probably not have missed his apparent delusions of grandeur in these excerpts from his writings. His imperiousness is unfortunate and detracts from his work; however, he feels that he is one of few to have had such an experience and he only has Zarathustra to relate to in this context. This is perhaps just and forgivable to the extent that he would have had no one to discuss such matters with, nor would it have been written of in any text that he readily had access to; certainly none of the philosophers of his day had openly achieved what he had. As was the case with Jung, and even more so today, there is easy access to a vast amount of information on a diverse range of subjects. Had he lived in a later age he would have known that he was not alone.

4 Carl Gustav Jung and his 'experience'

Carl Gustav Jung travelled widely in Africa, North America and the Orient and was an erudite man of great introspection. He perhaps represents best what can be described as that combination of academic study, meditation and resultant 'experience', which leads to oneness or *Atman*. He was a student of a variety of subjects including the work of Poe, Byron, Shakespeare and Nietzsche, and also of Sanskrit, Hindu and Egyptian myths, Greek and Norse legends, the Bible, the Church Fathers, Mithraism, Gnosticism and Aztec mythology, all of which are cited in his book *Jahrbuch* published between 1911 and 1913. There was debate with Freud regarding Akhenaton, the Egyptian Pharaoh who temporarily changed Egypt into a monotheistic society, and also study of the I Ching.

This diverse study is also referred to in the foreword by June Singer, a Jungian analyst, to the book *Jung and the Lost Gospels* by Stephan Hoeller: where she relates his interests in ancient literature to his profession of psychiatry and the motives behind how people think and believe:

It was C.G. Jung who discovered for himself and became enraptured by the literature of the Jewish and Christian Gnostics, whose writings included the Lost Gospels ... as a psychiatrist Jung was interested in why people think as they think and believe what they believe. He sought for clues in the mythology, especially for that which gives rise to religious and spiritual traditions ... When he became interested in pursuing the study of the ancient Gnostic texts, it was to support and

Carl Gustav Jung (1875–1961).

amplify his own experience ... He used it freely when it illuminated such issues as the necessity of reclaiming an interior view of oneself and the world in which we live.

The 'Lost Gospels' referred to here are the *Dead Sea Scrolls* and the *Nag Hammadi Library*, discussed previously.

Jung's obsession with Nietzsche's experience
At university, and subsequently, Jung became, to an extent, obsessed with Nietzsche and conducted a detailed analysis of him in the late 1920s to early 1930s. As Frank McLynn writes in his biography of Carl Gustav Jung, the reading of *Thus Spoke Zarathustra* was as much a revelation to him as *Faust* had been. Zarathustra was clearly Nietzsche's 'No.2', and, as Jung saw it, Nietzsche had been driven mad by two things: unlike Jung he had discovered his 'No.2' late in life; and he had 'fearlessly and unsuspectingly let his No.2 loose upon a world that knew and understood nothing about such things'. (Jung asserted that there were two personalities within an individual but he was wary of

the pathological interpretation of the No.1 and No.2 personality which had nothing to do with a split or dissociation in the ordinary sense but was something that was played out in every individual.)

McLynn goes on to comment how Jung was alarmed by the model of Nietzsche's insanity and how he strove to avoid a similar breakdown in himself:

> [Jung] was perfectly well aware how closely his experience resembled that of the great German [Nietzsche] who died in an insane asylum ... It was this fate that he feared above all, having survived madness by the skin of his teeth; he was often to say that the experience gave him a unique insight into the forces that carried off Nietzsche ... For at least four years he lived in a state of constant tension and near-breakdown, and he often reflected, with justifiable pride, that it was only his immense toughness that pulled him through. As one mental storm succeeded another, he frequently had to force himself to do yoga exercises to keep his emotions in check ... Jung practised yoga simply to give himself the strength to *return* to the fearsome world of the unconscious.

The 'experience' is not an easy one and is often bewildering, and in an explanation of this potential 'madness' McLynn writes:

> Nietzsche had been overwhelmed by madness because he did not retain a strong enough impression of the difference between the external world and his own fantasies. Jung insisted on seeing patients right through 1913–1916, even though the therapeutic process was presumably more from them to him than vice versa ... he took great comfort from his family: he repeated over and over to himself, 'I have a medical diploma from a Swiss university. I have a wife and five children. I live at 228 Seestrasse, Küsnacht.'

In other words, throughout the duration and process of his 'experience' Jung, unlike Nietzsche, was able to remain grounded.

Jung and 'Individuation'
The following excerpts are selected from McLynn's biography which highlight the points of interest that initiated Jung's journey and his

process of individuation. This is the harmonisation of the conscious and the unconscious and when the ego is decentralised. Perhaps, as McLynn goes on to suggest, this process of 'individuation' all started from Jung's study of the human 'psyche' and the 'collective unconscious'.

His study of dreams, the fantasies of schizophrenics, the beliefs of primitive peoples and the recurring motifs in the myths of civilisation after civilisation, Jung came to the conclusion that there existed something very like what Plato called in the *Timaeus* the 'world soul'. Jung's term for this core of actual and potential human mental dispositions he called 'the psyche', though he sometimes muddied the waters by using 'psyche' in the normal sense referring to the totality of the *individual's* psychic make-up. If the psyche was the 'world-mind' - in the sense that at the deepest level ... every individual was identical to all other selves – the true task of psychotherapy and all other Jungian-inspired journeys was to find the Self – that the level of the unconscious where the individual consciousness merged with the psyche, as a river flowing into a mighty ocean.

The unconscious, then, was collective, and because of its collective nature the human mind was predisposed to respond to situations through fixed patterns Jung called archetypes ... These archetypes manifested themselves in images and symbols, found in dreams, fantasies and myths. The recurrent and universal motifs found in all the world's mythologies pointed to their common origin in archetypes in the collective unconscious.

An archetype in psychology is a model of a person, personality or behavior. In Jung's psychological framework, archetypes are innate, universal prototypes for ideas and may be used to interpret observations.

Jung's system was centripetal, aimed at the still point where ego merged with Self ... a well-balanced individual, moving towards this fusion with the Absolute – or what the Buddhists call *Atman*.

The confrontation of the Self, and what Jung described as individuation, as mentioned, is the harmonisation of the conscious and unconscious and tapping into the true self. McLynn relates this to a self-regulating process in the individual and in the probing of the depths of the 'Self'.

> The journey into the collective unconscious in 'individuation' is accompanied by a self- regulating process ... As the individual descended into the unconscious in individuation, it was essential that the analyst kept the patient's conscious and unconscious balanced ... Probing deeper and deeper levels until the final encounter with the Self ... has been compared to the epic descent in Jules Verne's *A Journey to the Centre of the Earth*, often hailed by the Jungians as a metaphor for the individuation process.

> Once the archetypes of the spirit had been encountered, all that remained was the final stage of the journey, confronting the archetype of the archetypes: the Self. The patient on the journey of individuation knew he was approaching the centre of the maze in his dreams, fantasies or active imagination were characterised by mandalas, universal religious symbols such as Christ, Buddha, Anthropos and Adam and increasing experience of the deity as the 'God-image'.

McLynn goes on to say that it was the paradox of individuation that a person was most himself or herself after fusion with the world-mind or objective psyche. Repeatedly, Jung stressed that the Self had nothing to do with 'self' as used in ordinary language; for this he always used the word 'ego'. Jung's Self can be roughly approximated to the Buddhist *Atman*. As Jung stated, 'the experience of the Self is always a defeat for the ego.'

> The individuation process also meant coming to terms with death ... Shrinking from death robbed the second half of life of its significance, for an old man who could not bid farewell to life was as pathetic as a young man who could not embrace it.

'Self-knowledge' in Jung's last work: Mysterium Coniunctionis
The following excerpts are from Jung's *Mysterium Coniunctionis* which was Jung's last great work, on which he was engaged for more than a decade and which was finished in his eightieth year. It forms a

culmination of all his thoughts and research, and refers to his 'experience'. These should further elucidate individuation and the challenging process leading to this experience:

> The structure of wholeness (*Atman*) was always present but was buried in profound unconsciousness, where it can always be found again if one is willing to risk one's skin to attain the greatest possible range of consciousness through the greatest possible self-knowledge – a 'harsh and better drink' usually reserved for hell ... For self-knowledge – in the total meaning of the word – is not a one-sided intellectual pastime but a journey through the four continents, where one is exposed to all the dangers of the land, sea, air, and fire ... Nothing may be 'disregarded'... The fullest possible 'realisation' of the object of contemplation ... The aim of mystical peregrination is to understand all parts of the world, to achieve the greatest possible extension of consciousness.

Jung asserts that this understanding is necessary in order to appreciate the revelations of the spirit embodied in dogma:

> The limitations of human knowledge which leave so many incomprehensible and wonderful things unexplained do not, however, exempt us from the task of trying to understand the revelations of the spirit that are embodied in dogma, otherwise there is a danger that the treasures of supreme knowledge which lie hidden in it will evaporate into nothing and become a bloodless phantom, an easy prey for all shallow rationalists.

> It is the real experience of a man who has got involved in the compensatory contents of the unconscious by investigating the unknown, seriously and to the point of self-sacrifice.

Jung goes on to state that it is after the process of individuation that consciousness is renewed through the descent into the unconscious and when and how the two are joined.

The 'uroboros' is the emblematic serpent of ancient Egypt and Greece represented with its tail in its mouth, continually devouring itself and being reborn from itself. As a Gnostic and alchemical symbol, the uroboros expresses the unity of all things, material and spiritual.

Jung used the uroboros as a dramatic symbol of the integration and assimilation of the opposite, i.e. of the shadow. This 'feedback' process is, at the same time, a symbol of immortality, since it is said of the uroboros that he slays himself and brings himself to life, fertilises himself and gives birth to himself. He symbolises the One, who proceeds to the clash of opposites, and he therefore constitutes the secret of the prima materia, as a projection, unquestionably stems from man's unconscious.

Jung stated, however, that a mental union was not the culminating point, but merely the first stage of the procedure. The second stage is reached when union, that is, the unity of spirit and soul, is conjoined with the body. The third stage, and a consummation of the mysterium coniunctionis, can be expected only when the unity of spirit, soul, is made with the original 'unus mundus'. Unus mundus literally means 'One world', the concept of an underlying reality from which everything emerges and returns to.

In addition to knowledge of the unknown, essential to the process was the self-knowledge, the goal of which is the 'unio mentalis', 'the attainment of full knowledge of the heights and depths of one's own character.' Jung suggests that, 'Even adult persons often have no idea how to cope with the problem of living, and on top of that so unconscious in this regard that they succumb in the most uncritical way to the slightest possibility of finding some kind of answer or certainty.'

In the *Mysterium*, within the section titled Self- Knowledge, Jung refers to the confusing effect of the 'shadow' (the unconscious) in the search for self-knowledge:

> Self-knowledge is an adventure that carries us unexpectedly far and deep. Even a moderately comprehensive knowledge of the shadow can cause a good deal of confusion and mental darkness ... Even for modern psychology the confrontation with the shadow is not a harmless affair, and for this reason it is often circumvented with cunning and caution. Rather than face one's own darkness, one contents oneself with the illusion of one's civic rectitude.

Jung's 'shadow' is the aspect of one's own personality that an individual has preferred not to look too closely at and he uses the term 'shadow' for the unconscious part of the personality.

The importance of meditation
Essential for the 'experience' and self-knowledge is the employment of meditation of which Jung comments:

> The ego personality's coming to terms with its own background, the shadow, corresponds to the union of the spirit and soul in the *unio mentalis*, which is the first stage of the coniunctio. What I call coming to terms with the unconscious the alchemists called meditation ... the shadow, as we know, usually represents a fundamental contrast to the conscious personality.

Jung also comments on the indifferent or negative attitudes to meditation in the western world:

> In general, meditation and contemplation have a bad reputation in the West. They are regarded as a particularly reprehensible form of idleness or as pathological narcissism. No one has time for self-knowledge or believes that it could serve any sensible purpose. Also, one knows in advance that it is not worth the trouble to know oneself, for any fool can know what he is ... Self-knowledge is one of the most difficult and exacting of the arts.

> Since earliest times, therefore, men have had recourse in such situations to artificial aids, ritual actions such as dances, sacrifices, identification with ancestral spirits, etc., in the obvious attempt to conjure up or reawaken those deeper layers of the psyche which the light of reason and the power of the will can never reach, and to bring them back to memory.

Jung suggests that he would 'counsel the critical reader to put aside his prejudices and for once try to experience in himself the effects of the process of individuation he described, or else to suspend judgment and admit that he understands nothing.' For thirty years he studied these psychic processes under all possible conditions and had assured himself that the alchemists, as well as the great philosophies of the East, are referring to just such experiences, and that it is chiefly ignorance of the psyche if these experiences appear 'mystic'.

The benefits, Jung claims, for one who has gone through the process of individuation is that the person enjoys greater self-confidence in his or her beliefs and possesses an 'inner certainty'.

> [That person] alone has a genuine claim to self-confidence, for he has faced the dark ground of his self and thereby has gained himself. This experience gives him faith and trust, the *pistis* in the ability of the self to sustain him, for everything that menaced him from inside he has made his own. He has acquired the right to believe that he will be able to overcome all the future threats by the same means. He has arrived at an inner certainty which makes him capable of self-reliance, and attained ... the *unio mentalis*... [which]as a rule this state is represented pictorially by the mandala.

Mysterium Coniunctionis, along with *Aion*, is regarded as the most esoteric and impenetrable of all his writings, but some of his disciples claim them as the supreme masterpieces in his *oeuvre*. The title, *Mysterium Coniunctionis*, means a kind of wedding, whereby the soul attains its missing half and achieves wholeness, and was Jung's *magnum opus*. He was satisfied that he had succeeded where Goethe and Nietzsche had both failed. The full title of the work is *Mysterium Coniunctionis – An Inquiry into the Separation and Synthesis of Physic Opposites In Alchemy*. However, alchemy had little pertinence in the work – the thing that convinced Jung that alchemy was a kind of allegory for the analytic process was the uncanny parallel between the individuation process and the passage from *unio mentalis* to *unus mundus* in alchemy. The mandala as pictorially representative of *unio mentalis*, was the empirical equivalent of the metaphysician's *unus mundus*.

Jung's experience and 'mandala' symbols

As we can see, an aspect of the 'experience' and of individuation is the presence of mandalas, the Sanskrit word meaning circle. The typical mandala features a quaternity, with a circle containing a cross, a star, a square, or an octagon. Mandalas feature in ancient religions such as Tibetan Buddhism. In all major Buddhist tantric systems, the mandala is described as a visual representation of the components of the enlightened mind. For a period in Jung's life he began the habit of drawing mandalas in his notebook each morning. Jung himself described the mandala in the *Mysterium Coniunctionis* as portraying 'the self as a concentric structure, often in the form of squaring the circle.'

The mandala structure includes many different kinds of secondary symbols, most of them expressing the nature of the opposites to be united. The structure is invariably felt as the representation of a central state, or of a centre of personality essentially different from the ego. McLynn also states that it is of numinous nature:

> The idea is that the mandala is part of Nature's self-healing and compensates for the confusion. So, in later young Jungian language, the squaring of the circle is an archetype of wholeness, whose symbol is invariably the quaternity, as in the three Synoptic Gospels being 'compensated' by John's Gnostics one.

It is my assertion here that Jung's 'experience' was fully articulated in his *Mysterium Coniunctionis*. The initial point of process or embarkation is cited by McLynn, 'He noted the exact date when he 'let himself go.' It was 12 December 1913. This pertains to his spiritual journey and period of deep introspection and all the mysteries of the 'experience'.

The 'experience' itself is described consistently by Jung and, on many occasions, as 'numinous', meaning the indication of 'the presence of a divinity, spiritual or awe-inspiring', and he states that this would be recognised only by someone who had known it themselves. He declares that:

> Anyone who has experienced anything of the sort will know what I mean, and anyone who has not had the experience will not be satisfied by any amount of descriptions. Moreover there are countless descriptions of it in world literature. But I know of no case in which the bare description conveyed the experience.

In Jung's view, any attempt to gain an adequate understanding of the numinous experience must be made of parallel religious or metaphysical ideas which have not only been associated with it from ancient times, but are constantly used to formulate and elucidate it, a point which I have tried to make in this book. Jung goes on further to say that investigations of such experiences convinced him 'that previously unconscious contents then break through into consciousness and overwhelm it and that even Jesus appeared to his followers in that *light.*' Jung states that these images and ideas were not thought up or invented by the inspired person but 'happened' to them as experiences, and they became, as it were, their willing or unwilling victim. A will transcending his consciousness seized hold of him, which he was quite unable to resist. Naturally enough he feels this overwhelming power as 'divine'.

Jung and the alchemical allegory
In the epilogue to *Mysterium Coniunctionis* Jung writes of his 'experience' and also why he used the alchemical allegory to explain it:

> We can see today that the entire alchemical procedure for the uniting of opposites ... could just as well represent the individuation process of a single individual ... and that if he wanted to be understood that he would have to count on a reader whose experience was similar to his own. Alchemy therefore has performed for me the great and invaluable service of providing material in which my *experience* could find sufficient room, and has thereby made it possible for me to describe the individuation process as least in its essential aspects.

In this section, we see Jung's explanation of the process of individuation citing profound introspection and confrontation of the Self as an essential device which leads to this 'numinous' or awe-inspiring 'experience'.

5 Plato and his 'experience'

This chapter is titled *The Spiritual Philosophers* in an effort to demonstrate that these individuals were of profound thought and in my commentary they are shown to have been such. This is despite the reputation traditionally held that Goethe and Dante, with superficial philosophical knowledge, are considered more as poets, and Jung is perhaps best known as a psychiatrist. However, in addition to Nietzsche in the context of recognised 'philosophers', there is another who had a similarly profound experience: Plato. The evidence of such an experience in relation to Plato was suggested to me by Dr Raymond Moody.

The reference to Plato's 'experience' can be found in *The Thirteen Epistles of Plato* and in the seventh in particular. This Seventh Letter was a turning point in Plato's life; he was disillusioned with politics after the execution of his mentor, Socrates, and devoted himself thereafter to philosophy. Plato was also a well-travelled and learned man travelling to Egypt to study the discoveries of Pythagoras (580–500 BCE) who preceded him. Pythagoras was the founder of a religious and philosophical movement whose discoveries in mathematics, music, astronomy and metaphysics made a significant impact on Plato. It was after this journey and visiting Italy and Sicily that Plato returned to Athens to found the Academy, the modern day university, for the pursuit of philosophical and scientific inquiry.

In an introduction to the collection by L.A. Post, he asserts that the work can be compared with the letters of St. Paul (Paul will be mentioned in the next chapter). Post states that in this work of Plato's we find, 'The confident tone of a seer, the fervid outpouring of an enthusiast who has seen a vision – a vision that compels him to devote his life to propagating a divine truth amongst all mankind.'

The Seventh Epistle is the longest in the collection and the most valuable of the Platonic letters. Whilst there is debate over how genuine the letters are, even critics who dismiss some of the other letters accept the seventh as authentic.

Plato alludes to the experience, referring to and treating the 'subject' rather mysteriously and circumspectly. He does, however, employ the rather specific aspect of 'light' in his mention of it. Its attainment, Plato

146

Plato (428/427–348/347 BCE).

asserts, is for one who is genuinely devoted to philosophy, is a man of God and sees in the course marked out a path of enchantment which he must strain every nerve to follow, or die in the attempt. Provided that the individual does not relax their efforts, they are crowned with the final accomplishment. Plato suggests that, when this conviction has taken possession of the individual, they should continue in whatever occupation they engage, but never cease to practise philosophy and such habits that make them most effective in ensuring them an intelligent and retentive student. Plato continues that acquaintance of it must come after a long period of attendance on the subject and then 'suddenly, like a *blaze* kindled by a *leaping spark*, it is generated in the soul and at once becomes self-sustaining'.

Plato states that he has composed no work in regard to it nor will he ever do so for there is no way of putting it into words like other studies. He suggests that writing on such a subject is best avoided by others and, were such treatise to be produced, he would do it best. However, he goes on to state:

147

[If he thought] it possible to deal adequately with the subject in a treatise or lecture for the general public, what finer achievement would there have been in my life than to write a work of great benefit to mankind and to bring the nature of things to light for all men?

Plato and the revelation of 'light'

Of study and knowledge, Plato states that the study of virtue and vice must be accompanied by an enquiry into what is false and true of existence in general and must be carried on by constant practice and throughout a long period after scrutinising 'with benevolent disputation by the use of question and answer without jealousy, at last in a flash of understanding of each *blazes* up, and in the mind, as it exerts all its powers to the limit of human capacity, is flooded with *light*.'

Plato speaks of his reverence for the subject and states that there is no danger of anyone forgetting it since, once the mind grasps it, it is contained in the briefest of statements.

Plato was vehemently against writing of such matters. He did not feel that an attempt to tell mankind of these matters would be 'a good thing', except in a few instances where certain individuals were capable of discovering the truth for themselves with a little guidance. Of the rest, however, it would excite in some an unjustified contempt in a thoroughly offensive fashion and 'in others certain lofty and vain hopes, as if they had acquired some awesome lore.' On this matter, Plato adds that, 'no serious man will ever think of writing about such serious realities for the general public so as to make them a prey to envy and perplexity.' (Perhaps this is a remonstrance to myself for doing just that!)

Conclusion

It is hoped that I have been able to shed some light (yes, pun intended!), on the works of some of the best known philosophers in history. Some of these works have sometimes been considered as impenetrable; hopefully this book may provide new perspective on their writings. It would have been possible to write an entire book on Spiritual Philosophers, and perhaps even a book on any one of the authors mentioned above. However, this chapter was intended (much like *Esoteric Spiritual Texts*), to describe a specific occurrence and experience which surpasses metaphor, is based in reality and is consistently associated with 'light'.

It has been identified that this particular 'experience' is a result of the combination of academic study and dissection of the self by meditation and introspection. This approach is not, in principle, contrary to Hegel's dialectical method. That is, inherent within any phenomenon, the thesis, there are contradictory aspects, the antithesis, which require a journey with aim of resolution (synthesis). The parallel can be seen as the amalgamation of the conscious with the unconsciousness, resulting in *Atman* or oneness which is achieved with this 'experience'.

The individuals cited here were profoundly moved by this 'experience', the explanation of which in the following chapter will provide a fuller and more accurate perspective. Goethe portrayed the experience in a fictional work, as did Dante, so the academics would suggest, although I believe that Dante was recounting his own personal experience. Nietzsche lived it but did not rest well after his experience. Jung embraced it, not only by employing 'mental toughness' but also by being afforded a support structure in that he could see his thoughts and experiences mirrored in cultures and mythologies of antiquity. This support was further strengthened by his professional study of individuals including Nietzsche and his psychoanalysis of patients, and he found comfort, unlike Nietzsche, in the fact that many had gone through a similar experience, whether they knew how to cope with it or not. Plato alluded to it and, in doing so, also employed 'light' when writing about the subject.

Summary

This chapter has shown that these notable individuals had a profound experience, having employed intense study, contemplation and introspection. In recounting this experience we see again the constant association of 'light' in their articulation and explanation of it.

Goethe brought it to light in a fictional work, though the passion and detail of the work could conceivably lead one to wonder if he did not have the experience himself.

Dante provided articulation of it beautifully in Paradiso, the writing of which contains a superfluity of the mention of 'light'.

Nietzsche had such an experience and also mentions 'light'; unfortunately so powerful to him was his 'experience' that it affected him detrimentally.

Jung described his experience as 'numinous' or awe-inspiring but, despite this, he noted the difficulty in articulating the experience afterwards and suggested that only one who has had the same experience would fully understand what he meant. Jung was also careful to maintain a hold on himself, having studied and being aware of the negative impact of Nietzsche's own experience.

Plato was reluctant to speak of the experience and suggested that he could be the only one to fully present a treatise of it, but deferred actually writing or speaking of it. In his allusions to the experience he too refers to 'light'.

6

Kundalini: The Light at the End of the Tunnel

In the world there are many different roads but the destination is the same. There are a hundred deliberations but the result is one.

Confucius (551–479 BCE)

It is my assertion that the 'experience' referred to in the chapter on esoteric spiritual texts and experienced by the individual spiritual philosophers is 'Kundalini'. The experience is also known as 'samadhi' or 'total self-collectedness'. In Hindu and Buddhist philosophy, it is regarded as the climax of all spiritual and mental activity, a state of rapture and beatitude. It is also otherwise known as the 'Serpent Power' and it was Sir John Woodroffe, a High Court Judge in Calcutta, who was one of the first to bring the notion of Kundalini to the West. He published a book titled *The Serpent Power* and described the experience of Kundalini as such. The literal meaning of Kundalini in Sanskrit is 'coiled up' and is illustrated as a serpent coiled at the base of the spine; the symbol of Kundalini is the 'caduceus' or the staff of Hermes; entwined by two serpents (as shown at the beginning of the book). It has also been interpreted as the force that opens up the knowledge of the oneness of life, a divine energy leading to inner illumination.

My own experience of Kundalini

It is a most profound and unique experience. Once it has been experienced it cannot be forgotten, for there is nothing like it. It is neither equal to, nor parallel or even similar to any previous human

151

experience. In my case, it represented both the empiric proof, which I found comforting, and also the confirmation of all the study that had previously been imbibed. It offered all that blind religious faith and convenient scientific tenets failed to provide.

Whilst it is an ecstatic and beatific experience, it also creates a great deal of bewilderment and confusion. There was a period afterwards where I felt that something had broken within my mind and that I would perhaps go the way that Nietzsche had (this knowledge of Nietzsche was in hindsight, however, since I had not approached his works at that time). It is documented, as in the case of Nietzsche, that there are instances when the experience can potentially verge on the negative. One of the positives, however, is a profound sense, a knowledge indeed, of the existence of 'something else' and, perhaps resulting from this, a distinct lack of fear of the unknown, or indeed death.

It was about six o'clock in the evening and I had been looking through a number of spiritual and academic books that I had been cross-referencing. I was just sitting and idly reflecting, on what exactly I cannot remember, perhaps where my study would go next.

The moment was not even a period of the meditation which I had been undertaking throughout my course of self-imposed study, and my mind was completely open. Then, all of a sudden, I was seized, as though by some invisible and intangible force. It was an extraordinary feeling, utterly unique and totally different from any sensation that I had felt ever before. To add to the barrage of the senses came with the experience a constant whirring sound, which would not abate and remains with me today. This onset of sudden energy seemed to flood the whole of my person and the dominant impression, and what was so amazing and beautiful, although thoroughly confusing at the time, was the unmistakable sensation of *light*. The whole experience seemed to create an incredible luminescence which is almost impossible to describe as it was nothing like how one would usually envisage light, whether from the light of the sun or from an electricity bulb.

The whole experience did not, I don't think, last more than a couple of minutes, and quite probably less, although sitting through it at the time it felt as though it was an eternity. During the time it lasted, I remained absolutely motionless. It is difficult to say whether this was because of being constrained by the overwhelming activity around me or, if I did have a choice, whether I myself really wanted to continue to be part of this almost terrifying but nonetheless beautiful and quite unique experience. It seemed that what now 'constituted me' was *total consciousness*; the focus of my being was entirely of the 'soul', for want of a better description. It was as if the entire experience represented moments of revelation where 'everything' was made known and comprehended, although in a rather indefinable way. Yet, despite the bewilderment and confusion, I felt the presence of an absolute and profound sense of peace which was beyond anything I had ever known previously. And then, quite suddenly, it ended, just as suddenly as it had begun, with a discernible 'return' of my normal self and my normal thoughts.

The feeling of confusion afterwards is as difficult to describe as the experience itself, and I was left extremely shaken and wondering what in heaven's name had just happened. My own recall is that, whilst there were many sensations and thoughts, such as the seemingly enhanced clarity of the senses especially afterward, the dominating one was of an overwhelming sense that we, all of us, all of humanity on the planet and beyond, are somehow inextricably linked together.

For several weeks afterwards, the experience did return, but on these occasions it was in no way as powerful as the first time. It was not clear to me whether I was just tapping into the residual effects of the first instance, or whether whatever was occurring was 'finishing off' the whole experience, so to speak. In addition to this it has also 'lightly' occurred when visiting several of the ancient sites that I have since travelled to.

I am conscious that my description of this experience falls short of conveying adequately the intensity and impact of the entire event, although even as I write this today the hairs all over my body still stand on end at the memory of it.

My later reactions
Since that time I have, at best, only alluded to this experience and this is the first time in over a decade that I have spoken of it. The main reason is that it is such a profound experience that it is particularly difficult to describe – and who would listen anyway? Even if they did, would they believe me? And if they did listen, and perhaps even believe it, what would they think of me? It was at this time, and for these reasons that I

wrote a collection of works, four sets of writings which, for me, was the only way of expressing, or perhaps venting, all that came before and after it had occurred. This catharsis was an attempt to reconcile myself with the experience. Thereafter, however, the reconciliation was only really afforded by reading the texts previously referred to and those cited here, finding common ground and similar experiences. In fact, I had read many of the books mentioned in the last two chapters prior to my experience and, whilst I was aware of the numerous references to 'light', it was on re-reading them that I found I had a new perspective on their content, purely because of my experience. The provision of this new frame of reference made these texts much more meaningful to me.

Unlike Nietzsche, I was able to seek comfort by the realisation that I was by no means alone and that nothing was indeed 'broken'. My experience was, for me, just like when the hairs on the back of your neck stand up after some shock or revelation. But now multiply that several million times and extend its sensation over the whole of your body. It is still difficult today to describe how it is that, without either choice or intent, one is simultaneously physically apprehended and mentally invaded, whilst at the same time exploding, as it were, along with experiencing a profound sense of a great luminescence surrounding you that you are part of. This is not due to a lack of memory but due to the unique nature of the experience, which is, by its very nature, highly irrational and does not easily lend itself, if at all, to explanation or definition.

Kundalini: a parallel experience from Gopi Krishna

In reading further to understand and make sense of my experience, I happened to find a description of Kundalini and an explanation of it that mirrored so closely my own experience that I explored it further. I came across the name of Gopi Krishna, who has perhaps written most on this subject, in books such as: *Secrets of Kundalini in Panchastavi, Higher Consciousness and Kundalini, The Secret of Yoga, The Awakening of Kundalini* and *Kundalini – The Evolutionary Energy in Man*.

Gopi Krishna (1903–1984) was born in Kashmir and later resided in the Punjab region of India. He was an individual who, for many years,

Gopi Krishna (1903–1984).

practised unsupervised meditation and who, at the age of 34, suddenly experienced the awakening of Kundalini during his morning practice. His autobiography, *Kundalini – The Evolutionary Energy in Man*, recounts his own experience of Kundalini and tells of his struggle to find balance from the tumultuous experience and to overcome a variety of powerful, confusing and bewildering elements of it.

Perhaps the most notable author on the Kundalini experience, he stated that there is an absence of accurate knowledge and lack of unanimity in the writings about the experience itself. Furthermore, he believed that no amount of intellectual exercise could draw an accurate picture of this state and that language used to describe normal experiences was wholly inadequate to describe that of Kundalini. It was particularly difficult, in his view, to find words that would sufficiently describe this amazing experience of another plane of consciousness which would be intelligible to others. He used the analogy of someone who was blind trying to describe the colours of the rainbow to those with sight or indeed those with sight trying to describe the colours of the rainbow to those who are blind.

This comparison is also echoed by Jung when he writes in the *Mysterium*: 'Anyone who has experienced anything of the sort will know what I mean, and anyone who has not had the experience will not be satisfied by any amount of descriptions ... I know of no case in which the bare description conveyed the experience.

Parallels can also be drawn from Dante's epic poem, as quoted in the last chapter:

High in that sphere which takes from Him most light
I was – I was! – and saw things there that no one
Who descends knows how or ever can repeat.

Krishna's description of the experience
Of the experience itself, Krishna gives a very detailed description of its sensory effects, with its 'shining halo', 'luminous glow' and 'shimmering pool of light' and the strange noise accompanying it:

[I]perceived a luminous glow within and outside my head in a state of constant vibration, as if a jet of an extremely subtle and brilliant substance rising through the spine spread itself out in the cranium, filling and surrounding it with an indescribable radiance. This shining halo never remained constant in dimension or in the intensity of its brightness. It waxed and waned, brightened and grew dim, or changed its colour from silver to gold and vice versa. When it increased in size or brilliance, the strange noise in my ears, now never absent, grew louder and more insistent, as if drawing my attention to something I could not understand. The halo was never stationary but in a state of perpetual motion, dancing and leaping, eddying and swirling, as if composed of innumerable, extremely subtle, brilliant particles of some immaterial substance, shooting up and down, this way and that, combining to present an appearance of a circling, shimmering pool of light.

Gopi Krishna: *Kundalini – The Evolutionary Energy in Man*

In another text Krishna elaborates on this to describe how 'he was taken by surprise' and how the experience created the sensation of being surrounded by 'waves of light' and then of becoming 'a vast circle of consciousness on which the body was but a point' and 'in a state of exultation and happiness'.

> Entirely unprepared for such a development, I was completely taken by surprise; but regaining self-control, I remained sitting, keeping my mind on the point of concentration. The illumination grew brighter, the roaring louder – I experienced a rocking sensation and felt myself slipping out of my body, entirely enveloped in a halo of light. It is impossible to describe the experience accurately. I felt the point of consciousness that was myself, growing wider, surrounded by waves of light. It grew wider and wider, spreading outward while the body, normally the immediate object of its perception, appeared to have receded into the distance until I became entirely unconscious of it. I was now all consciousness, without any outline, without any idea of corporeal appendage, without any feeling or sensation coming from the senses, immersed in a sea of light simultaneously conscious and aware of every point, spread out, as it were, in all directions without any barrier or material obstruction. I was no longer as I knew myself, to be a small point of awareness confined in a body, but instead was a vast circle of consciousness in which the body was but a point, bathed in light and in a state of exaltation and happiness, impossible to describe.
>
> Gopi Krishna: *Kundalini: Path to Higher Consciousness*

Krishna further discusses 'the abnormal physiological reactions and the existence and extraordinary behaviour of the luminous vital currents in the body, which to the uninitiated and unprepared subjects like me are sure to bring host of terrors in their wake.' In another of his books he states that there is no appreciable effect on the body and that the whole phenomenon – the lights seen, the voices heard, the joy experienced, the knowledge gained, the wisdom acquired and the contact with Divinity were all purely mental or spiritual occurrences without any relation to the physical frame of man. Of the light itself, Krishna has described it variously as: an unearthly shine, celestial light, beaming splendour, indescribable glory, a flaming radiance, a flood of lustre, bright effulgence. The effect of Kundalini is the entry of a marvellous flood of light into the whole area of the mind, leading to a radiancy of thought and imagination which must be experienced to be believed.

After the experience, Krishna mentions his sense of bewilderment and how he 'remained in utter uncertainty about his strange condition for a long time, utterly at a loss to put meaning to the occurrence.' He suggests that, before the fateful morning in December when he saw the fabulous Kundalini in action, had he been told of such an experience by someone else, he would 'have placed him in that class of intelligent but credulous men who, while most accurate and conscientious in all other matters, exhibit a streak of puerility in respect of the supernatural.' Because of this feeling of incredulity that others might have about it, Krishna delayed any public mention of it for a very long time:

> [He]hesitated for nearly twenty years in making the experience public because in the first place, I wanted to make myself completely sure about my own condition, and secondly, I was entirely averse to exposing myself to the criticism of well-meaning friends and the ridicule of opponents. The story that I had to relate was so out of the ordinary and so full of strange episodes that I was very doubtful about its being accepted as a truthful account of an experience which, extremely rare has always remained wrapped in mystery from times immemorial.
>
> Gopi Krishna: *Kundalini – The Evolutionary Energy in Man.*

His perceptions after the 'experience'

While, according to Krishna, after the experience the senses function as before and there is absolutely no blurring or distortion in perception, the universe is no longer perceived to be a gigantic creation with its unimaginably vast size, reducing the observer to a state of utter insignificance and helplessness. On the contrary, it now appears like an island in a luminous sea of being where the observer is no longer a small insignificant puny creature made of flesh and surrounded by a cosmos which dominates the individual.

Gopi Krishna's graphic accounts of his experiences are the clearest and most elaborate documentations of this experience that I have read. Whilst being honest in his descriptions of the difficulties and dangers of the spiritual path, Krishna is not a guru in the traditional sense; it was his intention that the documenting of his experience would be helpful to others who encounter this extraordinary experience. Gopi Krishna suggested the establishment the Kundalini Research Foundation in 1970, an organisation to which I wish to express great gratitude for the information that they have provided to me.

Krishna believed that the Kundalini experience was an evolutionary step in mankind's progress and urged the scientific community to at least give some consideration to the experience, if not study it in some depth. His view was that 'it [the Kundalini experience] provides the only method available to science to establish empirically the existence of life as an immortal, all-intelligent power behind the organic phenomena on earth.' Moreover, he further claimed another potential effect if that research would establish that an evolutionary mechanism, ceaselessly active in developing the brain towards a predetermined state of higher consciousness, really does exist in man.

Dr Bonnie Greenwell on Kundalini

Krishna's descriptions of the Kundalini experience are echoed by another writer, Dr Bonnie Greenwell, in her book *Energies of Transformation,* which is a synthesis of eastern and western perspectives of the ancient phenomenon of Kundalini. It includes 23 studies sourced from individuals who have had this experience and a commentary which seeks to help those individuals with the understanding of it and the ability to integrate the experience physically, spiritually and emotionally.

She gives a telling account of the experience and the sensation of intense energy that is released throughout the body, moving from the spine to the crown of the head, and stemming from 'the deepest roots of the Self':

> Often the first flush of Kundalini is felt as energy moving up from the base of the spine where, according to esoteric literature, it has been coiled into a latent form since birth. It may flood the body like a geyser, crawl slowly upward in a spiral motion like a snake, or flow in a steady stream up the spine and through the crown of the head. The body vibrates or feels charged by energetic and (if fortunate) ecstatic sensations. The nervous system may be overwhelmed by

intense heat, sounds, or light … this 'radical' spiritual experience seems to arise from the deepest roots of the Self, and sweeps one into revolutionary personality and physiological changes. The intensity of this movement has been described in some yogic scriptures as the rush of a divine goddess, Shakti, who is released and charging upward through the system to be reunited with her lover, Siva, the universal consciousness that awaits her … initiating a struggle to free human consciousness from worldly thoughts, producing a wide range of psychic and physiological phenomena promotes ecstatic experience and agonising self-confrontation, and demands the reorientation of one's life.

Bonnie Greenwell: *Energies of Transformation*

William James on the 'mystic' experience

William James (referred to in Chapter 4) also discussed this experience at length in his book, *The Varieties of Religious Experience: A Study in Human Nature (Varieties)*, which is an empirical enquiry into the history of human consciousness. The entire text is full of examples of those individuals who have had a similar experience and associated it with the presence of light.

James' description of the 'mystic' experience strongly parallels previous descriptions. He states that:

It is natural that those who have personally traversed such an experience should carry away a feeling of its being a miracle rather than a natural process. Voices are often heard, *lights* seen, or visions witnessed; automatic motor phenomena occur; and it always seems, after the surrender of the personal will, as if an extraneous higher power had flooded in and taken possession. Moreover the sense of renovation, safety, cleanness, rightness, can be so marvellous and jubilant as well to warrant one's belief in a radically new substantial nature.

It is further described as an 'original and unborrowed experience' from a 'higher controlling agency' and from 'some influence from without'.

James explains that in these 'mystic' states individuals become 'one with the Absolute and we become aware of our oneness'. This is not dissimilar to that described in Paradiso as where 'our human nature is at one with God', where 'what we hold in faith, not argued through but known for what it is, as the primal truth that all believe'(*Paradiso: Canto 2*).

James lists four characteristics of the 'mystic' experience:

Ineffability
The subject of it immediately says that it defies expression and that no adequate report of its contents can be given in words. It follows from this that its quality must be directly experienced; it cannot be imparted or transferred to others. In this peculiarity, mystical states are more like states of feeling than states of intellect. No one can make clear to another who has never had a certain feeling, in what the quality or worth of it consists.

James also states that, 'it is probably difficult to realise their intensity, unless one has been through the experience one's self.' This mirrors similar thoughts from Krishna and Jung on the experience.

Noetic quality
Although so similar to states of feeling, these mystical states are also states of insight into depths of truth:

> Mystical states seem to those who experience them to be also states of knowledge. They are states of insight into depths of truth unplumbed by the discursive intellect. They are *illuminations*, revelations, full of significance and importance all inarticulate though they remain; and as a rule they carry with them a curious sense of authority for after-time.

Transiency
According to James, mystical states cannot be sustained for any length of time, from half an hour to two hours seem to be the limit, after which the experience fades. Thereafter, the quality of the experience can be imperfectly reproduced in memory, but when it recurs it is recognised.

Passivity

Of the experience itself, James describes how the individual is overwhelmed and how when 'the characteristic sort of consciousness once has set in, the mystic feels as if his own will were in abeyance, and indeed sometimes as if he were grasped and held by a superior power.' Of the same characteristic James also comments, 'throughout the height of it he undoubtedly seems to himself a passive spectator or undergoer of an astonishing process performed upon him from above.'

The further characteristics seem to be: a loss of all worry, a sense of perceiving truths not known before and a third peculiarity, which is the 'objective change which the world often appears to undergo. An appearance of newness beautifies every object.'

Within the testimonies of various individuals that James presents we have similar descriptions such as:

He sees, but cannot define the *light* which bathes him and by means of which he sees the objects which excite his wonder.

All the glory of God shone upon and round about me in a manner almost marvelous ... A *light* perfectly ineffable shone in my soul...

Like a ton's weight being lifted from my heart; a strange *light* which seemed to light up the whole room.

The work of conversion, the change, and the manifestations of it are no more disputable than that *light* which I see, or anything that I ever saw.

These are just a few of the many testimonies of the instance of *light* associated with the experience given in *Varieties* and seem to be further confirmation of the shared characteristics of these 'mystic' or 'Kundalini' experiences.

Similar descriptions of 'experiences' from Nietzsche, Jung, Gopi Krishna and others

It is my belief that these descriptions also refer to what Jung termed his 'numinous' or awe-inspiring experience, and lend credence to all that Nietzsche experienced, as related in this extract from his writings:

> One is merely incarnation, merely mouthpiece, merely medium of overwhelming forces. The concept of revelation, in the sense that something suddenly, with unspeakable certainty and subtlety, becomes *visible*, audible, something that shakes and overturns one to the depths, simply describes the fact ... a thought flashes up like *lightning* ... I never had any choice. An ecstasy whose tremendous tension sometimes discharges itself in a flood of tears while one's steps now involuntarily rush along, now involuntarily lag; a complete being outside of oneself with the distinct consciousness of a multitude of subtle shudders and trickles down to one's toes ... a superfluity of *light*. Everything is in the highest degree involuntary but takes place as in a tempest of a feeling of freedom, of absoluteness, of power, of divinity.
>
> Friedrich Nietzsche: *Ecce Homo*

This aspect of the experience, a ringing in one's ears, I initially found particularly irritating but, after some time, I became able to manage it. It never goes away, it seems, and after a while you merely learn to live with it. Bonnie Greenwell makes several comments on this aspect and Krishna called it 'the strange noise' in his ears and also described it as the buzzing of a swarm of bees. He suggests that this element is written of in the *Panchastavi*, which is a collection of devotional hymns divided into five cantos and dedicated to 'The Divine Energy' or Kundalini. Within the first verse of the *Panchastavi*, Kundalini is said to be the nature of light and sound where the sound is variously described and its mystery diversely explained. The sacred syllable 'Aum' is said to be greatest of the mantras and the quintessence of the Vedas, and it is prone to variation in different states of contemplation and different conditions of the body. Indeed many ancient esoteric spiritual texts mention sound alongside that of light although not in as great a volume. Additionally you can find mention of concordant tones within the works of the spiritual philosophers, as for example in Dante's *Commedia* (Paradiso):

With harmonies,
proportionate and clear, made me attend,
the skies of heaven ... The newness of the sound and that great light
Kindled in me a desire to know the cause
Sharper than any I have ever felt.

Krishna claims that the awakening of Kundalini is an activity for which a provision already exists in the human frame. He compares it to an electric wire with many twists and loops, each slightly different but charged with the same electric current. He claims that all kinds of religions or disciplines aiming at a form of mysticism, and indeed all types of magic or sorcery, derive originally from Kundalini.

Kundalini in the Bhagavad Gita *and* the Upanishads
There is substantiation of the point made earlier in Chapter 5 that both the *Bhagavad Gita* and the *Upanishads* refer to the Kundalini experience. Krishna firmly believed this and he provided an example from the *Upanishads* '"I am Brahma (the Absolute)", says one of the seers of the Upanishads. "The Light that shines in the sun shines in me also," echoes another. "This soul of mine and Brahman (the Absolute), are one," says a third.' Krishna thought that this has been so for thousands of years and that the very same idea, in different ways and under different names, has been echoed and re-echoed by at least a hundred generations of 'illuminated' sages and Yoga saints of India to this day.

Similarly, there is further confirmation of my earlier argument that Jung was indeed also referring to the experience of Kundalini, as he gave a lecture on the subject to the Psychological Club in Zurich in 1932. At this time, Jung said:

Expressed in psychological terms, that would mean that you can approach the unconscious in only one way, namely by a purified mind, by a right attitude, and by the grace of heaven, which is the Kundalini. Something in you, an urge in you, must lead you to it ... these experiences are secret; they are called mystical because the ordinary world cannot understand them.

One cannot even talk about them, and of such a kind are the experiences of the Kundalini yoga. That tendency to keep things secret is merely a natural consequence when the experience is of such a peculiar kind that you had better not talk about it, for you expose yourself to the greatest misunderstanding and misinterpretation.

C.G. Jung: *The Psychology of Kundalini Yoga:*
Notes of the Seminar Given in 1932

Is the Kundalini experience really as mysterious as it is made out to be?

However, the question arises: is the Kundalini experience really as arcane as it seems to be when we find this definitive experience presented in a great variety of philosophical and historical content? In addition to the several spiritual philosophers mentioned here, there is the fictional case of Goethe's *Faust* and his particular experience when meeting his first spirit:

A curious change affects me in this sign:
You, kindred Sprite of Earth, come strangely nearer;
My spirits rise, my powers are stronger, clearer,
As from the glow of a refreshing wine.
I gather heart to risk the world's encounter,
To bear my human fate as fate's surmounter,
To front the storm, in joy or grief not palter,
Even in the gnash of shipwreck never falter.
The clouds close in above me
And hidden is the moon;
The lamp dies down.
A vapour grows – red quiverings
Dart around my head – there creeps
A shuddering from the vaulted roof
And seizes me!
I know, dread spirit of my call, 'tis you.
Stand forth, disclosed!
Ah, how my heart is harrowed through!
In tumult of feeling
My mind is riven, my senses reeling

165

To you I yield, nor care if I am lost.

This thing must be, though life should be the cost.

(He seizes the book and pronounces the secret sign of the Spirit. A reddish flame shoots up, and the Spirit appears in the flame)

Faust: Part 1

Faust's speech here seems to echo many of the sensations of Kundalini described above, particularly in the phrases like 'a shuddering from the vaulted roof … seizes me', 'how my heart is harrowed through!' and 'my mind is riven, my sense reeling'. Perhaps Goethe had more awareness of this Kundalini experience than is generally recognised.

Enoch's experience in *The Book of Enoch*

In *The Book of Enoch,* it is recounted how Enoch, having being petitioned by the Sons of Heaven (those who had sinned with the daughters of men), sat down by the waters of the Dan in the land of Dan and then his 'experience' occurred:

Behold, in the vision clouds invited me and a mist summoned me, and the course of the stars and the lightnings sped and hastened me, and the winds in the vision caused me to fly and lifted me upward, and bore me to heaven. And I went in till I drew nigh to a wall which is built of crystals and surrounded by tongues of fire; and it began to affrighten me. And I went into the tongues of fire and drew to a large house which was built of crystals; and the walls of the house were like a tessellated floor (made) of crystals, and its groundwork was of crystal. Its ceiling was like a path of the stars and the lightnings, and between the fiery cherubim, and their heaven was (clear) as water. A flaming fire surrounded the walls, and its portals blazed with fire. And I entered the house, and it was hot as fire and cold as ice: there were no delights of life therein: fear covered me, and trembling gat hold upon me. And as I quaked and trembled, I fell upon my face.

Translation R.H. Charles: *The Book of Enoch*

Again, there are similar references to 'fire' and 'lightnings' and how his body 'quaked and trembled', which reflects aspects of the other experiences of Kundalini.

'Illuminated' spiritual individuals and their experiences of enlightenment

Buddha and the path to Enlightenment
Buddha is perhaps the most notable and acknowledged *enlightened* being or 'illuminati', literally meaning a person who has been enlightened. Within *The Teaching of Buddha*, we find so definitive his experience that to it is applied the date of 8 December when he was aged 35. It is described as follows:

> He gave up the practice of asceticism ... attempted yet another period of meditation ... It was an intense and incomparable struggle for him. He was desperate and filled with confusing thoughts, dark shadows overhung his spirit, and he was beleaguered by all the lures of the devils. Carefully and patiently he examined them one by one and rejected them all. It was a hard struggle indeed, making his blood run thin, his flesh fall away, and his bones crack.

> But when the morning star appeared in the eastern sky, the struggle was over and the Prince's mind was as clear as the breaking day. He has at last, found the path to Enlightenment. It was December the 8th, when the Prince became a Buddha at thirty-five years of age.
> Bukkyo Dendo Kyokai: The Teaching of Buddha

The 'light' of Muhammad
In the *Qur'an* there is constant reference to the 'light of Muhammad' and description of the prophet as 'an illuminating lamp'. Mohammad often meditated alone for several weeks in a cave called al-Hira in the Mountain of Light (Jabal al-Nur) near Mecca. (Some accounts name the mountain as al Hira.) Indeed he was aged 40 and it was in the month of Ramadan that he received his first revelation from the angel Gabriel, which was associated with mysterious seizures. The *Encyclopaedia of*

167

Muhammad as sometimes depicted, surrounded by flame or 'light'.
This detail is from a larger painting of Muhammad as he meets the prophets Ismail,
Is-hak and Lot in paradise. Taken from the *Apocalypse of Muhammad*, written in
1436 in Herat, Afghanistan (Bibliothèque nationale de France).

Islam suggests that Muhammad received a sudden 'prophetic call'
which transformed his whole consciousness and filled him with a
spiritual strength that decided the whole course of his life. Regarding
the mysterious seizures, it states that:

> Such moments may be regarded as genuine since they are unlikely to
> have been invented by later Muslims. These mysterious seizures must
> have afforded to those around him the most convincing evidence for
> the superhuman origin of his inspirations.

It is uncertain whether he had such experiences before he began to see
himself as the prophet of Allah or for how long he had these

experiences. Much like the fictional Faust and the biblical Enoch, he too, was presented with visions and like Enoch was taken on a 'tour' of the heavens, a journey known as the Mi'raj in the *Qur'an* and in the supplemental writings of the Hadith. As in Dante's epic poem, he tours the circles of heaven before returning to earth to recount the journey.

Abu Hamid Muhammad ibn al-tusi Muhammad al-Ghazali
Within the context of the Islamic world there is, I believe, another example of an 'illuminated' spiritual individual as parallel elements to the others certainly seem to be in place. Al-Ghazali may not be as well known in the West as others listed here. However, some of his writings are considered classics in the Middle East.

Al-Ghazali (mentioned in Chapter 4 in connection with Sufism) was born in modern day Iran in 1058 CE and died in 1111 CE (or 450 AH to 505 AH respectively, according to the Islamic calendar). Over four hundred texts are ascribed to al-Ghazali and forty books were devoted to the doctrines and practices of Islam and how these could be made the basis of a profound devotional life leading to higher spiritual levels by way of Sufism or mysticism. It is in his 'spiritual autobiography', *al-Munqidh min al-Dalal* (Deliverance from Error) that we can find evidence of his illumination.

From the earliest years of his life, al-Ghazali possessed a thirst 'for grasping the real meaning of things ... it was an instinctive, natural disposition placed in [his] makeup', which was not of his 'choosing and contriving'. He questioned blind religious conformism and he felt that everyone was born with the 'fitra' (original disposition) and thereafter their parents impose some religion or other on them. 'Consequently [he] felt an inner urge to seek the true meaning of the original *fitra*,' beliefs and knowledge. He resolved to find the answer to the question 'How do I know religion is true?' and spent eleven years in seclusion (1095 to 1106 CE) following this path.

To do this, al-Ghazali gave up much; he was a highly revered professor lecturing to some three hundred students at the Nizamiyah College in Baghdad. He states that the truth could only be found by fleeing from his 'preoccupations and attachments' and that he was applying himself to 'sciences unimportant and useless in this pilgrimage to the hereafter'. He later states that it is a 'very stupid and ignorant man who would wish to discover in them a wisdom by means of reason' and that faith in prophecy is to acknowledge the affirmation of a stage beyond reason. This departure was not easy for him, resolving one day to leave and then changing his mind the next. Al-Ghazali claims that it was God who made it easy for him to depart by placing 'a lock upon [his] tongue so that he was impeded from teaching.' He left the city after distributing what wealth he had and entered into 'seclusion and solitude and spiritual exercise and combat with a view to devoting himself to the purification of [his] soul.'

Al-Ghazali studied many disciplines in this endeavour 'making a thorough study of the views of these groups,' which included the sciences, philosophy and the teachings of the Batinites and of the Sufis. The Batinites or Batiniyah were Muslim sects, particularly the Ismailis, which interpreted religious texts to find their hidden or inner meaning (*batin*) as opposed to their literal meaning (*zahir*).

After a decade of this intense searching he came to *taste* of the truth. He stated that for 'ten years in that condition,' and 'in the course of those periods of solitude, things impossible to enumerate or detail in depth were disclosed to [him]. This much [he] shall mention, that profit may be derived from it.' He states that all 'motions and quiescences, exterior and interior, are learned from the *light* of the niche of prophecy. And beyond the *light* of prophecy there is no *light* on earth from which illumination can be obtained.' He further seeks to describe the 'state' or 'fruitional experience' as 'being totally lost in God' and comments on the ineffability of the 'state' when he writes 'stages beyond the narrow range of words: so that if anyone tries to express them, his words contain evident error against which he cannot guard himself.'

Further descriptions providing evidence to place him solidly in this category of illuminated individuals can be found in his references to 'light': 'the prophetic power is an expression signifying a stage in which man receives an "eye" possessed of a *light*, and in its *light* the unknown and other phenomena not normally perceived by the intellect become visible.' This 'state beyond reason', this 'phenomena not in accord with normal data of reason' was 'the effect of a *light* which God Most High cast into [his] breast. And that *light* is the key to most knowledge.'

Zarathustra 'the First Prophet'
Remaining in Persia, we can look to Zarathustra for further evidence. As one will recall, Nietzsche was a great advocate of Zarathustra or Zoroaster as he was known to the ancient Greeks. Mary Boyce (1920–2006) was a British scholar and a recognised authority on Zoroastrianism and it is from her work, *Zoroastrians: Their Religious Beliefs and Practices* that I include this evidence which entails light. It is contended by Mary Boyce that the Persian Zarathustra founded the Zoroastrian religion over 3,500 years ago and, due to this, it is perhaps the most difficult of faiths to study. Zoroastrianism still exists today, in modern Iran in isolated areas and in India, where Persians, the descendants of Zoroastrianism, immigrated and who are known as Parsis or Parsees. However, due to its antiquity, Zoroastrianism has suffered much, including the destruction of their ancient sacred literature when Alexander the Great burned their books and killed their priests.

The general consensus of opinion today places the existence of the prophet Zarathustra at 1,200 BCE, which would place him, like Moses, in the late Bronze Age. There is, however, also a school of thought which places him between 1,500 BCE to1,700 BCE and more in line with Abraham towards the middle of the Bronze Age, hence he is often referred to as 'the First Prophet'. This account, therefore, is perhaps the earliest recorded account of the Kundalini or 'mystic' experience.

Zarathustra is known to us primarily from the *Gathas*, seventeen hymns which he composed believing that he had been entrusted by God with a message for all mankind. These were not compositions of instruction, but inspired, passionate utterances with the intention of reaching an ultimate goal of restored perfection. He described himself as a 'vaedemna', or 'one who knows', and, according to Zoroastrian tradition, he too spent years in a wandering quest for truth.

Whilst much knowledge of this religion has been lost, one account that has endured the test of time is the one of the first instance of revelation.

According to tradition, Zarathustra was thirty when the revelation came to him. This defining moment is alluded to in one of the *Gathas* (Y 43) and is briefly described in a Pahlavi (Middle Persian language) work (*Zadspram* XX–XXI). It is said that Zarathustra was attending a gathering to celebrate a spring festival and went to a river to fetch water.

He waded in to draw it from midstream and, having emerged from the water, he had a vision. The accounts goes on to mention that, on the bank of the river he saw a 'shining Being, who revealed himself as Vohu Manah, 'Good Purpose', and this Being led Zarathustra into the presence of Ahura Mazda (God) and five other radiant figures, before whom 'he did not see his own shadow upon the earth, owing to their great *light*.' And it was then from this great heptad (group of seven), that he received his revelation.

It was after this revelation that Zarathustra began preaching of Ahura Mazda as the one uncreated God, breaking with the tradition and accepted beliefs of the time and of his people. Boyce suggests that one could not hope to retrace the steps leading to Zarathustra's exalted belief, but that it seems probable that he came to it through meditation.

The above account is the first of several occasions that Zarathustra saw Ahura Mazda in a vision. It is interesting to note here that of this monotheistic religion, Ahura Mazda is also referred to as the Lord of Wisdom, Truth and Light. Of the six 'radiant Beings', it is said that Ahura Mazda is either to have been their 'father' or to have 'mingled' himself with them, and, in one Pahlavi text, his creation of them is compared with the lighting of torches from a torch. According to the author S.A. Kapadia, in the *Khordah-Avesta*, the prayer book of the Parsis, he is described as 'the *Light* and the Source of *Light*'.

The Temptation of Christ
We find similar events happening to Jesus in the story of the Temptation of Christ. Jesus, of course, is attributed with many references to 'light' such as from John 8:12, when Jesus says, 'I am the *light* of the world.'

The Temptation of Christ occurs after Jesus has been baptised by John the Baptist and when he retreats into the desert for forty days and nights. According to Sanders in *The Historical Figure of Jesus* it is intrinsically likely that, from time to time, Jesus sought solitude for prayer and meditation. In the desert, Satan speaks to Jesus and shows him a vision of 'all the kingdoms of the world'. Once the temptations by Satan have concluded, the narrative has the devil depart and Jesus being 'ministered' to by angels.

The Temptation is also related in the gospels of Matthew, Mark and Luke immediately after the baptism by John, where we find further relevance in Matthew 3:16:

And Jesus when he was baptised, went up straightway out of the water: and lo, the heavens were opened unto him, and he saw the spirit of God descending like a dove and *lightening* upon him.

The Temptation in these gospels is a continuation of the baptism, that is to say, the experience seems to be encompassed by both instances and, as with Muhammad, occurred on more than one occasion.

The Transfiguration of Christ
It is, however, in what is known as the Transfiguration of Christ that we see the clearest instance of the experience. It is recounted in Matthew, Mark and Luke but there were three who were privileged to actually witness the phenomenon. These were Peter, James and John and two of them, Peter and John, alluded to it in the Bible. The verses tell that Jesus took the three disciples to what is thought to be Mount Tabor, where he was transfigured before their eyes.

From Matthew, 17:2:

There in their presence he was transfigured: his face shone like the sun and his clothes became as dazzling as light.

From: Mark, 9:3:

There in their presence he was transfigured: his clothes became brilliantly white, whiter than an earthly bleacher could make them.

From Luke, 9:29:

And it happened that, as he was praying, the aspect of his face was changed and his clothing became sparkling white.

This instance was also alluded to in the other gospels of John and Peter:

John, 1:14:

And we saw his glory, the glory that he has from the Father.

2 Peter, 1:16–18

> When we told you about the power and the coming of our lord
> Jesus Christ ... He was honoured and glorified by God the Father ...
> We ourselves heard this voice from heaven, when we were with him on
> the holy mountain.

Jesus is often depicted in paintings with a halo above his head or an
aureole, the latter derived from the Latin, *aurea,* meaning 'golden'. This is
the radiance of luminous cloud which, in paintings of sacred or
spiritual individuals, often surrounds the entirety of the figure and, in
this instance, can often also be called a 'mandorla'.

When it appears as a luminous disc around the head, it is called a
halo or nimbus. The halo is used in Christian art to represent the logos
of Christ, that is, his divine nature, true word or wisdom of God.
However, it is in the earliest of representations, prior to the fifth

The upper part of the Transfiguration of Jesus by Raffaello Sanzio (Raphael)
(1483–1520), focusing on the 'luminosity' of the event.

174

Russian icon of the transfiguration. Jesus is shown surrounded
by a light blue aureole with white flashes of lightning
(fifteenth century, attributed to Theophanes the Greek, Tretyakov Gallery, Moscow).

century, that Jesus was depicted with a halo and specifically after his
baptism by John. The halo, aureole or mandorla has been widely used
in the portrayal of sacred and spiritual individuals in not only Christian
but also in Egyptian, Greek, Roman, Buddhist and Indian art.

Judas Iscariot: in the context of the Gospel of Judas
One of the greatest accounts of the Kundalini experience lies in the
Gospel of Judas. This is an apocryphal scripture from the Codex Tchacos
and composed in the second century CE. It is attributed to the apostle
Judas Iscariot and, though lost for centuries, it was long known to have
existed at this time, being mentioned by St Irenaeus of Lyon in 180 CE.
It was rediscovered in the 1970s in Egypt and the translation was made
public in 2006. My reference is taken from the *Gospel of Judas,* edited by
Rodolphe Kasser, Marvin Meyer and Gregor Wurst in collaboration with
François Gaudard and published by the National Geographic Society.

175

Like the *Dead Sea Scrolls*, the *Gospel of Judas* is a Gnostic text, representing an early form of spirituality that emphasises gnosis, or 'knowledge' – mystical knowledge, knowledge of God and the essential oneness of the Self with God. In the middle section of this gospel, Jesus teaches Judas the mysteries of the universe and is principally a teacher and revealer of wisdom and knowledge. Jesus imparts to Judas the knowledge that can eradicate ignorance and lead to an awareness of oneself and God. He tells Judas that, in the beginning, there was an infinite transcendent deity and, through a complex series of emanations and creations, the heavens became filled with divine light and glory. This infinite deity is so exalted that no finite term can adequately describe the deity; even the word God is insufficient and inappropriate.

Here, Judas is seen as a positive figure and not the quintessential traitor who betrays Jesus. He is portrayed as a close confidant of Jesus, betraying Jesus not only knowingly but also at the sincere request of Jesus. This betrayal allows Jesus to be liberated from the flesh in order that he is able to discard his body and free his divine self, so that he might return to his heavenly home. The true home of Jesus is not this imperfect world below but the divine world of light and life. Judas does nothing that Jesus does not ask him to do and he listens to Jesus and remains faithful to him. Jesus says to Judas, 'You will exceed all of them. For you will sacrifice the man that clothes me.'

It is near the conclusion of the gospel that we find evidence of the Kundalini experience, when Judas is transfigured and enlightened in a luminous cloud and Jesus asks Judas to look up at the heavens and see the stars and display of light.

From the beginning of the scripture it is immediately clear that Judas has unique insight into the divine nature of Jesus. He says,

> I know who you are and where you have come from. You are from the immortal realm of Barbelo (the divine realm above and is the son of God). And I am not worthy to utter the name of the one who sent you.

Jesus then takes Judas aside to tell him of 'the mysteries of the kingdom' and that it is possible for Judas to reach it. In so doing, Jesus recounts that, among these secrets or hidden things, 'there exists a great and boundless realm, whose extent no generation of angels have seen, [in which] there is [a] great invisible [Spirit], And a luminous cloud appeared there.'

Judas, having been told all these matters, was asked by Jesus to lift up his eyes and look 'at the cloud and the light within it and the stars surrounding it. The star that leads the way to your star'. Judas lifted up his eyes and saw the luminous cloud, and he entered it.

This can be described as the transfiguration of Judas, much like that of the transfiguration of Jesus. It leads on to another similar instance of Kundalini, that of Paul the Apostle.

Paul the Apostle and the road to Damascus
A missionary and theologian, Paul the Apostle is perhaps the most powerful individual in the history of the church, and Christian theology owes much to Paul's epistles which provided its foundations.

He was from Tarsus, originally a Pharisee, a sect that embraced the Law of Moses and whose original Hebrew name was 'Saul'. He was strictly trained in Jewish law and traditions and, most likely, never met Jesus. However, he would have known much of the Christian movement and considered it initially a threat to Pharisaic Judaism, to the extent that he became an ardent persecutor of the church, approving of stoning and the going from 'house to house arresting both women and men and sending them to prison.'

It was on the road to Damascus when he had his experience, which resulted in his conversion to Christianity. In Acts 9 Saul [his name at that time] was to arrest any Christian, man or woman on the way to Damascus.

It was when he was approaching the city that 'suddenly there shined round about him a *light* from heaven' and, as he fell to the ground, he heard a voice ask 'Saul, Saul, why persecutest thou me?' When Saul asks whose voice it was, the response was 'I am Jesus whom thou persecutest.' Saul was then told to go on to Damascus and that he would be told what to do. Saul got up and, when he opened his eyes, he found that he was blinded. The men travelling with Saul stood speechless as they had heard the voice but saw no one and they led Saul to the city, where Saul remained blinded for three days.

There was a disciple in Damascus by the name of Ananias who received a vision instructing him to seek out Saul, and that he was to lay his hands on him and thereby give Saul back his sight. Ananias objected, citing the reputation of this man Saul and his actions

Paul blinded by the 'light' on his way to Damascus.
Painting by Caravaggio (1571–1610).

against Christians. The Lord replied saying that Saul was the chosen instrument to bring his name before gentiles and kings, and before the people of Israel. Ananias obeyed, found Saul, laid his hands on him, explaining his actions and that he was sent to recover Saul's sight and so that Saul would be filled with the Holy Spirit. Saul got up and he was immediately able to see again and was baptised.

After his conversion, or experience, Paul [as he then became known], much like Jesus, spent a period of solitude during his time in Arabia, before becoming one of the most notable early Christian missionaries. It is sometimes contended that Paul's account was a result of some inner conflict; however, it is clear that his previous life was free from such struggle, insofar as he excelled in his zeal for the Law and, by its standards, his life was blameless.

Whatever the case, this account of his instance of revelation enjoys no less than three accounts in Acts 9, 22 and 26 and I am convinced that it is an expression of the Kundalini experience.

The 'radiance' of Moses

I have often wondered if Moses himself did not have a similar experience. This Hebrew prophet was probably born in 1,200 BCE and was considered by some early Jewish and Christian traditions to have been the author of the *Torah*. God appeared to Moses in Exodus 3 in the form of a blazing bush, 'the bush burned with fire'. However, it goes on to say that the bush itself was not consumed.

In the account of Moses' return from God, there is another mention in the context of light. In Exodus 34:29 it states, 'And it came to pass, when Moses came down from Mount Sinai with the two tablets of testimony in Moses' hand, when he came down from the mount, that Moses 'wist not that the skin of his face shone while he talked with him [God].'

The account then goes on to say that when Aaron his brother and all of the children of Israel saw Moses, the skin of his face shone and that they were afraid to go close to him. This 'radiancy' seems to be very similar to the transfiguration of Jesus, as witnessed by Peter, James and John.

Another interesting and possible parallel is with the caduceus symbol and Moses' staff. It is after Moses questions (in Exodus 4) who has appeared to him and is commanding him, that God asks what is in his hand, to which Moses answers 'A rod' and God said 'cast it on the ground.' Moses 'cast it on the ground and it became a serpent.' The parallels here appear to be very close with the symbol. All these examples suggest thought and consideration that goes beyond coincidence and the use of metaphor.

Ezekiel and his 'vision'

In *Esoteric Spiritual Texts*, Jewish mysticism was discussed and it was noted that the ma'aseh merkabah movement, predecessors of the

Ezekiel's vision portrayed by Gustave Doré, the vision is surrounded by radiance; the divine presence (the figure on the throne) is seen. The impression is one of awe, and Ezekiel prostrates himself before it.

Kabbalah, based their mysticism on Ezekiel's vision. Within the *Nevi'im* (and the *Old Testament*), in the Book of Ezekiel, there are examples of remarkably similar imagery when the hand of the Lord came upon Ezekiel the priest. Ezekiel looked and 'a stormy wind came sweeping out of the north-a huge cloud and flashing fire, surrounded by a radiance; and in the center of it, in the center of the fire, a gleam as of amber.' Toward the end of the vision, Ezekiel sees what looks like a throne and the appearance of a man upon it. He saw 'from what appeared as his loins down, [I] saw what looked like fire. There was a radiance all about him. Like the appearance of the bow which shines in the clouds on a day of rain, such was the appearance of the surrounding radiance. That was the appearance of the semblance of the Presence of the Lord.'

As mentioned previously, it was this vision which the ma'aseh merkabah mystics focused on as a way to gain a fuller understanding of God. Indeed, of the theories and practices shared between the two movements, one is the idea of an ecstatic experience in which ones communes with God.

The 'experience' at the very foundations of our religions and spiritual thought
It does appear that this Kundalini or 'mystic' experience has occurred at the very beginnings of our religions and spiritual movements. I have already cited examples (in no particular order) from within Judaism, Buddhism, Islam, Sufism, Zoroastrianism, Christianity and Hinduism. In every instance, there exists a sudden onset of an experience, always entailing 'light', resulting in revelation and a compelling influence on the individual to articulate and share this unique and unusual experience. The individual nearly always seems to have gone through a previous period of deep introspection, contemplation and meditation in some search for 'truth'. This is not at all dissimilar to the experiences of *The Spiritual Philosophers* of the last chapter or at variance with the commentary given in *Esoteric Spiritual Texts*.

William James suggested that a personal religion will prove itself more fundamental than either theology or ecclesiasticism, and that, 'Churches, when once established, live at second-hand upon tradition; but the *founders* of every church owed their power originally to the fact of their personal communion with the divine.' Of these transformational figures and forerunners of religious and spiritual thought, James comments on how the experience transcends such individuals and quotes an author whom he does not name but states that this individual has made a careful study of the phenomena. The unnamed author comments on how the spiritual insight always comes suddenly, and in an overpowering way:

> How, one after another, the same features are reproduced in the prophetic books. The process is always extremely different from what it would be if the prophet arrived at his insight into spiritual things by the tentative efforts of his own genius. There is something sharp and sudden about it. He can lay his finger, so to speak, on the moment when it came. And it always comes in the form of an overpowering force from without, against which he struggles, but in vain.

Kundalini in other ancient cultures

In his writing on the presence of Kundalini in many other cultures, Gopi Krishna supports the contention of the world-wide nature of the instances of its occurrence:

> The Christian mystics who have seen the illuminating glory surrounding the vision of God; the Sufis and the splendour or Noor, emanating from their Divinity; the Taoists and their circling light, the blazing radiance of a multitude of suns that marks the Brahman of the Hindus and the shining halo of light around Buddha are all but different expressions used to designate the same phenomenon of inner illumination experienced on the entry of Kundalini into the brain.

Similarly, William James also suggests that, of 'mystic' consciousness, Hindus, Buddhists, Mohammedans and Christians have all cultivated it methodically. In India, training in mystical insight has been known under the name of yoga, yoga literally meaning the 'experimental union of the individual with the divine'. The follower of true yoga practice ultimately enters into the condition termed Samadhi and 'comes face to face with facts which no instinct or reason can ever know.' According to James, Samadhi is identical with 'the Atman or Universal Soul'. He also includes Sufism (discussed earlier).

Krishna further claimed that impartial assessment of the monuments left by the ancient Egyptians makes it increasingly clear that they possessed an absolutely intuitive knowledge of the laws and nature which science is only now finding out through laborious observation and experiment. He contends that there is no other explanation for the remarkable skill and ingenuity that was employed in the construction of the Great Pyramid and other archaeological wonders of antiquity. He believed that scientific study of Kundalini will lead ultimately to the same conclusion and that it will be found that nineteenth century science gravely blundered in drawing conclusions all too hastily about life and the state of knowledge in the ancient world. He also firmly believed that every revealed religious scripture of the world, 'the ancient religious literature of India, the esoteric doctrines of China, the sacred lore of other countries and faiths' was the direct result of this powerful experience.

This argument on the link between the Kundalini experience and ancient world cultures is echoed by Bonnie Greenwell in *Energies of Transformation*:

> Allusions to such experiences (Kundalini) can be found in the mystical teachings and practices of many cultures – Assyrian, Egyptian, Celtic, Greek, Taoist, Tibetan, Judaic, Native American, Alaskan, Australian, Hawaiian, Latin and African. Shamanism, Gnosticism, Sufism, and Christian mysticism reflect the use of these tools (practices to awaken Kundalini). Theosophists, Freemasons, Rosicrucians and the alchemists also reportedly have had secret practices for awakening (the) energy.
>
> *Energies of Transformation*

Indeed, alchemists pursued a search for the secret of life and a transformative substance which could turn base metals into gold. Undoubtedly they sought Kundalini, the life force which could transform the ordinary conditions of human embodiment. As Carl Jung believed, they were 'projecting upon matter and chemical transformation the whole gamut of the deep unconscious.' Bonnie Greenwell also cites the Hopi (see Chapters 2 and 3) as having 'always known of Kundalini'.

Evidence of Kundalini in South and Latin America?

Although no texts exist, as they were destroyed by the Spanish conquistadores, there remain indications of similarities with Kundalini in South and Latin America.

South America and the Inca
In Chapter 2 of Peru and the Incas I mentioned the venerated Viracocha, the universal creator and master of all and who is referred to as Illa or 'Light'. The Incas believed that Viracocha, the creator deity, left the daily working of the world to the surveillance of the other deities that he had created.

There is however, more contemporary evidence provided by Nicholas Griffiths in his book *The Cross and the Serpent* when he discusses the shamans of Peru. Griffiths states that in two communities studied by anthropologists, there are several categories of religious specialist. These religious specialists are distinguished by practices and methods which are typical of shamans. In both communities studied, the specialist who stands at the highest point of the religious hierarchy is the 'alto mesayoq'. What is pertinent is that the feature which characterises such a shaman most clearly is that individual's selection by the deity Ruwal by means of a *lightning bolt*. Ruwal is synonymous with the 'apus' or mountain spirits and this is the preferred method of conferring powers on the human representative of the apus.

The origin of the word mesayoq is derived from mesa, or strange-shaped stone of special powers, which the shaman is left with as proof of his or her selection after awakening from unconsciousness. It is after this initiation that the shaman is able to communicate directly with the deities Ruwal and Pachamama. Pachamama is usually translated as 'Mother Earth', but a more literal translation would be 'Mother Universe'.

Latin America and the Maya
Hunbatz Men is a Mayan and an authority on the history, chronology and calendars of Mayan civilisation. He states in his book, *Secrets of Mayan Science/Religion*, that the Maya refer to the spirit as 'k'inan', meaning 'solar origin', and that the Maya defined the spirit as originating from this source. He points to the fact that the Maya employed meditation, citing figurines in a typical meditative position similar to the Buddhists except that, in the Mayan position, the hands are placed across the chest, rather than on the knees as in Buddhist meditation. He also explains that the Maya worshipped the serpent as a symbol of movement and measure, cosmic synthesis, and presents another figurine from Costa Rica where 'the four marks on the lower part of the figure,' called 'can' in Mayan, represent the number 'four' and 'the serpent' and that, 'We know that in this area is centred the great power that awakens the Kundalini.'

He further explains that, 'The Mayan masters teach that we are the integration of the seven powers of *light*, travelling in the form of the serpent, undulating eternally with movement and measure.' The word 'cizin' esoterically implies a manifestation of our energies, i.e., a practical application of knowledge. A flowering *radiation* is visually represented by the serpent symbol of solar energy.

There is a pyramid in South America which I have visited on many occasions called El Castillo, a name ascribed to it by the Spanish, but it is in fact the Temple of Kulkulcan (the Mayan deity) at the beautiful site of Chichen Itza in Mexico. As the book, *The Mysteries of Chichen Itza* describes:

> The engineering of the Castillo is so exact that with the arrival of either equinox, seven triangles of sunlight are projected down the north-face staircase. When the serpent's head at the base (of the staircase) is added, the illusion is that of a snake dropping from the skies and slithering down the stairs.
>
> Adalberto Rivera: *The Mysteries of Chichen Itza*

Now this is perhaps a rather tenuous argument, but it is possibly more than coincidence that the interplay of light and serpent, two associations with Kundalini, are employed to create this effect. Indeed the author goes on to say that the concepts at work here, and the forces to which they refer, have been recognised by men of wisdom in every major civilisation the world has ever known (Kundalini yoga being perhaps the best-known example). This argument however, becomes more convincing when you know that the pyramid is built over an existing pyramid. This 'overlaying' of pyramids and temples was a common practice for the Mayans and as Adalberto Rivera cites in *The Mysteries of Chichen Itza*, in the upper portion of this inner pyramid is a vertical relief showing intertwining snakes ascending the wall; at the base of the relief is a lotus flower and at the top a pair of wings all very much like that of the caduceus symbol.

Are there Kundalini links to DNA through the caduceus symbol?

The corroboration of other instances in the world can also be viewed in *The Cosmic Serpent* by Jeremy Narby, which shows that ancient peoples from the Aborigines to the Egyptians, have known for millennia about the double helix structure (DNA), only discovered by conventional science in 1953. He cites the similarity of a shape which shamans the world over described as a ladder, vine, rope, spiral staircase or a twisted rope ladder which connects heaven and earth and with which they gained access to the world of spirits. He compares this closely to the shape of the double helix, which was also often so described: 'I had looked up DNA in several encyclopaedias and had noted in passing that the shape of the double helix was most often described as a ladder or twisted rope ladder, or a spiral staircase.' Moreover, Narby suggests that the similarity between the caduceus symbol and the representation of DNA was unmistakable. He quotes from Campbell's *Occidental Mythology* regarding omnipresent snake symbolism:

> Throughout the material in the Primitive, Oriental and Occidental volumes of this work, myths and rites of the serpent frequently appear, and in a remarkably consistent symbolic sense. Wherever nature is revered as self-moving, and so inherently divine, the serpent is revered as symbolic of its divine life.
>
> Jeremy Narby: *The Cosmic Serpent*

Narby continues by saying that the caduceus, formed by two snakes wrapped around an axis, can be found from the most ancient of times in countries from India to the Mediterranean. Also not only did the Ancient Egyptians, the Aztecs, the Amazonians and the Australians employ serpent symbolism, but the Taoists represented the caduceus with the yin-yang symbol in addition to the Shipibo-Conibo tribe of the Peruvian Amazon and their depiction of a ladder around which is coiled a cosmic serpent.

The 'experience' and its symbol of the caduceus seems to be reflected in every culture and philosophic system of antiquity and, with the evidence of my own eyes, I can certainly attest to the existence of the caduceus symbol on and from ancient sites in Mexico, Malta, Cambodia, Egypt and Greece.

Meditation leading to the awakening of the energy

On the awakening of the energy in the Kundalini experience, Krishna said that the deepest levels of the cerebrospinal system are involved in the process of illumination. The change at these levels occurs through intense meditation, devotional prayer, worship, pranayama (control or regulation of breath) with concentration and other yogic and religious disciplines practised from immemorial times. It is not the place here to provide a teaching of the attainment of Kundalini nor do I wish to. It suffices to say that it is essential and that associated with the awakening of this energy is a concentration and focus on matters profound. Whilst a teacher or guide may be beneficial, initiation of all must be by the individual, no matter what the course of action. The quotation from Confucius at the beginning of this chapter can be applied here. 'In the world there are many different roads but the destination is the same. There are a hundred deliberations but the result is one.'

Importance of the freedom from psychological or emotional conflicts
Bonnie Greenwell explains the relevance of meditation and a concern about the meaning of life as a consistent factor among those reporting the Kundalini experience; that it can also be achieved among those with an openness of mind and an absence of psychological and emotional conflicts:

> After centuries of hiding in nearly every culture on the globe as a secret esoteric truth, the Kundalini experience is reported more and more frequently among modern spiritual seekers and appears to be occurring even among people who do not follow spiritual practices ... exposure to many practices, especially meditation, and deep concern about the meaning of life – are found in the histories of people who report Kundalini symptoms. Yet one can never predict who will awaken this energy. Openness of mind, heart and/or body seems to promote it. This means that it is helpful if psychological and emotional conflicts are minimal and the body is free of blocks and tensions. It is well to have few attachments regarding worldly concerns.
>
> Bonnie Greenwell: *Energies of Transformation*

The importance of study and contemplation with meditation
While not wishing to provide a teaching of this awakening of Kundalini, as mentioned previously, it seems clear to me that it is from the concentration of profound philosophical, spiritual matter and of the Self that leads to the awakening of the energy. Certainly, the incorporation into one's life of study, contemplation and meditation seems to be essential. This appears to be the case if you find validity in the evidence presented by the spiritual philosophers, spiritual texts and prophets of the world throughout history. On the process of meditation there are a number of forms and suggestions by various teachers and schools of thought on the matter, and it is for the individual who wishes to pursue its practice to decide which form might suit them best. Perhaps there is an approach of no form at all, which is to say that with endeavour and practice, it is possible to clear the mind.

Other aspects of achieving meditation
Some other aspects in attempting the practice of meditation include those such as finding a peaceful location, use of a mantra, employing a constant rhythm of breathing, and the free flow of thoughts.

Peaceful location
In my view it is extraordinarily difficult to ask a novice to think solely of the black dot in the middle of the forehead and of absolutely nothing else. Finding yourself in a physical location which is as peaceful and quiet as possible is essential. A mantra may be beneficial, though not essential; this is the utterance of a syllable, word or verse sounded either out loud or internally and either continuously or merely once. My personal choice is not to use a mantra.

Letting thoughts flow over you
Breathing is the most important factor, maintaining a constant and deep rhythm. Permit all thoughts to flow over you, whatever they may be, whether troubling or insignificant, and allow these thoughts to have their time and for as long as it might take for them to 'settle', do not disallow them in an effort to attain total quietude. Allow further thoughts to take their place, once contemplated upon to their extinction,

should they return again permit them to have their time. No matter the volume of thoughts, no matter how bothersome, positive or negative, accept them. The more often you practise, the less the volume of thoughts appears and, what is more, there will be reconciliation of previous thoughts and perhaps action in the physical realms of your life, which assist in the achievement of such. As time and practice progress there will eventually be a peace, a quietude, once you place yourself in a position with the intention of meditation; with more practice the more immediate the state and this will only take place over time. This is not a matter, in any way, to be rushed. You will eventually find your place, a peace within yourself, comfortable and unchallenged and possess a greater sense of who you are. You will find eventually all that is right and wrong, positive and negative, all that you have been and all you wish to be, a vision of yourself in absolute clarity.

The *Bhagavad Gita* articulates all this in a similar way, with practice of the 'harmony of the soul' in 'a restful place' to find 'a soul in peace and all fear gone':

> Day after day, let the Yogi practise the harmony of the soul; in a secret place, in deep solitude, master of his mind, hoping for nothing, desiring nothing.
>
> Let him find a place that is pure and a seat that is restful, neither too high nor too low, with sacred grass and a skin and a cloth thereon.
>
> On that seat let him rest and practise Yoga for the purification of the soul; with the life of his body and mind in peace; his soul before the One.
>
> With upright body, head and neck, which rest still and move not; with inner gaze which is not restless, but rests still between the eyebrows;
>
> With soul in peace, and all fear gone, and strong in the vow of holiness, let him rest with mind in harmony, his soul on me, his God supreme.
>
> The Yogi who, lord of his mind, ever prays in this harmony of soul, attains peace of Nirvana, the peace supreme that is in me.

Mascaró, translator of The *Bhagavad Gita* and The *Upanishads*, also comments on this:

> Meditation is the means, contemplation is the end: the one is the path and the other is the end of the path. Even as the vessel is still and at rest when it has arrived in port, when the soul has reached contemplation through meditation it should cease its toil and inquiries; and happy in the vision of God, even as if He were present, be one in feelings of love, of wonder, of joy or other such.

At a point in *Varieties*, James states that, 'Even the least mystical of you must by this time be convinced of the existence of mystical moments as states of consciousness of an entirely specific quality, and of the deep impression which they make on those who have them.'

Dr Richard Bucke on Kundalini and 'Illumination' or 'Cosmic Consciousness'

There is one further and highly interesting body of evidence on the prevalence of the Kundalini experience (although given a different name), in the writing of another author who has developed his own interpretations of it.

In seeking to research consciousness from both a philosophical and scientific perspective I came across the title *Cosmic Consciousness: A Study in the Evolution of the Human Mind* by Dr Richard Maurice Bucke.

It is a particularly interesting text because it recounts the author's own experience of Kundalini, except that he describes it under the name of 'Illumination' or 'Cosmic Consciousness'. In *Varieties* William James cites Richard Bucke as one who has had the 'mystic' experience.

Richard Bucke maintains that 'Cosmic Consciousness' is a third form of consciousness that is superior to that of self-consciousness, as possessed by the human race and which itself is superior to simple consciousness, as possessed by the upper half of the animal kingdom. The prime characteristic of 'Cosmic Consciousness', states Bucke, is a consciousness of the cosmos, that is, of the life and order of the universe.

Dr Richard Maurice Bucke (1837–1902).

Bucke also suggests that only a personal experience of it, or a prolonged study of individuals who have had this experience, will enable us to realise what it actually is. He expected his work to be useful in two ways: first, the broadening of the general view of life and second, he hoped to furnish aid to individuals in a far more practical and important sense. He took the view, that, sooner or later, humans would reach the condition of 'Cosmic Consciousness' as a race, just as in the past our ancestors passed from simple to self-consciousness. He also believed that this step in evolution was being made, and suggested that more and more individuals were having this experience. His view was that intelligent contact with individuals of cosmic conscious minds would benefit those of self-consciousness minds in their ascent to this higher plane. He hoped that his book would facilitate such contact and assist men and women in making the almost infinitely important step in question.

Bucke's own career

Bucke provides a background to his life and experience of what he calls 'Cosmic Consciousness'. He was born of good middle-class English stock and grew up almost without education on a backwater Canadian farm. As a child, he tended to livestock, worked in the hay field and undertook other such menial tasks. He never, as a child, accepted the doctrines of the Christian church and, as soon as he was old enough, he began to dwell on such matters as conscious identity and whether it would be preserved after death. Bucke writes that he thought on such matters more than anyone would suppose but perhaps no more than other introspective fellow mortals. At the age of ten, he longed to understand the secrets of what lay beyond and that they might be revealed to him. At the same age he read the book *Faust* by Reynolds.

Bucke left home at 16 and wandered over the North American continent, working on railways and steamboats and leading a physically challenging existence. After five years of travelling, he returned home and, with money inherited from his mother, embarked on study. Some four years after his return he graduated with high honours. In addition to his syllabus, he read widely and many books such as Darwin's *The Origin of Species*, Tyndall's *Heat* and *Essays*, poems by Shelley and many others. His life, he described, was, for some years, one passionate note of interrogation, an unappeasable hunger for enlightenment on the basic problems and, after leaving college, he continued this search with the same ardour. He also taught himself both French, so that he might be able to read French authors such as Auguste Comte, Victor Hugo and Renan, and also German, so that he could read Goethe, especially *Faust*.

Bucke's experience of 'Illumination'

Bucke then goes on to describe his own 'experience'. It was early spring at the age of 36 and he had spent an evening with friends discussing Wordsworth, Shelley, Keats, Browning and Whitman. They parted ways at midnight and he had a long drive home. His mind was full of the ideas, images and emotions derived from the reading and conversation of the evening and he was in a state of calm, almost passive enjoyment. Suddenly, and without warning, he found himself 'wrapped around as it were by a *flame*-coloured cloud'. For a moment he thought of fire and the next 'he knew that the *light* was within himself'. Immediately afterwards, he felt a sense of exultation and immense joyousness, accompanied by an intellectual *illumination* quite impossible to describe. Into his brain stem, Bucke continues, streamed one momentary *lightning-flash* of Brahmic Splendour, which has ever since *lightened* his life and thereafter has been always remembered as 'a taste of heaven'. He saw and knew that the Cosmos was not dead matter but a living presence, and that the soul of man is immortal. He states that he saw, and knew, that the universe is so built and ordered for the good of all and that its founding principle is what we call love. Bucke claims to have learned more in that brief period, and that the illumination had made more of an impression on him, than his previous years of study.

The illumination only lasted a few seconds in time but its effect was indelible, to the extent that it was impossible for him ever to forget what he saw and knew from that moment, and that he could never doubt the truth of what was presented to his mind. Bucke later describes 'the instantaneousness of the *illumination* as one of the most striking features. It can be compared with nothing so well as with a *dazzling flash of lightning* in a dark night, bringing the landscape which had been hidden into clear view.'

This account seems very close to the other experiences described in *Caduceus*. I consider it to be one of the most succinct accounts of Kundalini, or 'illumination' or entrance into 'Cosmic Consciousness', as Bucke describes it, that I have read and further supports my contention on the world-wide prevalence of Kundalini.

Up to this point, my case has been based on the experience of Kundalini by providing examples of it both in the context of spiritual texts of some antiquity and the writings of great thinkers. I then provide a foundation to my argument by paralleling these descriptions with those provided by the Kundalini commentators, Gopi Krishna and Bonnie Greenwell. The aforementioned are relatively contemporary publications on the subject of Kundalini. Krishna was first published in 1970 and Greenwell in 1990. Yet Bucke's *Cosmic Consciousness* was first published just over one hundred years ago in 1901.

Bucke's bewilderment and apprehension after the 'experience'
Bucke writes of the bewildering and confusing nature of the experience. Individuals who enter into this experience of 'Cosmic Consciousness'

are, at first, more or less excited by apprehension and they then ask themselves if what they see and feel represents reality or whether they are suffering from a delusion. He suggests that they doubt whether the new sense may not be a symptom or form of insanity, and suggests that Muhammad was greatly alarmed, as was Paul. The fact that the new experience seems even more real than the old teachings of simple self-consciousness does not seem to reassure them. He goes on to say that each person who has the experience eventually believes in its teachings, accepting them as absolutely as any other doctrine.

Like others, Bucke also suggested that the experience was particularly difficult to describe. It is interesting that his comments are also reflected in Bonnie Greenwell's assertion that there would be increased numbers of individuals who would have the experience. His own hypothesis was that cases of 'Cosmic Consciousness' would become more numerous from age to age, not only this, but they should become more perfect and more pronounced. Indeed Bucke, much like Krishna, believed that the experience is a manifestation of an evolutionary change in mankind's existence. This step in evolutionary change, he claimed, was being made so that his descendants would sooner or later reach the condition of 'Cosmic Consciousness' or 'Elevated Consciousness'.

Bucke's own interpretations of individuals experiencing Cosmic Consciousness
In support of my own arguments on 'light', Bucke reconciled himself with the illuminating experience years afterwards in finding examples of this subjective light in others. Indeed, the bulk of the content of *Cosmic Consciousness* consists of naming and providing descriptions of other 'illuminated' individuals and instances of 'Cosmic Consciousness'. His list includes Buddha, Jesus, Paul, Muhammad and Dante, who, as I have described previously, experienced Kundalini. Obviously, Bucke predated Nietzsche and Jung, and the *Gospels of Judas* would not have been available to him, but had he been aware of them I would like to think that they would have been included. Interestingly, Bucke names individuals including Francis Bacon, William Blake and Balzac in his list and others such as Moses, Isaiah, Wordsworth and Tennyson within the category of lesser, imperfect or doubtful instances.

Bucke's aim in his book *Cosmic Consciousness* was to point out that there have lived in this world certain individuals, who, not out of an extraordinary development of any or all of the ordinary mental faculties, but in whom the possession of a new consciousness, peculiar to themselves and non-existent (or at least undeclared) in ordinary people, see, know and feel spiritual facts and experience physical phenomena, which being veiled from, are still of most vital importance to, the world at large.

Bucke makes an interesting point and one with which I agree and have based this book on. Of the individuals that he has listed and the ones that I have described here, with some overlap, Bucke suggests that if one or two of these individuals are studied to the exclusion of the others, the result would be inadequate and unsatisfactory, compared to the study of all of them. If all are read, and their testimonies compared, new light is thrown upon their accounts and these supplement and strengthen those of the others. I have stated earlier that this should also be applied to the ancient spiritual texts. In the same vein, Bucke comments on the slight discrepancies in accounts of the experience and on doubts thrown on the reality of the experience. He uses an analogy of the sight of a tree across a field, half a mile away, which one knows to be real and not a hallucination because all other persons having the sense of sight also see the tree. If it were a hallucination no one would see it but you. By the same method of reasoning, Bucke establishes the reality of the experience. If three individuals saw the tree and were asked half an hour later to draw or describe the tree, their representations would not tally in detail but would in general outline. Bucke further believes that there is no person who has had the experience who would fail to recognise or deny the experience described by another.

A further interesting point Bucke makes is that Westerners would benefit more from reading Buddhist and Muhammadean scriptures, than by reading Jewish or Christian scriptures. This would apply also to individuals in Southern Asia who were born Buddhists, Brahmans or Muhammadeans; they could benefit more readily and be more profoundly stirred by the Gospels or other 'western text' than by the Vedas or by the books that owe their inspiration to the teachings of Buddha or Muhammad.

Bucke's account of individuals who experienced Kundalini in terms of 'Cosmic Consciousness'

Bucke's own accounts of the individuals that I have mentioned have common elements: for example, a loss of the fear of death, an element of the experience that Bucke describes, is consistent with a great many cases and indeed consistent with my feelings. There is one interesting point that Bucke has identified which I had not previously considered in my research and that is the proximity of the ages of these illumined individuals when the experience occurred, generally ranging from 30 to 40 at the time.

Bucke's accounts and interpretations of those individuals experiencing 'Cosmic Consciousness' that overlap with those individuals mentioned in earlier chapters are shown below.

On Buddha and 'the light that expels darkness'
Bucke relates how Siddhartha Gautama abandoned asceticism and, shortly afterwards, at about the age of 35, attained illumination under the celebrated tree. The *Dhamma-Kakka-Ppavattana-Suta* was a summary of the words of the great Indian thinker and reformer and proclaimed his new ideas. In it, Gautama the Buddha declares that the 'noble truths' taught within were not 'among the doctrines handed down' but that 'there arose within him the eye to perceive them, the knowledge of their nature, the understanding of their cause, the wisdom that lights the true path, the light expels the darkness.' Bucke asserts that Gautama is a clear case of 'Cosmic Consciousness', not least because the initial character of his mind seems to have been ardent, earnest and aspiring, which usually, if not always, precedes the experience.

On Jesus and the moment of baptism from John
Bucke suggests that the age of 'illumination' for Jesus took place when he was 33. He too cites the transfiguration and provides description of the moment of baptism: 'And straightaway coming up out of the water, he saw the heavens rent asunder, and the Spirit as a dove descending upon him: and a voice came out of the heavens saying thou art my beloved son in thee I am well pleased'. This is the earliest and probably most authentic account of the 'illumination'. Bucke states that Jesus

going to John to be baptised shows that his mind was directed toward religious thought. However, one need not suppose that illumination necessarily took place immediately upon the baptism. He also states that the impulse which drove Jesus into solitude after his illumination is usual if not universal. In addition, Bucke further claims that the accounts given in the synoptic gospels of the transfiguration of Jesus can only be explained by supposing that he was seen while in the condition of 'Cosmic Consciousness'. He also refers to the way that 'his face did shine as the sun' and his countenance whilst praying 'was altered and his raiment became white and dazzling,' claiming that there is no known human condition that would account for these words except illumination or 'Cosmic Consciousness'.

On Muhammad and 'celestial light'

Bucke describes this case, both overall and in detail, as marvellously complete. He suggests that the disposition of Muhammad prior to his experience on Mount Hara (Hira) was serious, devout, earnest and deeply religious, as is the essential prerequisite for the attainment of 'Cosmic Consciousness'. He discusses Muhammad's solitude in a cave on Mount Hara and his endeavouring by fasting, prayer and solitary meditation to elevate his thoughts to the contemplation of divine truth. It was here, in the month of Ramadan in his fortieth year that, according to Bucke, Muhammad, wrapped in a cloak, heard a voice calling upon him; uncovering himself, a flood of *light* broke upon him of such intolerable splendour that he swooned away and, on regaining his senses, he beheld the angel (Gabriel). Muhammad instantly felt his understanding was illuminated by 'celestial light'.

In Bucke's view the *Qur'an* is a book of greatness, power and spirituality which must be considered in the context of its impact on the world and that no effect of it is greater than its cause, that of the originating experience from which it is derived.

On Paul: five aspects of his experience

Bucke was so convinced that Paul the Apostle was also a case that he proclaimed that this was as clear and certain as 'Caesar was a great general'. He believed that this case meets all the elements of probability and proof. He cites Paul's earnestness and enthusiasm for the religion in which he was brought up and suggests that Paul was four or five years younger than Jesus and that his illumination, which Paul himself describes as his conversion, took place at the same age as that of Jesus.

Bucke refers to the three separate accounts of his experience and, in summing up, lists the elements regarding Paul's experience: (a) the characteristic suddenness of the experience, (b) the instance of subjective light which is very clearly and strongly manifested, (c) the intellectual illumination of the most pronounced character, (d) the instance of strongly marked moral exaltation and (e) the conviction, the sense of immortality, the extinction of the sense of sin and the extinction of the fear of death.

On Dante and his entry into Cosmic Consciousness

Bucke explained that, whilst knowledge of Dante's outward life and personality was all but lost to him in the nineteenth century, it was said by Boccaccio that Dante was taken by the sweetness of knowing the truth of the things concealed to him in heaven and sought a state of mind where no part of philosophy would remain unseen to him and that with his acute intellect he plunged into the deepest recesses of theology and by assiduous study came to know of the divine essence. Bucke believes that Dante's contemplativeness, studiousness and earnest nature is consistent with individuals who attain illumination.

He discusses the *Divine Comedy* and suggests that Inferno and Purgatorio are realms of self-consciousness, whilst Paradiso is the realm of 'Cosmic Consciousness' and is comparable to Nirvana. On this point, Bucke quotes several passages from the *Divine Comedy* and particularly of entering into 'Cosmic Consciousness':

The glory of him who moves everything penetrates through the universe and shines in one part more than in another less. In the heaven that receives most of its light I have been, and have seen things which he who descends from there above neither knows how nor is able to recount[72:1]

On a sudden day seemed to be added to day as if he who is able had adorned the heaven with another sun. [72:4].

Bucke suggests that this is the same subjective light as seen by Muhammad and the others discussed by him.

Dante's age at the time of 'illumination' was 35 and it was after this illumination that he wrote the *Divine Comedy*.

On Moses: an imperfect example of illumination?

Bucke mentions Moses as a lesser or imperfect example of 'illumination'. He quotes the burning bush which was not consumed by fire and suggests that the shining of Moses' face when he descended from Mount Sinai could be the transfiguration characteristic of 'Cosmic Consciousness'. He states that Moses was, at or near, the usual age of illumination and that he was alarmed at the 'fire' or light, as is usually the case.

Bucke's 14 cases of Cosmic Consciousness

In his book Bucke discusses 14 cases of 'Cosmic Consciousness'. Five I have already mentioned and the remaining nine cases that Bucke provides include: Plotinus, Las Casas, John Yepes, Francis Bacon, Jacob Behmen, William Blake, Honoré De Balzac, Walt Whitman and Edward Carpenter.

I have read Walt Whitman's *Leaves of Grass: The First Edition (1855)* and I am in no doubt that he too had such an 'illuminating' experience. I especially like how he refers to his experience as 'the merge'. Having read many of William Blake's works, I have always had a deep sense that he himself had such an illuminating experience. However, whilst his writings lend to this opinion, I have been unable to indentify enough specific quotations from his writings to provide convincing evidence for inclusion as a separate example in this book.

Bucke's view of William Blake and his 'Imaginative Vision'

Bucke's view is somewhat different in that he asserts that William Blake seems to have entered into 'Cosmic Consciousness' at the age of just over 30, but he can point to nothing of the occurrence of subjective light in Blake's case. Bucke does say that Blake also possessed a sense of immortality, which is consistent with all of those who have had the 'experience'. He provides several extracts of his work, which he says almost prove that Blake had such an experience which he called

'Imaginative Vision'. Furthermore, while there do not appear to be any exact details of his entrance into 'Cosmic Consciousness', his writings may be fairly allowed to prove the fact of possession. An example would include the preface to *The Jerusalem*. Blake speaks of this composition being 'dictated' to him, and that he regarded it as a revelation of which he was scribe, rather than it originating from his own mind. Blake contended that it was 'the grandest poem that this world contains.' While there is still a dearth of specific details, Bucke maintains that a study of his writings and drawings convinced him that Blake *was* a genuine, and probably a great, case for 'Cosmic Consciousness'.

Having read Bucke's *Cosmic Consciousness* and found such overlap and corroboration of his various cases with my own, I have gained a greater sense of confidence and comfort in the presentation of my own assertions (not that I was in much doubt prior to reading it!).

Kundalini as a unifying force among all religions

As the quotation from Confucius at the beginning of this chapter suggests, there are many ways to approach not only the attainment of Kundalini, but also a state of peace and consciousness. There must be a change in the present world consciousness and, whilst its initiation comes from individuals, it is imperative that this change be worldwide.

As Krishna explained it:

> The awakening of Kundalini is the greatest enterprise and the most wonderful achievement in front of man. There is absolutely no other way open to his restless searching intellect to pass beyond the boundaries of the otherwise meaningless physical universe.

He thought that this represented the first and not the final ladder of evolution and should be seen as the path to lead the human race to a much improved, and presently unknown, state of consciousness. His view was that this elevation is the real aim of all religious disciplines and faiths of mankind and that, owing to intellectual speculation and incorrect presentation, the real purpose of faith and the true aim of spiritual discipline have been lost.

According to Krishna, the real and initial goal in front of man is to know himself and I couldn't agree more. This sentiment has also been echoed elsewhere, of course; Jesus said 'Man know thyself', and in Ancient Greece the inscription 'Know Thyself' stood on the Temple of Apollo. (It is interesting here to note that Apollo was the God of light and the sun and was originally a deity of radiant purity.)

Kundalini and its effects may be covered in greater detail in some future book. However, the particular beauty of my experience is defined by the fact that I did not know of Kundalini prior to the experience. It was by the focusing of an enquiring mind on profound and meaningful matters, combined with meditation, that it was encountered or indeed imposed upon me. It was not sought, there was no prior knowledge of it, so one cannot declare that my subconscious yearned for it and therefore it came to pass. Whether or not the reader believes my personal experience is not of great consequence. It was my experience that led me to write this book. However, were you to take my experience out of it, I hope that my assertions and contentions still stand by the variety and volume of anecdotal evidence there is. At the very least, I hope that I have provided the identification of constant, consistent and transcendent evidence that this experience exists.

With this transcendent evidence, there may be reason for hope for the future. Could Kundalini as this shared experience be a light at the end of the tunnel? In addition to the benefits outlined in this chapter, it is clear that this 'light' is a potentially unifying element for *all* religions. After all, there are glaring overlaps in the spiritual texts of religions and spiritual movements cited in esoteric spiritual texts. It is evident in the formation of these religions and spiritual movements the originators had undeniably, and remarkably, parallel experiences. The very instances of their initiation were virtually identical. Should we not view within this ever-present source a unifying element and the 'oneness' of them all? Can we seize this opportunity to dispense with ingrained prejudices and redundant conflict between them, having identified this most profound common ground? Could this unifying 'oneness' now become the light at the end of the tunnel?

Summary

We identified and confirmed that ancient spiritual texts in Chapter 4 and the spiritual philosophers in Chapter 5 pointed and referred to the experience of Kundalini.

There are striking similarities of the experience of Kundalini in testimonies by Gopi Krishna and Dr Richard Maurice Bucke, as well as commentary by William James and Dr Bonnie Greenwell.

The Kundalini or 'mystic' experience, 'illumination' or 'Cosmic Consciousness' are all, by definition, the very same.

The elements of the Kundalini experience were described as being:

- Suddenness of the experience
- Subjective light
- Prior nature of individual being of introspection, contemplation, meditation with earnest endeavour and in general seeking of knowledge and wisdom.
- Loss of fear of death

The question was posed as to why the Kundalini experience might be as unacknowledged and 'mysterious' when the evidence for it has been presented in so many forms, philosophy, religions, spiritual texts and in relation to a number of notable individuals since time immemorial.

There were also similarities of the Kundalini experience among spiritual individuals, prophets and messiahs such as Enoch, Moses, Jesus, Muhammad and Buddha, in addition to more contemporary individuals such as Nietzsche and Jung.

To attain this state demands deep introspection, self-knowledge, a focus and study of profound and spiritual matters and the employment of meditation.

The worldwide nature of the experience and, more pertinently its potentially unifying benefits across all the various religions of the world were emphasised.

7

'Light' at the End of Life?

For certain is death for the born
And certain is birth for the dead;
Therefore over the inevitable
Thou shouldst not grieve.

The *Bhagavad Gita*

At various times I have heard anecdotes of individuals who have had a Near-death experience. In these anecdotes, the common factor has often been an occurrence of 'light'. These experiences occurred among individuals who have either found themselves in a life-threatening situation or who have been declared clinically dead and subsequently been resuscitated. So, in writing this book, I decided to research the subject and I was amazed to find the remarkable similarities between the Kundalini experience and accounts of these Near-death experiences. It seems possible that the 'light' in both scenarios is exactly the same, of the same origin and source but accessed from different angles.

Accounts in Plato's writings

There is very little historical reference of being close to death and thereafter being revived. This may well have something to do with the advances of medical technology which today enables doctors to 'bring people back from death', whereas previously such considerations would not have been possible.

Plato's The Republic

One of the first accounts of dying, the return to life and what occurred in between, including the occurrence of light, can be found in Plato's *The Republic* in Part Eleven. Titled; The Immortality of the Soul and the Rewards of Goodness, it recounts in section 3 The Myth of Er, a Greek soldier who was killed in battle along with many of his comrades. The bodies of the slain were collected on the tenth day, however, while the other bodies were decomposing, Er's was 'still quite sound'. Er was taken to his home to be buried on the twelfth day but as he lay upon the funeral pyre 'he came back to life again and told the story of what he had seen in the other world.'

Er recounted that his soul left his body and travelled in the company of other souls until they came to a wonderful place where there were two gaping chasms close to each other, and between which sat a panel of judges. Er, however, was not judged and was told that 'he was to be a messenger to men about the [this] other world.' He saw how souls rose out of the earth stained with the dust of travel and others descended from heaven, pure and clean. These souls, after their long journey, encamped in a meadow and spent seven days there. They set out on the eighth day and, after four more days, came to a place where they could see a 'shaft of light' stretching from above straight through heaven and earth, like a pillar, closely resembling a rainbow, only brighter and clearer. They reached this after a further day's journey and saw there in the middle of the light stretching from the heaven the ends of the bonds of it. It goes on to say that this light was 'the bond of heaven and holds its whole circumference together.'

In addition to the instance of light, further stories of the souls are recounted, including what he learned on how man should lead his life and, relevant to our theme, the importance of knowledge and wisdom. The Myth of Er states that it should be our first care to 'seek and study that which will show us to perceive' and that those who 'during his [their] earthly life faithfully seek wisdom,' for 'not only happiness in this life but for the journey from this world to the next and back again that will not lie over the stony ground of the underworld but along the smooth road of heaven.' Er eventually returns to life suddenly opening his eyes, still lying on the pyre, unsure 'by what manner of means he returned to his body.'

In *The Republic* we find accounts of this recurring theme of light and the importance of wisdom and knowledge.

Plato's Phaedo

To my mind there is no greater discourse than that of Plato's *Phaedo* on the matter of the separation of the soul and the physical body after its demise. The events in 399 BCE in this text centre on Socrates' last day and his execution after his conviction by a court in Athens on charges of impiety. He was sentenced to death by poisoning. Plato was an admirer of Socrates and used Socratic discourses not merely as devices to reproduce the conversations that he heard, but also as a vehicle to support his own philosophical ideas.

Early on in the discussion, they seek to conclude whether there is a tendency of the body to hamper the soul in its quest for truth. In addition to this, it is largely accepted that the soul is a spiritual substance, which is present during life and is separated from it at death, able to exist thereafter in a disembodied state. In some instances of the discussion, the soul is the 'true self' or 'real person', which is absolutely distinguishable from the 'physical body'.

The souls Socrates describes resemble the divine and are different from the physical body:

> [The] soul is most similar to the divine, immortal, intelligible, uniform, indissoluble, unvarying and constant in relation to itself; whereas [the] body, in its turn, is most similar to what is human, mortal, multiform, non-intelligible, dissoluble, and never constant in relation to itself.

The soul, Socrates asserts, is what constitutes our well-being and should be the most important part of our lives, which should be cared for in this life and for the life to come.

Two further thoughts can be extracted from the discussion: that the soul, just like human reason or intellect, motivates us in the seeking of truth and wisdom and that the soul provides life to the body that it occupies and is limited to these intellectual and reasoning functions. The thought is the 'separation of soul from the body' and this appears in the first and last arguments for immortality.

Socrates argues that not only does the soul continue to exist after death, but that it existed prior to birth. This assertion is based on 'recollection', on what is really the regaining of the knowledge which the soul possessed in a disembodied state before birth. In using our senses, we 'regain' knowledge possessed before birth. 'Our learning is actually nothing but a recollection,' and later, '... having got them (pieces of knowledge), before birth, we lost them on being born,' and 'using the senses about the things in question, we regain those pieces of knowledge that we possessed in some former time; in that case wouldn't what we call "learning" be the regaining of knowledge belonging to us?'

I interpret this to mean regaining a knowledge and wisdom that is already present within us that needs to be drawn out, and this can be best achieved by the study of matters profound.

While we will be looking at some contemporary evidence for reincarnation later, this theme is also discussed by Socrates who states that:

> There is an ancient doctrine, which we have recalled, that they [souls] do exist in that world, entering it from this one, and that they re-enter this world and are born again from the dead, yet if that is so, if living people are born again from those who have died, surely our souls would have to exist in that world? Because they could hardly be born again, if they didn't exist.
>
> Plato: *Phaedo*

The Tibetan Book of the Dead

Another source of some antiquity dating back to the eighth century is *The Tibetan Book of the Dead*. This text also refers to the existence of light after the instance of death and the transference of consciousness or the soul.

It provides the most detailed and compelling description of the after-death state in world literature and is a comprehensive guide to both living and dying. It was collated by Buddhist sages and traces its origins to one of the oldest schools of Tibetan Buddhism, derived from the first wave of Buddhist teachings in Tibet. It provides written guidance and practices for the transformation of our daily lives, how to address the process of dying and the after-death state, in addition to helping a dying person by making them aware of the unusual and wondrous phenomenon as they experience death.

In particular, it recounts the mind or soul of the dying individual as it departs the body and what happens to it until rebirth. This phase, *The Tibetan Book of the Dead* describes as an 'Intermediate State of Reality', which arises after the *intermediate state of the time of death* (`chi-kha'i bar-do*) and before the *intermediate state of rebirth* (*srid-pa`i bar-do*). It is during this period that *The Tibetan Book of the Dead* makes numerous references to the 'soul', encountering 'radiant light' along its path to rebirth.

This is an example from the *Aspirational Prayer which Rescues from the Dangerous Pathways of the Intermediate States*:

O, as I roam in cyclic existence [driven] by deep-seated aversion,
May the transcendent lord Vajrasattva draw me forward,
Leading me on the path of *radiant light*,
Which is the mirror-like pristine cognition.
May the supreme consort Buddhalocana support me from behind,
And thus [encircled] may I be rescued
From the fearsome passageway of the intermediate state,
And be escorted to the level of an utterly perfect buddha.

The Tibetan Book of the Dead

Contemporary research: *Life After Life* by Dr Raymond Moody

Whilst there is a dearth of historical accounts of the experience close to or after death, there is a considerable amount of contemporary research on the phenomenon. It is Dr Raymond Moody who coined the phrase, Near-death experience (NDE), in the 1970s and who published *Life After Life* in 1975. This best-selling book, which sold in excess of 13 million copies, was based on his pioneering research and is acknowledged as the standard/foundation of the experience by many authors on this subject. Moody, although an advocate of the experience, suggests that, unfortunately, the idea of near-death experience belongs more to our 'superstitious' past than to our 'scientific' present.

Moody first came to the subject when he was an undergraduate studying philosophy. A clinical professor of psychiatry in the School of

Medicine whom he met related the story of how he had died on two occasions about ten minutes apart, and what had happened to him while he was 'dead'. Several years later Moody gained his PhD in philosophy and was teaching in a university. He was urging his students to read Plato's *Phaedo*, a text where immortality is discussed (see above). One student asked whether they might discuss immortality in class because his grandmother had died during an operation and, after being resuscitated, had recounted an amazing story. To Moody's surprise, the student related almost the same series of events after death as had been recounted by the psychiatry professor. Moody's interest increased and he included readings on the subject of human survival of biological death in his philosophy courses, careful not to mention the two near-death experiences in his courses. Adopting this wait-and-see approach, he was amazed to find that in every class of approximately 30 students, at least one student would relate to him a personal near-death experience.

In *Life After Life* Moody states that the experiences that he has since come to study fall into three categories:

1. The experiences of persons who were resuscitated after having been thought, adjudged, or pronounced clinically dead by their doctors;

2. The experiences of persons who, in the course of accidents or severe injury or illness, came very close to physical death;

3. The experiences of persons who, as they died, told them to other people who were present. Later these other people reported the content of the death to Dr Moody.

He goes on to state that, whilst he found the reports of the third type complementary to the first and second, he dropped this third type to focus on first-hand reports.

Similarities with the Kundalini experience
It is important to say here that no two experiences are exactly the same in Near-death experiences as they are also not the same with the Kundalini experience. There are however, many similarities between

the Kundalini experience and the Near-death experience, not least of which is the occurrence of light and/or beings of light.

In *The Day I Died* by Tammy Cohen, a collection of 20 testimonies of Near-death experiences, thirteen of the accounts had encounters with light and/or beings of light. However, the similarities go much deeper. Dr Moody relates that there are 15 elements to the experience, which I have shown as a comparative table with the Kundalini experience, commentary is provided on each of the shared characteristics.

Comments on the comparisons
Ineffability
Moody suggests that the understanding of language depends on the existence of a broad community of common experience, in which most of us participate. Those who have had Near-death experiences lie outside of our community of experience and, as a result, have some difficulty in expressing what has happened to them. Individuals involved uniformly characterise their experience as ineffable or inexpressible. Several people have suggested that there are just no words to describe this experience and there are no adjectives or superlatives to convey its effect.

This is similar to the Kundalini experiences described earlier of Krishna, Jung, al-Ghazali, James, Bucke and also myself. Krishna pointed out the innate difficulty of finding any appropriate description of such an experience:

> No amount of intellectual exercise can draw an accurate picture of the state. It would be like the attempt of one denied sight to explain the colours of the rainbow to others, or like one who sees a rainbow and its colours to convey his impressions to a group of sightless people.

And Jung also emphasised this difficulty of finding a meaningful description for it:

> Anyone who has experienced anything of the sort will know what I mean, and anyone who has not had the experience will not be satisfied

Elements of Near-death Experience	Similarity to Kundalini Experience
Ineffability, inability to describe	Yes
Hearing yourself pronounced dead	Not applicable!
Feelings of peace and quiet	Yes
The noise	Yes
Seeing or being in a dark tunnel	Yes?
Out of the body	Yes?
Meeting others (spiritual beings)	Yes
The existence of light	Yes
The review	Yes
The border or limit	Uncertain
Coming back (return to physical body)	Yes
Telling others: frustration and lack of inclination to	Yes
Effect on lives	Yes
New views on death; losing fear of death	Yes
Corroboration	Too subjective for comparison

Table showing comparisons between the Near-death experience
and the Kundalini experience.

by any amount of descriptions ... I know of no case in which the bare description conveyed the experience.

Furthermore, al-Ghazli, said that this experience is difficult to describe beyond the narrow range of words that are available to us, 'so if anyone tries to express them, his words contain evident error against which he cannot guard himself.'

In addition, Richard Bucke in his text, *Cosmic Consciousness* also mentioned that his illumination was 'quite impossible to describe'. William James cited this aspect as his first characteristic of the 'mystic' experience:

> The subject of it immediately says that it defies expression that no adequate report of its contents can be given in words. It follows from this that its quality must be directly experienced; it cannot be imparted or transferred to others. In this peculiarity mystical states are more like states of feeling than like states of intellect. No one can make clear to another who has never had a certain feeling, in what the quality or worth of it consists.

Hearing the news

Moody suggests that numerous individuals have told of hearing their doctors or other spectators pronounce them dead. Thankfully this is not applicable to my own experience or to the Kundalini experience that happened to others!

Feelings of peace and quiet

There are descriptions of extremely pleasant feelings and sensations during the early stages of the experience. Moody provides examples of individuals with a severe illness or who had 'died' feeling warmth, comfort, peace, ease, quietness and being relaxed.

In my experience it was (on reflection) such a shock that I had no choice but to 'go with the flow' and resign myself to the experience. In this sense it was peaceful and comfortable; there was certainly no sense of chaos or discomfort, not that I was what can be described as particularly conscious at the time. William James notes this as number four in his list of the characteristics of the 'mystic' experience which he titles *Passivity*: 'The characteristic sort of consciousness once it has set in, the mystic feels as if his own will were in abeyance, and indeed sometimes as if he were grasped and held by a superior power.' Of the same characteristic, James also comments, 'Throughout the height of it he undoubtedly seems to himself a passive spectator or undergoer of an astonishing process performed upon him from above.'

The noise

Moody states that, in many cases, unusual auditory sensations are reported to occur at or near death. He provides descriptions such as a buzzing noise, loud ringing, a whistling sound, bells tingling and a very rhythmic brrrrrnnnnng- brrrrrnnnnng- brrrrrnnnnng.

As mentioned earlier, this occurred both with Krishna and my own case and can be found in Dante's epic poem. Krishna comments: 'The Sound is variously described and its mystery diversely explained. The sacred syllable "Aum" is said to be greatest of the mantras and the quintessence of the Vedas.' Krishna also compared this element to the buzzing of a swarm of bees. And Dante's Paradiso in *The Divine Comedy* refers to the sound and light:

> With harmonies
> proportionate and clear, made me attend,
> the skies of heaven ...
> The newness of the *sound* and that great *light*
> Kindled in me a desire to know the cause
> Sharper than any I have ever felt.

The dark tunnel

There are descriptions of being pulled very rapidly through a type of dark space, described variously as a cave, a well, a tunnel, a vacuum or a void.

While I cannot myself attest to a physical tunnel, one feels constrained, a type of seizure that Nietzsche referred to as being pulled rapidly through a space, and that could be applied to this element.

Out of the body

Moody states that after an individual has their rapid passage through the dark tunnel, they might have an overwhelming surprise. They might

213

well find themselves looking at their own physical body from a point outside it as though they are a spectator, a third person in the room or as if watching events onstage or in a movie. Accounts have described individuals as feeling that they were of 'pure' consciousness and were weightless.

He goes on to provide examples of events where people who have 'died' or come very close to death actually observe events around their unconscious physical bodies such as the activities of doctors and nurses.

In my own experience, I did not actually feel as if I was physically there. I cannot say that I had left my physical body but another form was certainly dominant at the time. As explained previously, I too felt that my constitution at that time seemed to be that of consciousness and this description is also similar to that of Gopi Krishna.

Meeting others

At the point of dying, individuals became aware of the presence of spiritual beings in their vicinity. In many testimonies, this presence has been in the form of a family member or friend who had passed away and, in other instances, people have encountered what they described as their guardian spirits or spiritual helpers.

During the Kundalini experience, and in meditation prior to and after the experience, there are instances where one encounters such spiritual beings, but I would not say that they were family members or friends. James does state, however, that 'visions' are part of the 'mystic' experience.

The existence of light

According to Moody, the most incredible common element of Near-death experiences, and that which has the most profound effect upon the individual, is a very bright light. Initially this light is dim but it rapidly gets brighter until it reaches an unearthly and indescribable brilliance. Many individuals make the specific point that this light in no way hurts their eyes, dazzles them or prevents them from seeing other things around them. Not one person has expressed any doubt that this light has a definite personality and that they have an irresistible magnetic attraction to this light. The presence of this light is utterly invariable and the identification of the light changes from individual to individual. Moody then asserts that this seems to be a function of the religion of the individual, Christians identifying the light as the light of Christ, a Jewish man and a Jewish woman ascribed 'angel' to the light. At the same time, one woman who was a Christian felt no compulsion at all to call the light 'Christ'. The light is usually described as a very brilliant light, an illuminating white light, a huge beam and not of the kind of light that one can describe on this earth.

The instance of light in the Kundalini experience seems to be clearly established, but there may be one difference. In Near-death experiences, the individuals seem to approach the light; it seems dim at first and brighter as they get closer. In the Kundalini experience, one seems to *explode* into the light; it is not removed from you and you seem to be part of it. There are accounts of people who have had Near-death experiences being part of the light, as can be found within Cohen's *The Day I Died*. One individual related that he went into the light and, once in that light, realised what it felt to be completely a part of everything around him. Another individual realised himself to be the light that enabled him to see in the tunnel before he emerged into an indescribable pure white world of light. A further individual felt he was an integral part of an indescribable white light and, in yet another case, at that moment they became one with the light.

It is interesting to note that several celebrities have had Near-death experiences; Cohen gives several examples. Sharon Stone, after she almost died from internal bleeding caused by a tear in an artery at the base of her skull, described seeing a giant vortex of white light and being met by friends before recovering. Peter Sellers related a Near-death experience during the first of his eight heart attacks and described an incredibly beautiful, bright and loving light. Jane Seymour also saw a white light when she was undergoing an allergic reaction to an injection of penicillin and Bill Clinton described circles of light containing the faces of his wife and daughter, flying towards a 'brightness' during heart surgery. He said of the experience that he was not sure if it was a Near-death experience or a life-affirming one, and that it was perhaps a bit of both.

The review
Moody claims that the appearance of light leads to a moment of startling intensity when the individual is presented with a panoramic

215

review of their life. The intention, it seems, is to provoke reflection. Some individuals characterise this as an educational effort and, as they witness this display of light, it stresses the importance of two things in life: learning to love other people and acquiring knowledge. In one account, the individual is continually alerted to things concerning knowledge, that they had to continue learning, that there will always be a quest for knowledge and that this is a continuous process and one which continues after death.

In addition to following the theme of acquisition of knowledge over the last three chapters, there are also similarities here in that a review process is similar to the introspective and meditative process prior to the Kundalini experience. It is the process of individuation, if you will, and you do this review yourself. In terms of my own experience and search for and acquisition of knowledge, this book has been written as a result of it.

The border or limit

In a few instances, Moody suggests that people have described how, during their Near-death experience, they seemed to be approaching a 'border' or 'limit'. This is variously described as a body of water, a grey mist, a door, a fence across a field or simply a line. He suggests that, while this is highly speculative, it could raise the question of whether there might be the same basic root experience interpreted in different and subjective ways.

Moody provides no conclusion on this element and I cannot parallel it to the Kundalini experience, except to refer to the sensations of being restricted or seized, as with the element of the tunnel.

Coming back

Obviously all the individuals that Moody spoke to had to 'come back' in order to recount their experience. In some accounts, the person made initial attempts to return to their body and they experienced regret over their physical demise. However, once they reached a certain depth in their experience, especially those who reached the light, they did not want to return and may have even resisted a return to the body. This point is echoed in Cohen's book where, in certain cases, individuals had wanted to stay with the light in this 'other world', and had been frustrated at being 'sent back' and bitterly disappointed to find themselves back in this world.

The Kundalini experience is initially confusing and bewildering. However, over time this feeling subsides. There is reconciliation with the experience because of knowledge of its existence and the fact that others have had similar experiences. Once this occurs, there is a similar desire to 'return' and I have often referred to this other world as 'home'.

This return can be twofold; some individuals, at the end of their experience, went to sleep or lapsed into unconsciousness to awaken later in their physical bodies, while others were drawn speedily towards their physical bodies. In my own case, the latter would apply.

Telling others

A person who has gone through such an experience has no doubt whatsoever about its reality and its importance. Individuals insist that the experience is not a dream or hallucination, but are emphatic that it is an actual and absolute occurrence. In Moody's research, the individuals he interviewed are functional, well-balanced personalities, who do not recount their experiences as they would dreams but rather as real events. He further states that, after relating their experience, an individual can express profound relief when informed that others have reported exactly the same events.

Many have desisted from telling anyone of their experience, Moody says, because other people might think of them as being mentally disturbed. Others have resolved not to relate their experience to others as it was so indescribable and far beyond human language and human modes of perception and existence that it was fruitless even to try.

This, of course, parallels Kundalini in the ineffability of the experience. In the context of it being a real experience, which I recall vividly in flashes every so often, this most certainly was the case with me. Bucke, in *Cosmic Consciousness*, stated that 'It was impossible for him ever to forget what he at that time [his illumination] saw and knew; neither did he, nor could he, ever doubt the truth of what was presented to his mind.' Furthermore, he states that an individual who has had the experience will still, forty years afterwards, feel within themself the purifying, strengthening and exalting effect of the illumination.

William James also comments on this element in number two on his list of characteristics of the 'mystic' experience. This he calls the *noetic quality*. He states, that although so similar to states of feeling,

> mystical states seem to those who experience them to be also states of knowledge. They are states of insight into depths of truth unplumbed by the discursive intellect. They are *illuminations*, revelations, full of significance and importance all inarticulate though they remain; and as a rule they carry with them a curious sense of authority for after-time.
>
> William James: *The Varieties of Religious Experience*

Effect on Lives

Most people have related that their lives were broadened and deepened by the experience and that they became more reflective and concerned with ultimate philosophical issues. Again this book strongly bears out this similarity. As Bonnie Greenwell states, the Kundalini experience 'demands the reorientation of one's life'. James suggests that there is an 'objective change which the world often appears to undergo. An appearance of newness beautifies every object' and speaks of 'the sense of renovation, safety, cleanness, rightness, can be so marvelous and jubilant as well to warrant one's belief in a radically new substantial nature.'

According to Moody, in a very small number of cases people have recounted that after their experience they seemed to acquire, or to notice, faculties of intuition bordering on the psychic. Several of Cohen's accounts also confirm this, and I have read such accounts in the context of Kundalini. Apart from occasional flashes of intuition, however, the psychic element seems, in my case, to be no greater than that. At best, perhaps my own intuition was enhanced and it serves me well on occasion. I have certainly known at least two individuals more 'psychic' than I am who had not had the experience of Kundalini.

Moody reiterates that many have emphasised the importance of seeking knowledge and that this acquisition of knowledge continues even in the after-life. He also states that, after the experience, they were not left with feelings of instantaneous salvation or moral infallibility. Bucke also refers to this as it must not be supposed that because a man has 'Cosmic Consciousness', he is therefore omniscient or infallible.

New views on death

Almost everyone has expressed the thought that they are no longer afraid of death. Moody seeks to clarify that certain modes of death are undesirable and that none of these individuals actively seek death. He also states that all would dismiss suicide as a means to return to the realm of their Near-death experience.

I am in entire agreement on this. There is no fear of death, comfortable in the knowledge that there is something else. Bucke in *Cosmic Consciousness* cites the sense of immortality and the loss of the fear of death as elements of his illuminating experience. James comments on the loss of all worry and McLynn states of Jung and his individuation process:

> The individuation process also meant coming to terms with death ... Shrinking from death robbed the second half of life of its significance, for an old man who could not bid farewell to life was as pathetic as a young man who could not embrace it.

Corroboration

Another element which does not parallel the Kundalini experience is that of corroboration: whether there is any evidence of the reality of Near-death experiences which might be acquired and which are independent of the descriptions of the experiences themselves. Moody was surprised that, in quite a few instances, there was such evidence. For example, several doctors related to Moody that they were totally baffled how patients with no medical knowledge could describe in detail and accurately the procedure used in resuscitation attempts, especially when the doctors had assumed the individuals to be 'dead'. However, he is careful to state that this does not constitute proof.

With the Kundalini experience, it is so subjective that it cannot be similarly corroborated.

Conclusion on Moody's 15 elements

We find that out of Moody's 15 elements, one is not applicable (hearing yourself pronounced dead), there is no parallel with the corroboration element, and three are questionable, (the tunnel, out of body and the border), though these elements cannot be totally dismissed as lacking comparison. This leaves ten valid comparisons between the Near-death experience and the Kundalini experience. Both these experiences are unique by nature and in origin and yet remarkably similar.

Reincarnation

Moody states that none of the cases he has looked into are in any way indicative of reincarnation. He goes on to say none of these cases rule out reincarnation either and that, should reincarnation occur, it would be likely that an interlude in some other realm would take place between the time of separation from the old body and entry into the new one.

While accounts of reincarnation can be found in some ancient texts, especially those of the Hindus, one of the most compelling pieces of evidence that I have found to support belief in reincarnation is the research by Dr Ian Stevenson. His book, *Where Reincarnation and Biology Intersect*, centres on children who claim to remember past lives. Whereas his longer version, *Reincarnation and Biology: A Contribution to the Etiology of Birthmarks and Birth Defects*, considers some 225 cases, *Where Reincarnation and Biology Intersect* provides summaries of 112 cases, of which Dr Stevenson has examined all but eight himself.

Common features of cases of children with recall of past lives
These cases are of children who recall previous lives and have three features in common which Stevenson describes as 'universal'. These are: between the ages of two and four speaking about a past life; between the ages of five and eight ceasing to speak about a previous existence (it is difficult to judge whether memories fade at this point or remain but the child stops speaking of it); and a high incidence of violent death in the previous life.

Most children speak of this previous life with strong emotion and with such intensity that it surprises the adults around them. They do not distinguish past from present and may well use the present tense while referring to a past life. For example, they may say things like, they *have* a wife and two sons, or I *live* (wherever they have lived previously). Some children may make 50 or more different statements while others might only make a few but repeated, often tediously, many times.

In remembering the parents of the past life, the child may refer to their 'real parents' and often ask to be taken to the previous family.

The content of what the child may say often includes some account of the death in the previous life, especially if the death was a violent one and less so if it was a natural death. The proportion of cases with a violent death is 51 per cent.

Correlation of birthmarks with a violent death

The compelling aspect of Stevenson's research is the correlation of the birthmarks and birth defects of these cases with their oftentimes violent death. Stevenson states that these birthmarks and birth defects are important for three reasons:

(a) The birthmarks and birth defects provide an objective type of evidence which far surpasses the fallible memories of informants. Stevenson produces photographs showing these physical marks and, in many cases, has access to a medical document, usually a post-mortem report, that provides written confirmation of the correspondence between the birthmark or birth defect and the wound of the deceased individual of whose life the child, when it can speak, will claim to remember. Stevenson suggests that, while there are obvious difficulties in Western thought and modern science, the birthmarks and birth defects do not lend themselves easily to explanations other than reincarnation.

(b) Birthmarks and birth defects derive importance from the evidence they provide that an officially deceased individual who was still alive would not later influence a child that has made such a claim.

(c) The cases with birthmarks and birth defects provide a better explanation than is presently available as to why some individuals have such marks when others do not. Research suggests that the causes of birth defects can be attributed to genetic factors, some viral infections and chemicals such as thalidomide and alcohol. However, these and other causes account for less than half of all birth defects. Also, the cases Stevenson produces suggest that, for some birth defects, it can be said why a particular individual has a birth defect and why it might be in one particular location as opposed to another.

The latter relates more to birth defects than birthmarks; Stevenson suggests that almost everyone has birthmarks. According to one survey an individual has an average of 15 on their body. Despite a few rare instances of inheritance of birthmarks, nothing is known of the reason why individuals have birthmarks in one place instead of another.

Average birthmarks are generally small areas of increased pigmentation that are called nevi by physicians, better known as moles. Stevenson claims that, while some of the birthmarks in his cases are of this type, they are often larger than normal and often occur in unusual locations. Most, however, are hairless areas of puckered, scar-like tissue often raised above the surrounding tissue or depressed below it, and a few are areas of decreased pigmentation. Some are bleeding or oozing when the baby is born.

Examples of birthmarks in children related to cases of violent death
Examples of these instances would include the child born in Lebanon with increased pigmentation on his cheeks. As soon as he began to speak he recounted how a man who lived in a village some four kilometres away had shot him before he left for work. This story corresponded to the murder of a man who was shot by a mentally unstable person who had mistaken him for someone else. The bullet entered one side of his face and exited the other, damaging the tongue on the way. This resulted in his tongue becoming particularly swollen so as to necessitate a tracheotomy, making a hole in his windpipe in order for him to breathe.

Stevenson was able to examine the hospital record and found out that the birthmarks on the child's left cheek, the smaller of the two, corresponded to the entry wound while the larger on the right side corresponded to the exit wound. In addition to recounting the shooting, the child also recalled falling out of bed which resulted in his death due to his airway being obstructed by his injured tongue. He also asked his family to call him by the victim's name. The child also experienced difficulty in articulating properly, in particular the pronunciation of 's' sounds which require the elevation of the tongue, possibly as a result of a bullet having passed through it.

In another example, a child born in India possessed an extremely large birthmark of the port-wine type. This extended over her upper right chest and much of her right arm. In addition, she had three birthmarks on the lower right of her neck and the upper part of her chest. It was on a trip to a neighbouring village that the child recognised a man that she called her son and gave the man's name. It was after this that the child recounted details of her past life in this village and how she had been murdered there with a sword by professional killers, hired by her daughter-in-law. The post-mortem report of the individual whom she professed to be showed satisfactory correspondence between the sword marks on the murdered individual and the child's birthmarks. The child was noticeably frightened of this 'daughter-in-law' when she saw her, stating that she would kill her again.

Stevenson gives many such examples, and the fascinating thing is this: the skin of a normal-sized adult would comprise 160 squares, each 10 centimetres in size; therefore the odds that a single birthmark would correspond to the location of a single wound would be 1/160. There are instances of two birthmarks corresponding to two wounds and the odds immediately increase and become $1/160 \times 1/160$ or approximately 1/25,000. The assertion is that the likelihood of correspondence occurring by chance is greatly diminished.

Other aspects revealed by research
Phobias almost always related to the form of death in the previous life and occured in approximately 35 per cent of cases. For instance, a child who remembers the end of a previous life due to being shot might have a phobia of guns and loud noises, one who drowned might be afraid of being immersed in water. There seem to be no similar instances within the family unit and the child had no experience in childhood that would account for the phobia.

Philias (denoting an undue inclination or fondness or love for something) are also an aspect of his research. This would take the form of an undue fondness for certain foods or clothing that is not the norm for the family. There have also been instances of craving substances such as tobacco, nicotine and drugs, to which the previous personality used/was addicted.

There are what Stevenson describes as 'sex-change' cases in which the child remembers being of the opposite sex. They have tendencies to cross-dress and play games of the opposite sex, and may display attitudes typical of the opposite sex. Whilst one such case has become homosexual and a few have remained fixed to the sex of the previous life, in many cases these drives, as with phobias, fade.

Stevenson's research is world-wide, but cases are more often found in non-Western regions such as the Hindu and Buddhist countries in South Asia, the Shi'ite peoples of Lebanon and Turkey and the tribes of West Africa and the north west of North America. There are many cases from Europe and North America, but the non-European cultures possess a strong belief in reincarnation and are inclined to allow a child who wishes to speak of a previous life to do so.

His investigative method requires that one or more informed adults testify that he or she noticed the birthmark immediately after the child's birth, or within a few weeks of the birth. He begins with interviewing the child, its family and others, provided that they can provide first-hand testimony regarding the child's statements and any unusual behaviour. Then, he examines and photographs the birthmark or birth defect and secures any documents that provide exact records of dates such as identity cards. Next, they go to the family of the claimed previous life, if that information is available, and conduct a series of interviews with the members of that family. These individuals must be also able to provide first-hand testimony.

An important part of Stevenson's investigation is to find out any previous acquaintance of the two families in an effort to exclude, as best he can, the possibility that the child might be influenced in any way. In the cases of birthmarks and birth defects, he has spared no effort in obtaining post-mortem reports of the deceased individual. He claims that he has only published those cases which he felt to be authentic; similar independent investigations have increased his confidence in the authenticity of cases of children recalling previous lives.

Stevenson's conclusion

After rejecting unlikely scenarios such as discarnate entities possessing a child and imposing memories of its life on the child, Stevenson suggests that he can think of no other interpretation for these events other than reincarnation (especially in cases where the two families were previously unacquainted).

In his conclusion, Stevenson suggests that he cannot advance the merits of reincarnation as a contributory factor in the composition of human personality without exposing the limitations of genetics and environmental influences.

He identifies these limitations as genes which provide the instructions for proteins. However, he states that we have no idea as to how proteins develop their complex three-dimensional structure, and that there is even less knowledge of how protein and other metabolites become organised into cells and then into highly differentiated tissues and complicated organs that comprise our bodies. He further states that geneticists have allied themselves with biologists, who believe that natural selection provides a sufficient explanation of evolution. Stevenson suggests that we deduct nothing from Darwin's achievement by saying that his theory explains much but not all that we need to understand about evolution.

In terms of environmental influence, infancy and early childhood are formative times during which the human personality is shaped and may permanently influence the individual. The suggestion is that many psychologists and psychiatrists cling to this, but he questions whether there is evidence for such conviction. He believes there is a great body of data showing that reversibility of the effects of seemingly damaging events of early childhood is possible.

Stevenson does not propose that reincarnation replaces either or both of these factors in the composition of human personality. However, he feels that it should be a third factor that is considered, and that it may well fill gaps in the knowledge of human personality.

One of the most important consequences of the acceptance of reincarnation would be the acknowledgement of the duality of mind and body. He suggests that we cannot possibly imagine reincarnation without the corollary belief that minds are associated with bodies during our physical life, but are also independent of them to the extent of being fully separable from them and surviving the death of their associated body.

Tom Schroder, a writer, was the first journalist permitted to travel with Stevenson and accompany him around the world in his fieldwork and was changed from sceptic to believer. His book, *Old Souls,* is an account of his travels with Stevenson. It was his meeting with, and story on, Dr Brian Weiss, which led Tom Schroder to Dr Ian Stevenson. Weiss' work will be discussed next and segues nicely from this section to return to the subject of light.

Regression therapy and the 'Light'

Further anecdotal evidence on both reincarnation and the instance of light can be found in another bestselling book, *Many Lives, Many Masters,* by Dr Brian Weiss. A graduate of Columbia University and Yale Medical School, Dr Weiss is Chairman Emeritus of Psychiatry at the Mount Sinai Medical Center in Miami.

He was a traditional psychotherapist, whose mind was trained to think as a scientist and a physician, distrusting anything that could not be proven by scientific method. He was aware of parapsychology being conducted at major universities across the USA. However, this did not have any impression on him since it all seemed too far-fetched. Parapsychology is the study of mental phenomena outside the ordinary sphere of psychology and might include activities such as hypnosis, telepathy and so on (*para* in Greek meaning alongside, therefore alongside psychology).

Weiss's regression therapy treatment of his patient, Catherine
Weiss had a patient, Catherine, referred to him. Catherine was an attractive woman who worked in the same hospital in which Weiss was Chief of Psychiatry. She had taken months to make the appointment with Weiss, despite being strongly advised to do so by two staff physicians. Her life had been beset with fears and her symptoms included a fear of water, choking, airplanes, the dark and death. Her fears had begun to worsen and she suffered from insomnia. When she did sleep, she experienced nightmares and sleep-walking episodes. As these fears and symptoms increasingly affected her life, she sunk deeper into depression.

After eighteen months of conventional methods of therapy failed to overcome her symptoms, Weiss decided to employ hypnosis. Nothing had prepared Weiss for the results achieved. In a few short months, her symptoms disappeared, resulting in her resuming her life happier and more at peace. Weiss describes hypnosis as nothing mysterious, a state of focused concentration which, when under the instruction of a trained hypnotist causes the patient's body to relax and their memory to sharpen. He had used hypnosis on hundreds of patients previously, on occasion successfully regressing patients back to their childhoods, eliciting traumatic memories that were disrupting their lives.

This method was found beneficial in reducing anxiety, eliminating phobias, changing bad habits and recalling repressed material. He was surprised, therefore, when at first, Catherine's symptoms remained as severe as ever after this regression therapy. It was in a further session after this initial failure that, in regressing her back to the age of two and asking of symptoms that would have occurred prior to then, Catherine recounted a story of herself but as Aronda, an eighteen-year-old in the year 1863 BCE. He was amazed when, in a series of subsequent hypnotic trances, Catherine recounted 'past-life' memories which seemed to be the cause of her psychological symptoms.

During these sessions, she revealed many secrets of life and death and also acted as a conduit for information from highly evolved 'spirit entities'. These messages were given during her in-between states, that is, between past lives. These so called Masters provided Weiss during the sessions with various messages that he has since gone on to share. Weiss does not have a scientific explanation for what occurred during these sessions. He suggests that Catherine, whilst under hypnosis, might have been able to focus in on the part of her subconscious mind that sorted actual past life memories, or that she tapped in to what Jung termed 'the collective unconscious', described by him as the energy source that surrounds us and contains the memories of the entire human race.

Catherine was alleged to have had 86 previous lives in a physical state. Not all of these lives were 'remembered', as apparently it is only when it is important to remember that there is a memory of a particular life. None of these were particularly impressive in the sense that she was never a Cleopatra or a Catherine the Great, but had fulfilled more mundane roles in her previous existences. It seemed that the entire process of regression into past lives by hypnosis and the memories themselves seemed to provide a cure and eradicate the symptoms of her present life. For instance, as she 'remembered' a life where she had died a traumatic death, her fear of death diminished; where she recalled drowning in a previous life, her fear of water decreased and so on. As she 'saw' the events of past lives, it eradicated the symptoms in this life.

Catherine also became increasingly psychic and more intuitive as the sessions progressed and would often recognise individuals in her present life in past lives. For example, a friend in the present life was her father in a previous one, and her child in another previous life was her niece in the present one. Many individuals recurred life after life, but in different capacities.

In this, there was a message revealed by the Masters and that is that we are drawn to individuals of the same level as ourselves, and that we must learn to go not only to these individuals whose vibrations are the same, but also to those whose vibrations are not necessarily in sync with ours in order to help and assist these individuals. That way, we will reach a point where we are all equal.

Both Weiss and Catherine benefited from the revelations and messages from the Masters. The importance of learning, knowledge and wisdom are also mentioned several times. Wisdom was mentioned in the context that it is achieved very slowly because intellectual knowledge, though easily acquired, must be transformed into emotional or subconscious knowledge. Theoretical knowledge, without practical application, is not enough.

Catherine's encounter with the light
In its entirety *Many Lives, Many Masters* is a thoroughly interesting and compelling book, but it is the instance of light which is most relevant here. It appears that, at the end of each of her lives, Catherine encountered the light and there would be a wait of minutes in the same session before she found herself in another lifetime. She variously described this light as becoming 'brighter and more luminous, a wonderful energizing light and a light around ... and spirits, other people.' In one session, and in a hypnotic state, Catherine declared of the 'wonderful' light that it was brilliant, that everything came from the

light and that our soul immediately goes there upon death. It is like a magnetic force that we are attracted to.

In another hypnotised state when she saw the light, Weiss asked her whether the light gave her energy, to which she replied that it was like starting all over again, a rebirth. He also asked her how people in physical form can feel this energy, to which she responded, 'by their minds'. When asked how they achieve this state, she answered that the individual must be in a very relaxed state and that one can renew through light by no longer expending energy but renewing your own.

This seems an interesting link to the aspects of the light encountered in the Kundalini experience. It adds an extra perspective on its nature and whether, as described, it originates from a similar source.

Telephone interview with Dr Raymond Moody

So taken aback was I with the parallels between the Kundalini and the Near-death experience that I organised a telephone interview with Dr Raymond Moody. During this, it became immediately evident that Dr Moody was a modest man with a wonderful demeanour and insight and I would like to thank him for his helpful comments and suggestions both in general and with regard to specific texts in support of my contentions.

My main purpose in interviewing him was to find out if the parallels that I had identified indeed existed. To my surprise Dr Moody, whilst he declared that he was no expert on the subject of Kundalini, was familiar with the experience and had read about the subject. He also stated that, over the years, he had talked with and met several individuals who had an experience which would fall into parameters that could be described as Kundalini.

I mentioned the sense of confusion that often occurs after the event and the subsequent thoughts that one might feel that something detrimental may have happened to one's mental state. He said that this seemed to be a common response but that, being a psychiatrist as well as a philosopher, he had reassured individuals that it does not resemble any of the standard forms of mental illness. However, those who have had this type of experience, and who are endeavouring to understand it, may well consider it to have been a kind of mental illness for a period of time. Although I had some time ago come to this conclusion myself, I was rather reassured to hear these words.

I referred to anecdotes of Near-death experiences and its association with 'light' that had come to my mind and I felt that the subject was worth researching in more depth. I had read Dr Moody's book, *Life after Life*, and was quite amazed at the strong similarities there appeared to be.

Common elements in Near-death and Kundalini experiences
During the interview, we were able to discuss each of the 15 elements of the Near-death experiences and their similarities to those of the Kundalini experience.

Ineffability: The reason for agreement here, Dr Moody suggested, was general for mystical experience. He cited William James, mentioning that the primary characteristic of mystical experience is the nature of ineffability; despite how articulate one might be, it tends to lie beyond our power to verbalise or describe it.

Hearing yourself pronounced dead: We agreed there was no comparison.

Feelings of peace and quiet: There was also agreement on this characteristic and, again, Dr Moody cited William James, saying that whilst these mystical experiences might be brought on by some spiritual discipline, nonetheless, when the experience took place, it is experienced in a totally passive way.

The noise: On the element of the ringing in the ears, Dr Moody suggested that there might be a medical source for this, a condition by the name of tinnitus. Tinnitus is a medical mystery for which there is no real cure and is regarded as having little medical significance. My response was that I had heard of this condition and that, while I had not had myself medically checked, I had no recollection of it prior to the experience. I am convinced that in my case whatever the cause of the condition, whether medical or otherwise, it was initiated by my experience.

The tunnel: This was one of the questionable elements. Dr Moody's view was that while many had reported the feeling of being in a tunnel, not everyone experienced this particular sensation.

Out of body: This was another questionable element. Although I could not suggest that in any way at the time I was separated from my physical body, I felt that there was an element of not being myself, a focus of being at the time on the soul or consciousness. Dr Moody suggested the description 'transcendence of the ego' which I felt hit the nail on the head.

Meeting others: We both acknowledged the similarity here.

The review: We briefly discussed that my life review came both prior to and subsequent to the experience, as opposed to during the experience itself as occurs with the Near-death experience.

The 'border' or 'limit': We referred to the tunnel element and feeling of constraint.

Coming back: In a brief discussion we acknowledged the common factor here.

Conviction of the reality of the experience: Dr Moody suggested a description here which again was perfect, 'A sense of hyper-reality: more real than real.'

Telling others, frustration and lack of inclination: There was no discussion on this point since it was all very close to, and also covered by, the element of ineffability (mentioned above).

Effects on lives: Again, there was acknowledgement of the similarity of this effect.

New views on death, elimination of fear: There was complete agreement on this point.

Corroboration: We both agreed there was no parallel here due to the nature of the circumstances. Dr Moody suggested that, were it possible to be able to corroborate the Kundalini experience in near-death context, it would in effect destroy the distinction between this world and the next. While it was quite probably part of the experience, it cannot be verified empirically.

The element of light: This was left for the end of the discussion as clearly for me it was the crux of the matter. We were agreed on identifying the instance of light in both experiences. But I observed a possible difference, however, in the sense that in the majority of cases of Near-death experiences, these individuals seemed to *approach* the light whereas in the Kundalini experience individuals seemed to be *part* of that light. Dr Moody suggested that this could be partly due to the difficulty in articulation and said that many had recounted to him in various instances that the light was within, that they were part of the light, that they had become almost absorbed into it and that their identity becomes the light. As a result, we agreed that any difference that might exist might be a result of lack of the ability to articulate, rather than a difference in the experience itself.

Finally, I asked Dr Moody – 'Having met and interviewed the hundreds of individuals, what was your sense of what this light might be?' He replied that he had not drawn a definitive conclusion and that he would prefer to leave it open. He had a sense that it might not be possible, by the path of reason, to get to the truth of these matters while we are alive. He added that, nonetheless, his sense of approval for it is profound.

Anecdotal research into the Near-death experience

As a coda to the above discussion on the nature of near death experiences, I was subsequently able to carry out my own research into an anecdotal case.

The case of 'Jane'

As fate would have it, I was presented unexpectedly with the opportunity to speak to an individual who had had not one but two Near-death experiences. When I told my wife rather excitedly about my interview with Dr Moody, she mentioned it to my mother-in-law who said that she knew of someone who had had such an experience. It turned out that I had met this individual some two years previously in the south of France. I was given her telephone number and was able to contact her.

It turned out that 'Jane' had been admitted to hospital for what was supposed to be minor surgery. Due to details I will not disclose here, this operation went very wrong and quickly resulted in her heart stopping. 'Jane' described how she found herself 'in the wall', absolutely detached, watching as the doctors applied paddles in order to resuscitate her. She was then consumed by 'a great light' that she felt 'was part of her and that she was part of it.' It was a 'magical and wonderful' feeling and 'Jane' had a profound sense of being 'home'.

'Jane' returned to herself after she heard her deceased father's voice telling her to go back. She found herself back in bed, rather disappointed at having returned from this blissful experience. As is often the case, she was so bewildered at the reality and profundity of the experience that she did not speak of it, even to her husband, for some ten years.

A few years ago, 'Jane' again found herself in medical difficulty when a breakdown of her immune system resulted in kidney, lung and heart failure. She again found herself in hospital and, due to the severity of her condition, again out of her body. On this second occasion, she described how she felt herself 'float out of' her body and then in a tunnel of white light. The difference on this occasion was that she approached the light, albeit particularly rapidly. She had a sense of going home and, again, the feeling of being totally detached from her physical self and of extreme blissfulness. Again she was returned and again felt the disappointment of leaving. On this second occasion, however, she trusted in what had happened.

It also transpired that in 'Jane's' zeal to understand after the first experience, she had not only read a lot not only on Near-death experiences but she also became particularly au fait with the Kundalini experience. In our discussion, as with Dr Moody, we acknowledged and agreed on the similarities between the two.

So closely aligned are the two experiences that surely one is compelled to consider whether this 'light' is one and the same entity. It is in the profound detail of the parallels, much more than the instance of 'light' but the additional and derivative elements of both experiences, which must draw one to this conclusion.

Summary

We presented the Near-death experience as the phrase coined by Dr. Raymond Moody and listed the 15 elements of this experience as cited by him in his book *Life After Life*.

Comparison was made between the Near-death experience and the Kundalini experience identifying the instance of light and finding that many other derivative and associated elements of both experiences show parallels. Indeed, there are ten absolute parallels, three questionable parallels, which cannot be dismissed, out of the total fifteen elements.

Evidence for reincarnation, as offered by Dr Ian Stevenson's research, was discussed. If past lives can be accepted then we might consider the 'access' of them via regression therapy as is presented and provided by Dr. Brian Weiss' true story of past-life therapy. In this account his patient told of the encounter with 'light' at the end of each of her lives.

One element where there is an absolute parallel is the existence of 'light'.

8

A Last Word

I am not one who has been born in the possession of knowledge; I am one who is fond of antiquity, and earnest in seeking it there. Study the past if you would define the future.

Confucius (551–479 BCE)

Caduceus probably gives rise to more questions than it does answers, which, if it should be the case, would be desirable. However, I mentioned in the introduction that it would not be a definitive text. It should be considered as Japanese koan, a Buddhist technique to give the mind pause, to inspire thought and an aid to meditation. Examples of such would be: if a tree falls in the forest and there is no one there to hear it, does it make a sound? Or what is the sound of one hand clapping?

Throughout, there is a continuous and constant thread to the evidence provided. Within the esoteric spiritual texts discussed, there is the firm advice that one should seek truth, knowledge and wisdom. For me, it was asking the questions, researching and weighing the subject matter in terms of science and history and then subsequently in terms of religions and philosophy.

In the chapter on esoteric spiritual texts, it was proposed that 'light' was often a result of such a search for knowledge and meditation. In the chapter dealing with the spiritual philosophers, there were individuals of profound thought, of great contemplation and introspection who acted on such advice and, as a result, were compelled to write about their experience and, in particular, to describe their experience as awe-inspiring and also associate it with 'light'. In the chapter on Kundalini,

235

further notable individuals were identified who had had this experience and also associated it with 'light'. So powerful were these experiences that some of these individuals went on to found the religions and spiritual movements that we have today.

Furthermore, the Near-death experience is one which also solidly includes the element of 'light' as a part of it. William James suggested of the 'mystic' experience that, leaving aside the question of the truth of these, we should surely on the basis of the undeniable action and influence gathered from this information view it as, at least, worthy of consideration, but at best as amongst the most important, tangible and biological functions of mankind.

Plato used the discourses of Socrates to supplement his own philosophical ideas much like Lao Tzu, who used the maxims of earlier sages to illustrate his sentiments. I have similarly used a wide range of quotations, not only to provide substance to my assertions but also to serve as a mouthpiece for my contentions. Whilst there are many authors who have written on the specific subjects included in *Caduceus*, I felt that there was no one book 'out there' which brought all the elements together, as I have tried to do. I believe that it is only by taking a 'universal' view that we can come to something of any solidity closely aligned to 'the truth'.

The nature of this 'light'
So what, then, is this unifying and universal 'light'? That which seemingly can be accessed via the Kundalini experience or the Near-death experience? That which has been presented to us since time immemorial in so many spiritual and religious texts by so many individuals of a spiritual and/or philosophical persuasion.

Might this light be 'heaven' as recounted in Plato's *Myth of Er*, this 'shaft of light' which stretches from heaven to earth or, as it further suggests, that 'this light is the bond of heaven and holds its circumference together?'

Might it be God, a divine entity, an omniscient entity? It is seen in esoteric spiritual texts in various forms:

The *Tanakh*: God described as a 'consuming fire'.
The *New Testament*: God is light.

The *Qur'an*: God is the Light.

The *Bhagavad Gita*: the radiance of the Supreme Spirit is comparable to the light if a thousand suns rose in the sky.

The *Texts of Taoism* (Tao - 'the way'): describes the 'light' of the Tao

The Zoroastrians claim that God is the Light and the source of light. Indeed in scripture around the globe and within a vast majority of cultures and sects, such as the Gnostics, its respective omniscient entity or fundamental underlying principle of life is referred to as 'light'.

The question arises, do we just wave aside all these accounts of the experiences of the originators of the religious and spiritual thoughts and dismiss them as mere coincidence or metaphor?

The answer may best be left with the reader to respond by forming their own thoughts and opinions.

Some individuals who read spiritual texts like to be told what to do and how to act but one important conclusion here is that it is knowledge of the Self and knowledge gained by the individual that is essentially required. In this book, I have set out to provide as much transcendent evidence, albeit anecdotal, from a variety of sources and angles. It was Plato who suggested that reason will only take you so far. At some point, one has to take a new and all-encompassing perspective on what is available but, in my view, the preponderance of evidence suggests that, at the very least, there is 'something else'.

What is certain is that this 'light' has been at the emergence of all our religions and spiritual movements. James' comment was that 'the founders of every church owed their power (and influence) originally to the fact of their direct personal communion with the divine.' What also seems certain is that, when we consider the studies of Moody and others on the Near-death experience, this 'light' awaits us at the end of our physical life.

As James further stated, these experiences offer hypotheses which may form an insight into the meaning of life. These accounts:

tell of the supremacy of the ideal, of vastness, of union, of safety, and of rest. They offer us *hypotheses*, hypotheses which we may voluntarily ignore, but which as thinkers we cannot possibly upset. The supernaturalism and optimism to which they would persuade us may, interpreted in one way or another, be after all the truest of insights into the meaning of this life.

Self-knowledge and change from within

In an increasingly difficult world of fragile economies and of the ongoing deterioration of the world's ecosystem, a significantly different mental approach is essential. However, it is imperative that the initiation of such change must originate from deep within the individual. Only from a change to an individual's consciousness and conscientiousness will such a change on a global basis come about. A new approach, a new perspective, is demanded, along with the formation of a new reality.

The confrontation of the Self is of most importance, since it is only with that knowledge that there will be individual change and a shift in consciousness. Furthermore, it is only by this individual process that this essential shift in world consciousness will also arise.

A complete departure from this present global spiritual morass is needed because all that has been is not working now, to the extent that although it may have worked, it can most certainly be improved. Indeed, at times, it seems with the evolution of the human species that there has been devolution in consciousness.

It is, therefore, imperative that there must be significant change to the way that we approach life, individually and as a world population, and that we liberate ourselves from this worldwide spiritual quagmire in which we find ourselves. Even many self-described 'spiritual' individuals are not as comfortable as perhaps they profess to be and, while it is preferable that they exist for they have made steps in the right direction for those that need it, perhaps they will find some relevant foundation or context from the contents of this book.

We can no longer be complacent, our minds at rest with scientific tenets which, for many of us, provide little substance and comfort. Nor should we find a peace with a *blind* faith within one of many religious systems which all stem from undoubtedly one source. Neither system, religious or scientific, is fully formed in answering all that we lack in knowledge; the gaps in our psyche are not filled to any satisfactory degree. However, one cannot know one's self if there is no perspective, no knowledge of our present environment or from whence we came.

It is essential that we possess knowledge from antiquity to find the greatest truth, or at very least, the least corrupted, and this needs, like everything else in life, the requisite effort.

Theoretical knowledge without practical application is redundant. This knowledge must be absorbed into the subconscious. It is essential that, in attaining a more accurate perspective, we are aware of cultures of antiquity and ancient spiritual texts. We would all benefit from less escapism and a concentration on more meaningful and profound matters. Indeed, in my view, the world of non-fictional work is particularly fascinating with greater wonders to behold than that of fiction.

One might ask how in this fast-paced materially-based society are we ever to accommodate such an endeavour. Someone said that there is always time, it is only the lack of inclination that prevents us. It may be this is not for you and if so, then so be it. If one is willing, however, one can find the opportunities. Watch less television, read on your commute and if you drive, listen to audio books, and so on. Suffice it to say that the greater the endeavour, the greater the rewards, and the greater number of the world population that gets on board, the greater the transition, the more complete the shift in global and collective consciousness or, as Plato described it in the *Timaeus*, the 'world-soul'.

Carl Jung was once criticised on the grounds that only the privileged few can allow themselves the degree of introversion Jung allowed himself, and that to benefit fully from Jungian-like analysis one should be relatively affluent, well-read and familiar with Greek mythology, articulate and good at the visualisation of images, as well as having a relatively strong ego to be able to confront the instincts and images of the unconscious. In other words, that Jung's procedure, not dissimilar to that suggested here, was designed particularly for a leisured, cultivated, creative elite.

My response is that meditation costs nothing and today there is a vast amount of information available on the internet if one does not have access to libraries. Worldwide travel is also more available and affordable than it has ever been. At the same time, you do not need to become an ascetic, to give up everything and live just below the snow line in the Himalayas seeking alms. There is no greater reward than treading such a path and triumphing spiritually in this challenging and material world.

Juan Mascaró describes this in a striking way, comparing it to reaching the top of a mountain and having the path illuminated by glimpses of light:

> This is the great adventure and the great discovery. No one can do it for us. Until we have reached the top of the mountain we cannot see in full glory the view that lies beyond; but glimpses of light illumine our path to the mountain. These glimpses of light give us faith, because then we know, not with the external knowledge of reading books, but with that certainty of faith that comes from moments of inner life. But if in intellectual pride or in laziness of dullness we deny the light, thereby denying ourselves, how can we avoid being in the darkness?

Such studious endeavour may not provide definitive answers but, then again, neither does science, nor do the religious systems of today. Indeed, anything that is definitively systematic is a less valuable path. The greater the understanding of the Self by the Self, the greater the peace, the settledness, the perspective of the individual. It is better to rest and be within knowledge based on fact and best evidence. This provides more accurate perspective, rather than not being at peace, embracing imposed knowledge and parameters defined by tenets which provide none of this. Even if the scientific fraternity were to provide their holy grail, a unified theory, this would be of no greater benefit to mankind. Psyches remain the same, the global lack of consciousness and conscientiousness remain the same and its revelation would be of no material value or benefit in this conflicted world. As William James says in *Varieties*, 'Weight, movement, velocity, direction, position, what thin, pallid, uninteresting ideas!'

At one point in my research, I came across someone, I forget who, that suggested that it was the easy way out of the consideration of life to contemplate on matters spiritual and religious and to tread such a path. They suggested that the way science provided was of more 'solidity' and was more comprehensive. Naturally, I disagree and were I to see that individual now, I would say that the easy way out was the path of solely embracing scientific tenets. Today, I smile at such a comment, for the study I have undertaken was far more arduous and transcendent than a path of scientific thought could ever provide.

However, there were times when I wished that my mind could have rested cosily, comfortably and unchallenged within defined scientific tenets and not have had to apply the profound questions that I have put to myself and to the purpose of life – answers to which science could not begin to answer.

Again, William James summarises this point on science aptly when he states:

> [Science] has ended by utterly repudiating the personal point of view. She catalogues her elements and her laws indifferent as to what purpose may be shown forth by them, and constructs her theories quite careless of their bearing on human anxieties and fates.

Later he refers to the difference between a rational consciousness and other forms of consciousness:

> Our normal waking consciousness, rational consciousness as we call it, is but one special type of consciousness, whilst all about it, parted by the filmiest of screens, there lie potential forms of consciousness entirely different. We may go through life without suspecting their existence; but apply the requisite stimulus, and at a touch they are there in all their completeness.

Another similar view is given by the classic Islamic writer al-Ghazali, who stated that, 'Very stupid and ignorant would be the man who would wish to discover in them a wisdom by means of reason.'

But does one need to absolutely 'know all' by definition? Perhaps this is not meant to be, but we can, at the very least, find ourselves in a state of realised confusion, comfortable in the remaining mysteries, still always seeking and honing our thoughts and ourselves but comfortable in our being. The first stage is to cast our gaze backwards towards antiquity to enable us to make positive steps in the future.

Truth in ancient mythology versus science
To my mind, it is preferable to take from the mythology of antiquity and spiritual and philosophical subjects when cross referenced across the world, rather than from science, which seems to have a perpetual

241

line of thought that must conform, it seems, to some previous scientific tenet to the exclusion of all else. It is more concerned with proving and enhancing prior theory than the truth and the real essence of 'being'.

As Einstein said, the search for the truth and knowledge is one of the finest attributes of man, although often it is most loudly voiced by those who strive for it least. In *The World As I see It*, Einstein states that, 'It is not the fruits of scientific research that elevate a man and enrich his nature, but the urge to understand, the intellectual work, creative or receptive.' Surely an open and enquiring mind and that of transcendent thought, based upon the weight of evidence provided in antiquity, in fact offers a greater degree of truth about the nature of life. Indeed, the sole embrace of scientific tenets provides us with an excuse to escape from a thorough introspection and general inspection of things, rather than assisting in finding ourselves. It leads to non-action in discovering the Self.

Against this, Richard Rorty, the well-known contemporary American philosopher, has suggested an opposite viewpoint – that it is not whether our ideas correspond to some fundamental reality, but whether they help us carry out practical tasks and create a fairer and more democratic society. As you might expect, I do not accept this at all and hopefully this book has shown a variety of overlap in history, philosophical and religious thoughts and anomalies central to us the world over. It is solely when we are able to solidly identify world factors we all possess in common and founded in fact that there may be an end to the ridiculous, never-ending acrimony and conflicts across the globe. Only then will we be able to learn from the Cain and Abel biblical story and find that we are in mind and in deed our 'brother's [and sister's] keeper'. Only then will we find ourselves in a fairer and more conscientious global society.

There must be cessation of the physical and violent imposition upon neighbouring and foreign nations in an attempt to move them onto the path of democracy or some such. As we have seen time and time again, not only does this not work, but the ramifications of such acts are far more detrimental than the best of intentions provide. It is solely via education, the finding of common ground by all nations and religions and by the accurate knowledge and lessons of antiquity that a better existence for us all the world over will be availed.

What the future holds

Perhaps over and above all there would be great value in the imposition upon us all of the quotation, 'Do unto others as you would have them do unto you.' Surely then we would be closer to that ideal world existence and would better achieve an end to the spate of violence in crimes like paedophilia, rape, murder and wars and terrorism and all crimes against mankind, and generally achieve a greater level of conscientiousness, both individually and globally.

Unfortunately, should the suggestion presented in this book be initiated, there would be no room for procrastination. On the basis of change of ages and periods referred to earlier then this is believed by some perhaps to occur again and imminently. If the Mayans and the transition which they prophesied is accurate, this world will change again and there are schools of thought that suggest that the time of change might be less traumatic if we were better spiritually prepared and developed, resulting in a smoother transition stemming from a global shift in our collective consciousness.

Could Kundalini and in particular this 'Light', provide a unifying force for the world? From time immemorial to the present day, the world has been plagued by religious conflict, one group seeking violently to impose their beliefs and interpretations upon another.

The identification and study of Kundalini, as experienced by all religions and their messiahs and prophets, the forerunners of their respective religious thought, could provide us with a unique opportunity; indeed an opportunity to find a unity in belief and a common ground for relating to an omniscient entity.

It was William Blake who said that, 'All religions are one.' I agree entirely and feel that, at their very core, they are all essentially the same and of one source. Perhaps an even more pertinent comment here would be Mahatma Ghandi's, 'God has no religion.' If we choose to interpret and worship in our individual ways that is our prerogative, however, we should seize this opportunity to dispense with the ridiculous and vicious downward spiral as a result of the perceived differences of religious thought. I hope that there might be Light at the end of the tunnel.

The Beginning

Recommended Reading / Bibliography

Introduction:

Francis Fukuyama: *The End of History and The Last Man*: Penguin 1992
G.W.F. Hegel: *The Philosophy of History*: Dover Publications 1956
Edward O. Wilson: *Consilience – The Unity of Knowledge*: Vintage Books 1999

The Scientific Fraternity:

Alan Alford: *Gods of the New Millennium*: Hodder and Stoughton 1997
Michael J. Behe: *Darwin's Black Box – A Biochemical Challenge to Evolution*: Free Press 1996, 2006
Bill Bryson: *A Short History of Nearly Everything*: Black Swan 2003
Alice Calaprice: *The New Quotable Einstein*: Princeton University Press 2005
Michael A. Cremo and Richard L. Thompson: *Forbidden Archaeology – The Hidden History of the Human Race*: Bhaktivedanta Book Trust 1996
Charles Darwin: *The Origin of Species*: Penguin Books 1968
Richard Dawkins: *The God Delusion*: Black Swan 2006
Michael Denton: *Evolution – A Theory in Crisis*: Adler & Adler 1985
Albert Einstein: *The World As I See It*: BN Publishing 2007
Graham Hancock: *Supernatural*: Arrow Books 2005
Stephen Hawking with Leonard Mlodinow: *A Briefer History of Time*: Bantam Press 2005
J. Douglas Kenyon (ed), *Forbidden History* Rochester, VT 05767 Copyright © Inner Traditions / Bear & Co. 2005
Antony Latham: *The Naked Emperor – Darwinism Exposed*: Janus Publishing Ltd 2005
Jeremy Narby: *The Cosmic Serpent – DNA and the Origins of Knowledge*: Phoenix 1998
Michael White: *Isaac Newton – The Last Sorcerer*: Fourth Estate 1997: reprinted by permission of Harper Collins Publishers Ltd

Michael White: *Isaac Newton - The Last Sorcerer* (Copyright © Michael White, 1997) Reprinted by permission of A.M. Heath & Co Ltd.

Anomalies:

Robert Bauval and Adrian Gilbert: *The Orion Mystery – Unlocking the Secrets of The Pyramids*: Mandarin Paperbacks 1994

E.A. Wallis Budge: *The Book of the Dead – Hieroglyphic Transcript and Translation into English of the Ancient Egyptian Papyrus of Ani*: Gramercy Books 1999

David Hatcher Childress: *Ancient Micronesia & The Lost City of Nan Modal*: Adventures Unlimited Press 1998

David Hatcher Childress: *Technology of the Gods – the Incredible Sciences of The Ancients*: Adventures Unlimited 2000

Giorgio De Santillana & Hertha von Dechend: *Hamlet's Mill – An Essay Inverstigating The Origins of Human Knowledge and Its Transmission Through Myth*: David R. Godine 1969

English Heritage: *The Prehistoric Monuments of Avebury*: 1994

Rand Flem-ath and Colin Wilson: *The Atlantis Blueprint*: Warner books 2000

Raphael Girard: *Esotericism of The Popol Vuh – Sacred History of the Quiche Maya*: Theosophical University Press 1979

Robert Graves: *The Greek Myths 1&2*: Penguin 1960

Graham Hancock: *Fingerprints of the Gods*: William Heinemann Ltd 1995

Graham Hancock: *Heaven's Mirror – Quest for The Lost Civilisation*: Penguin 1998

Charles Hapgood: *Maps of The Ancient Sea Kings – Evidence of Advanced Civilisation in the Ice Age*: Adventures Unlimited Press 2000

Hesiod: *Theogony and Works and Days*: Oxford University Press 1988

J. Douglas Kenyon (ed), *Forbidden History* Rochester, VT 05767 Copyright © 2005 Inner Traditions / Bear & Co.

C. Scott Littleton: *Mythology – The Illustrated Anthology of World Myth and Storytelling*: Duncan Beard Publishers 2002

Donald A. Mackenzie: *Myths and Legends - China and Japan*: Senate 1994

Recinos Goetz Morley: *Popol Vuh – The Sacred Book of the Ancient Quiche Maya*: University of Oklahoma Press 1950

Chris Morton and Ceri Louise Thomas: *The Mystery of The Crystal Skulls*: Thorsons 1997: reprinted by permission of Harper Collins Publishers Ltd

Sister Nivedita & Ananda K. Coomaraswamy: *Myths and Legends – Hindus and Buddhists*: Senate 1994

Piri Reis and His Charts: Topkapi Museum ISBN 975-96278-2-5

R.A. Schwaller de Lubicz: *Esotericism & Symbol*: Inner Traditions Ltd 1985

R.A. Schwaller de Lubicz: *The Temple In Man*: Inner Traditions Ltd 1949

Zecharia Sitchin: *The Lost Realms*: Bear & Company 1990

Homer Sykes: *Mysterious Britain*: Cassell & Co. 2001

Peter Tomkins: *Mysteries of The Mexican Pyramids*: Thames and Hudson 1976

E.T.C. Werner: *Myths and Legends of China*: Dover Publications 1994

John Anthony West: *Serpent in the Sky: The High Wisdom of Ancient Egypt*: The Theosophical Publishing House 1993

Frank Walters: *Book of The Hopi*: Penguin 1963

David M. Wislon: *The Vikings and Their Origins*: Thames & Hudson 2003

Evidence of an Unknown Antediluvian Civilisation:

Bill Bryson: *A Short History of Nearly Everything*: Black Swan 2003

E.A. Wallis Budge: *The Book of the Dead – Hieroglyphic Transcript and Translation into English of the Ancient Egyptian Papyrus of Ani*: Gramercy Books1999

Michael A. Cremo and Richard L. Thompson: *Forbidden Archaeology – The Hidden History of the Human Race*: Bhaktivedanta Book Trust 1996

Ignatius Donnelly: *Atlantis – The Antediluvian World*: Dover Publications 1976

Graham Hancock: *Underworld – Flooded Kingdoms of The Ice Age*: Penguin 2002

Charles Hapgood: *Maps of The Ancient Sea Kings – Evidence of Advanced Civilisation in the Ice Age*: Adventures Unlimited Press 1996

J. Douglas Kenyon (ed), *Forbidden History* Rochester, VT 05767 Copyright © Inner Traditions / Bear & Co. 2005

Richard Laurence (Translator): *The Book of Enoch*: Wiz 1995

C. Scott Littleton: *Mythology – The Illustrated Anthology of World Myth and Storytelling*: Duncan Beard Publishers 2002

Recinos Goetz Morley: *Popol Vuh – The Sacred Book of the Ancient Quiche Maya*: University of Oklahoma Press 1950

Plato: *Timaeus And Critias*: Penguin Classics 1965

H.C. Randall-Stevens: *Atlantis to The Latter Days*: The Order of the Knights Templar of Aquarius 1981

W. Scott-Elliot: *Legends of Atlantis and Lost Lemuria*: The Theosophical Publishing House 1990

Zecharia Sitchin: *The Lost Realms*: Bear & Co. 1990

Lewis Spence: *The History of Atlantis*: Adventures Unlimited Press 1996

The Zohar: The Soncino Press 1984

Esoteric Spiritual Texts:

The Bhagavad Gita - Introduction by Juan Mascaro: Penguin 1962
The Chumash: Mesorah Publications Ltd 1993
Bart D. Ehrman: *Misquoting Jesus*: HarperOne 2005
Holy Bible: King James Version: Nelson 1989
William James: *The Varieties of Religious Experience: A Study in Human Nature*:
Longmans, Green and Co. 1902, reprinted by Penguin Classics 1985
The Koran: Penguin Classics 1997
James Legge (tr): *The Texts of Taoism Part I and Part II*: Dover Publications 1962
Mahabharata: Torchlight Publishing Inc. 1999
R.J. McCarthy (tr), *Al-Ghazali's Path to Sufism: His Deliverance from Error: al-Munqidh min al-Dalal*: S.J.: Fons Vitae 2006
Hunbatz Men: *Secrets of Mayan Science/Religion*: Bear & Co. 1990
Recinos Goetz Morley: *Popol Vuh – The Sacred Book of the Ancient Quiche Maya*:
University of Oklahoma Press 1950
The New Jerusalem Bible: Darton, Longman & Todd Ltd 1990
The Qur'an: Translation M.A.S. Abdel Haleem: Oxford World's Classics 2004
James M. Robinson (General Editor): *The Nag Hammadi Library – The Definitive New Translation of the Gnostic Scriptures Complete in One Volume*: Harper Collins 1990
E. P. Sanders: *The Historical Figure of Jesus*: Penguin 1993
St John of the Cross: *The Mystical Doctrine of St John of the Cross*: Continuum 2002
The Teaching of Buddha: Bukkyo Dendo Kyokai 1966
The Torah; The Five Books of Moses: The Jewish Publication Society of America 1962
The Upanishads - Introduction by Juan Mascaro: Penguin 1965
The Vedas: Sarvadeshik Arya Pratinidhi Sabha 1993
Geza Vermes(tr): *The Complete Dead Sea Scrolls in English*: Penguin 1998
The Zohar: The Soncino Press 1984

The Spiritual Philosophers:

Dante Alighieri: *The Divine Comedy 1: Inferno* - Translated and edited by Robin

Kirkpatrick: Penguin Classics 2006

Dante Alighieri: *The Divine Comedy 2: Purgatorio* - Translated and edited by Robin Kirkpatrick: Penguin Classics 2007

Dante Alighieri: *The Divine Comedy 3: Paradiso* - Translated and edited by Robin Kirkpatrick: Penguin Classics 2007

William Blake: *The Divine Comedy*: Bibliotheque de l'Image 2000

Richard Friedenthal: *Goethe His Life and Times*: Wiedenfeld & Nicolson 1993

Johann Wolfgang von Goethe: *Faust Part One*: Penguin Classics 1949

Johann Wolfgang von Goethe: *Faust Part Two*: Penguin Classics 1949

A. Hoeller, Forward by June Singer: *Jung and the Lost Gospels*: Stephan Quest Books 1989

C.G. Jung: *Aion – Researches into The Phenomenology of the Self*: Routledge & Kegan Paul 1959

Carl G. Jung (Er): *Man and His Symbols*: Dell Publishing 1964

C.G. Jung: *Mysterium Coniunctionis – An Inquiry into the Separation and Synthesis of Psychic Opposites in Alchemy*: Routledge & Kegan Paul 1963

C.G. Jung: *Symbols of Transformation*: Bollingen Foundation Inc. 1956

Christopher Marlowe: *Doctor Faustus (A- and B- Texts) and Other Plays*: Oxford World's Classics 1998

Christopher Marlowe: *The Tragical History of Doctor Faustus: a special version by Basil Ashmore, including the 1592 edition of the The History of the damnable life and deserved death of Doctor Faustus (translation; P.F. Gent)*: Blandford Press 1948

Frank McLynn: *Carl Gustav Jung*: Black Swan 1996 reprinted by permission of the Random House Group

Frank McLynn: *Carl Gustav Jung* © 1997 by the author and reprinted by permission of St Martin's Press, LLC (US)

Friedrich Nietzsche: *Ecce Homo*: Penguin Classics 1992

Friedrich Nietzsche: *Human, All Too Human*: Penguin Classics 1984

Friedrich Nietzsche: *The Birth of Tragedy*: Penguin Classics 1993

Friedrich Nietzsche: *Thus Spoke Zarathustra*: Penguin Classics 1961

Friedrich Nietzsche: *Twilight of The Idols*: Oxford World Classics 1998

Thirteen Epistles of Plato: Introduction, translation and notes by L.A.Post: Oxford University Press 1925

Voltaire: *Candide*: Penguin Classics 1947

Kundalini: The Light at the End of the Tunnel

Arthur Avalon (Sir John Woodroofe): *The Serpent Power: the secrets of tantric and shaktic yoga*: Dover Publications 1974

The Bhagavad Gita - Introduction by Juan Mascaro: Penguin 1962

R.H. Charles (Tr): *The Book of Enoch* SPCK 1997

Mary Boyce: *Zoroastrians: Their Religious Beliefs and Practices*: Routledge 2007

Encyclopaedia of Islam: E.J. Brill 1960 – 2005

Dr. Richard Maurice Bucke: *Cosmic Consciousness – A Study in the Evolution of the Human Mind*: Innes & Sons 1901

Johann Wolfgang von Goethe: *Faust Part One*: Penguin Classics 1949

Bonnie Greenwell PhD.: *Energies of Transformation – A Guide to the Kundalini Process*: Shakti River Press 1990

Nicholas Griffiths: *The Cross and the Serpent*: University of Oklahoma Press 1966

Holy Bible: King James Version: Nelson 1989

William James: *The Varieties of Religious Experience: A Study in Human Nature*: Longmans, Green and Co. 1902, reprinted by Penguin Classics 1985

C.G. Jung: *The Psychology of Kundalini Yoga – Notes of the Seminar Given in 1932 by C.G. Jung*: Princeton University Press 1996

S.A. Kapadia: *The Teaching of Zoroaster and the Philosophy of the Parsi Religion*: 1913

The Koran: Penguin Classics 1997

Gopi Krishna: *Ancient Secrets of Kundalini*: UBS Publishers 1995

Gopi Krishna: *Kundalini – The Evolutionary Energy in Man*: Shambhala Publications 1970

Gopi Krishna: *Kundalini: Path to Higher Consciousness*: Orient Paperbacks 1976

Al-Ghazali's Path to Sufism: His Deliverance from Error: al-Munqidh min al-Dalal: R.J. McCarthy, (Tr) *Al-Ghazali's Path to Sufism: His Deliverance from Error: al-Munqidh min al-Dalal*: S.J.: Fons Vitae 2006

Hunbatz Men: *Secrets of Mayan Science/Religion*: Bear & Co. 1990

Jeremy Narby: *The Cosmic Serpent – DNA and the Origins of Knowledge*: Phoenix

The New Jerusalem Bible: Darton, Longman & Todd Ltd 1990

M.P. Pandit: *Kundalini Yoga – A Brief Study of Sir John Woodroffe's 'The Serpent Power'*: Lotus Press 1993

Adalberto Rivera: *The Mysteries of Chichen Itza*: Universal Image Enterprise Inc. 1995

E. P. Sanders: *The Historical Figure of Jesus*: Penguin 1993
St John of the Cross: *The Mystical Doctrine of St John the Cross*: Continuum 2002
The Teaching of Buddha: Bukkyo Dendo Kyokai 1966
Walt Whitman: *Leaves of Grass: The First (1855) Edition*: Penguin Classics 1986

The Light at the End of Life:

P.M.H. Atwater: *The Big Book of Near-Death Experiences*: Hampton Road Publishing 2007
Tammy Cohen: *The Day I Died*: John Blake Publishing 2006
Raymond A. Moody: *Life After Life*: Rider Books 2001
Melvin Morse, M.D. *Closer to the Light*, Ivy Books 1990
Plato: *The Republic*: Penguin Classics 1955
Plato: *Phaedo*: Oxford University Classics 1999
Tom Schroder: *Old Souls*: Fireside 2001
Ian Stevenson, M.D.: *Where Reincarnation and Biology Intersect*: Praeger Publishers 1997
The Tibetan Book of the Dead: Introductory Commentary by His Holiness the Dali Lama, Penguin 2006
Dr. Brian Weiss: *Many Lives, Many Masters*: Piatkus 1994

A Last Word:

William James: *The Varieties of Religious Experience: A Study in Human Nature*: Longmans, Green and Co. 1902, reprinted by Penguin Classics 1985
Plato: *Timaeus And Critias*: Penguin Classics 1965
Richard Rorty *Philosophy and Social Hope*: Penguin 1999
St John of the Cross: *The Mystical Doctrine of St John of the Cross*: Continuum 2002
The Upanishads - Introduction by Juan Mascaro: Penguin 1965